Technology Enhanced Language Learning

Connecting theory and practice

Leanna Li
2020.3.

Also published in
Oxford Handbooks for Language Teachers

Technology Enhanced Language Learning

Connecting theory and practice

Aisha Walker | Goodith White

Leanna Li
J. 16. 2020.

OXFORD
UNIVERSITY PRESS

OXFORD
UNIVERSITY PRESS

Great Clarendon Street, Oxford, OX2 6DP, United Kingdom

Oxford University Press is a department of the University of Oxford.
It furthers the University's objective of excellence in research, scholarship,
and education by publishing worldwide. Oxford is a registered trade
mark of Oxford University Press in the UK and in certain other countries

ISBN: 978 0 19 442368 7

Printed in China

This book is printed on paper from certified and well-managed sources

ACKNOWLEDGEMENTS

*The authors and publisher are grateful to those who have given permission to reproduce
the following extracts and adaptations of copyright material*: p.xv Screenshot of
'Wordle', www.wordle.net. Reproduced by permission; p.54 Screenshot
from Inanimate Alice: Episode 4–Hometown, www.inanimatealice.com.
Reproduced by permission; p.70 Extract from 'Why I sent Oxford a rejection
letter' by Elly Nowell, The Guardian, 19 January 2012. Copyright Guardian
News & Media Ltd 2012. Reproduced by permission; p.70 OUP (Oxford
panoramic/John Woodworth/Vetta); p.90 Screenshot from 'Animate your
homework' from www.boxoftricks.net. Reproduced by kind permission of
José Picardo; p.99 Screenshots from www.wikipedia.org. Content available
under the Creative Commons Attribution-ShareAlike 3.0 Unported license:
http://creativecommons.org/licenses/by-sa/3.0; p.138 Extract from 'New
skills for new classrooms: Training tutors to teach languages online' by
Regine Hampel and Ursula Stickler, *Computer Assisted Language Learning*, 18:4,
311-326, 2005. Reprinted by permission of the publisher (Taylor & Francis
Ltd, http://www.tandf.co.uk/journals); p.144-5 Extract from 'The battle of
the boards' by Sarn Rich, *English Teaching Professional*, Issue 78, January 2012.
Reproduced by permission of the copyright holder, Pavilion Publishing and
Media Ltd. *Sources:* p.7 *Applied Linguistics Journal*, Oxford University Press.

Artwork supplied by Oxford Designers and Illustrators on pages: xv, 7, 8, 66, 70, 72,
90, 99, and 138.

*Although every effort has been made to trace and contact copyright holders before
publication, this has not been possible in some cases. We apologise for any apparent
infringement of copyright and, if notified, the publisher will be pleased to rectify any
errors or omissions at the earliest possible opportunity.*

CONTENTS

ACKNOWLEDGEMENTS

The authors would both like to thank our editors, Keith Layfield and Anna Cowper, for their great skill, enthusiasm, and patience. We would also like to thank Alan Carver in Orgiva for providing a peaceful haven and our colleague Richard Badger for his wisdom and friendship.

Goodith would like to thank the following for all their advice and help: Christopher Taylor, Peter Carlill, Kirsten Thompson (Leeds University); Kevin Balchin, Sarn Rich, Carol Wild, Glenis Lambert (Canterbury Christ Church University); and Stephen Bax (Bedfordshire University).

Aisha would like to thank the School of Education at the University of Leeds, and colleagues Penelope Robinson, Alice Deignan, Sue Pearson, and Gary Chambers for their support. I would also like to thank John Threlfall for his part in our work on assessment. Thank you also to Kalyan Chattopadhayay for his encouragement, and to Gilli, Lillian, Gemma, and Nick – you know why! Particular thanks to my family, especially to my husband, Keith, for being there.

LIST OF ACRONYMS

CALL	computer assisted language learning
CAT	computer adaptive testing
CLIL	content and language integrated learning
CMC	computer-mediated communication
CoP	community of practice
EAP	English for academic purposes
ESOL	English for speakers of other languages
ICT	information and communications technology
IELTS	International English Language Testing System
IWB	interactive white board
L1	first language
L2	second language
LMS	learning management system
PDA	personal digital assistant
PLP	personal learning pathway
SMS	short message service
TELL	technology enhanced language learning
TOEFL	Test of English as a Foreign Language
VLE	virtual learning environment

INTRODUCTION

The last few decades have seen an exponential growth in the use of technology for language learning and teaching purposes. Students use technology in their daily lives outside the classroom; educational institutions feel the pressure to invest in technology if and when they can afford it. Whilst some teachers feel immediately comfortable with using technology, others feel anxious about their ability to use it effectively in order to help their students learn, and advice about the use of technology for pedagogical purposes tends to focus either on the technical aspects of how to use particular software, or to describe interesting classroom activities. To us at least, there seems to be a dearth of reflection on how particular uses of technology relate to theories and practices of language learning, how they change contexts for learning, and how they affect language use.

This book attempts to bring together theory and practice with regard to using technology in the teaching of languages, particularly English. We feel that, all too often, books about technology focus on the practical aspects of what you can do with particular tools, yet the technology is transient and the specific resources available today will be outdated tomorrow. However, if teachers have an understanding of the theoretical underpinnings and issues involved in using technology with learners, any new use of technology which appears on the horizon can be integrated into teaching and learning in a principled way. In this book, we aim to provide reflection on the relationship between various uses of technology and theories of language learning. We recognize, however, that many readers may be less familiar with current technology than they would like, consequently each chapter contains practical tasks to illustrate different uses of technology and to help readers to become familiar with some currently useful tools. These reflective practitioner tasks often direct the reader to software and websites, the full references for which can be found on the website that accompanies this book, located at www.oup.com/elt/teacher/tell. At the end of each chapter there are suggestions for further reading.

Overall, we have chosen to focus on **language skills**, and include considerations of **syntax** and **lexis** within our discussion of those skills. We recognize the importance of focusing on grammar and vocabulary in language teaching and also that there are technological tools that can be extremely useful, for example corpus and concordancing tools like the British National Corpus (http://www.natcorp.ox.ac.uk/). Such tools search extremely large databases of language and can be used by learners to understand how lexical items occur in natural language contexts. However, we believe that technology radically changes the nature of the language skills (speaking, listening, reading, and writing) which learners use and need, so we have decided to emphasize this area in particular. For example, reading on screen is not the same as reading paper texts, and we now have a huge range of different screens for reading, from 'traditional' computers to mobile phones, **e-ink** readers, and tablets. In addition, digital texts differ greatly from paper texts. Paper text is static and consists of words with occasional images, whereas digital texts are **multimodal**, fluid, and combine words with images, video, and sound. There is an interaction and overlap between the different aspects of multimodal texts and this has implications for how learners read and make sense of digital documents.

How this book is organized

Chapter 1 presents an overview of the theories that underpin learning and language learning with technology. We consider issues such as the role of technology in the process of learning and situate technology enhanced language learning (**TELL**) in its historical context. We conclude this chapter with a new model that moves from computer assisted language learning (**CALL**) to TELL.

In Chapter 2, we move on to consider how technology provides new environments for language use and how this changes both the ways in which we communicate with each other and the language that we use. We also discuss some of the challenges that technologically-based language change poses for teachers, such as the conundrum about whether 'txt spk' should be considered as inaccurate use of language, or whether these words, abbreviations, and 'emoticons' are legitimate new linguistic forms that should be included in the language curriculum.

Chapter 3 covers speaking and listening skills. We look at the ways in which technology can provide opportunities for learners to practice oral language and how sometimes that practice may be in written form using text chat. We also consider the range of listening and speaking materials and tools available to learners and how these can be exploited effectively. However, digital tools are not only about taking and using what already exists; amongst the most powerful aspects of technology is the possibility for learners to create materials and practise speaking and listening in virtual spaces.

Chapter 4 is about reading. In addition to differences between traditional and **digital text**, we consider the problems facing learners when learning to read in a new language and the ways in which technological tools can be used to support them to develop the skills they need.

In Chapter 5, we move on to writing. In addition to asking how technology affects the processes and contexts of writing, we consider different approaches to teaching **L2** writing (**genre**, product, process). We also explore some of the tools that can support writing and the ways in which learners can use technology to publish their written work to new audiences.

In Chapter 6, we consider multimodality, especially the use of visual materials for language learning and teaching. We discuss the role of images in multimodal texts and examine how visual materials can be used to support language learning; for example, Figure 0.1 shows a 'word cloud' from Chapter 6 made with a tool called Wordle. The image provides an instant overview of the chapter content in a way that an abstract or summary consisting solely of words cannot do, and makes connections between words which go beyond the linear.

Figure 0.1 Word cloud of vocabulary from Chapter 6 (created from www.wordle.net)

Chapter 7 focuses on study skills and **EAP**. Digital technologies have had considerable impact on the way that students are expected to work, particularly in higher education, where they need to find materials on virtual learning environments **(VLEs)**, prepare and deliver presentations, submit assignments online, and work collaboratively using tools such as **wikis**. We also consider issues that students face such as managing their reading and referencing, evaluating information sources, or avoiding **plagiarism**, and look at some tools that may be helpful.

In Chapter 8, we consider young learners, particularly primary school children. Young learners are often described as 'digital natives' (an assumption that we discuss in Chapter 2) and in this chapter we examine the role of technology in the lives and education of children and in the school curriculum. We also consider the role of foreign languages in primary school and the tasks explore some ways that technology may be used to engage and support young learners. It is in this chapter that we discuss tactile interfaces (for example, **touchscreen** tablets) because, although these affect all users, we feel they have particular impact on the education of children.

Chapter 9 is about assessment. We examine the different reasons for assessing learners, analyse the different phases of the assessment processes, and consider how technology may be used within each phase. We also think about the different ways in which learners may be assessed, both summative and formative, and discuss both the benefits and potential drawbacks of technology-enhanced assessment.

Chapter 10 looks at technology use from the teacher's perspective, and considers the kinds of skills which teachers need to develop in order to use technology effectively with learners. We consider institutional uses of technology, such as VLEs, interactive whiteboards, and electronic voting systems, and we also discuss how teachers can be empowered to develop personal learning environments (PLEs), which may suit their own teaching style better. We also discuss how teachers can make use of new technology for their own professional development.

In Chapter 11, we discuss choosing and using TELL materials. We explore the ways in which TELL may be incorporated into an existing syllabus and how coursebook materials may be enhanced by technology. We also consider criteria for the selection of existing TELL resources or for designing your own and think about technology in the context of learner independence: technology gives learners more choice and influence over what they learn outside the classroom and this may have an impact on classroom teaching.

The final chapter, Chapter 12, summarises the main themes of the book and attempts to think about the future. We say 'attempts' because our crystal ball is not digitally enhanced and predicting the future of technology is extremely difficult as the opening quotation to Chapter 12 demonstrates. However, we hope that whatever new technological tools and resources the future brings, the theories and issues that we have presented throughout the book will help teachers to make effective use of them.

1

LEARNING

Learning without thought is labour lost; thought
without learning is perilous.
CONFUCIUS, philosopher

Change is the end result of all true learning.
LEO BUSCAGLIA, writer

Aims

In this chapter, we will try to give you some answers to the following questions:
- What role(s) does technology play in learning?
- What is digital competence?
- What are the differences between CALL and TELL?

Introduction

In this chapter, we look at theories underpinning approaches to learning with
technology, in particular, language learning and technology. We look at historical
models of computer assisted language learning and consider the various roles
that technology can play in learning in relation to theories of learning. We also
consider the notion of digital competence and its relationship to **communicative
competence** and conclude with an overview of how computer assisted language
learning has transformed into technology enhanced language learning.

Computer assisted language learning

In the year 2000, Warschauer and Kern argued that computer assisted language
learning (CALL) developed in three phases, which they aligned with dominant
paradigms of language learning and technology. Warschauer considered that there
were parallels between a changing view of language (leading to change in teaching
approaches) and the development of educational technology. Warschauer's model
can be critiqued (notably by Bax 2003) because it portrays development as linear,
each stage apparently superseded by the next. Bax's alternative model, which refers
to 'approaches to CALL' rather than phases, includes elements that Warschauer

does not consider, such as the location of computers (in the lab, in the classroom, 'in every pocket'), the role of the teacher, the type of activity, and the type of feedback provided within each approach.

Warschauer believed that the first phase consisted of 'structural CALL' which was based on a view of language as a formal system of structures (grammar, **phonology**, etc.) and focused on drill and practice methods to achieve accuracy (Castagnaro 2006). This echoes the grammar translation and audio-lingual approaches to teaching language which were popular at a particular time. Bax (2003) essentially concurred, but called this approach 'restricted CALL' because the types of questions, tasks, responses, and feedback tend to be closed, restricted to whatever is programmed into the system. Bax further argued that this approach is largely a historical artefact that is now rarely used. We would argue that this was not true in 2003 and is even less true now with the concurrent (but coincidental) developments in **Assessment for Learning** (AfL) and smartphones, given that many learning **apps** feature 'closed' tasks.

The second phase in Warschauer's model was called 'communicative CALL', with an underpinning view that knowledge about language is constructed in the learner's mind (rather than existing as an external system of rules) and with a dominant methodology of **communicative language teaching** (CLT). Bax (2003:18) suggests that this phase had, in fact, little to do with real communication or CLT. He also argues that CLT has not been superseded as an approach to language teaching (which the third phase of Warschauer's model appears to suggest). Bax proposed instead an approach called 'open CALL' which he argued had persisted from its introduction in the 1990s to 'today' (i.e. 2003). Open CALL, like communicative CALL, includes open-ended interactions with both computers and, occasionally, with other users.

The third aspect of the respective models is called 'integrated' by Bax and 'integrative' by Warschauer, but although these terms appear similar, they do not have the same meanings in the model. Warschauer talks about '**multimedia** and the internet' – applications that, in the earlier 21st century, were still tied to desk-based computers, whereas Bax foresees devices that are 'very different in shape and size from their current manifestations' (p23). Bax argues that 'integrated CALL' will be achieved when the technology is fully normalized (see below) and 'CALL' is no longer a meaningful construct because technology is an inseparable part of everyday life and teaching. In some respects, we could argue that we have reached Bax's third stage in that digital devices are very much a part of everyday life. However, in teaching, technology is still somewhat disruptive and there are many teachers who feel that educational technology is still an area that they need to learn. Indeed, the very existence of this book indicates that technology is still seen as something that is different from ordinary teaching and learning.

The concept of 'normalization' is central to Bax's argument with regard to 'integrated CALL', and is revisited in Bax (2011). Bax argues that when new technology is introduced, people react strongly, whether with alarm or with awe, and the new technology is seen as having the power to transform life as we know it. Indeed, exactly those reactions met the introduction of the Apple iPad (see Johnson 2010 and Richmond 2012). Woolgar (2002) called these extreme reactions **'cyberbole'** and we shall return to this in Chapter 12. However, as Bax says, as we become accustomed to something new, the technology itself recedes and becomes simply a normal part of the way that we do things. He argues (as does Woolgar) that social and cultural factors influence, even determine, the process of normalization. However, this is not a one-way process: technology also influences socio-cultural change, albeit incrementally rather than with the transformational leaps that pundits tend to predict. We believe, following the work of theorists such as Cole and Engeström (1993) and Nardi (1996), that technology needs to be seen within the context of the **activity system** that it mediates. Activity is carried out by people (subjects) working towards ends (objects) and mediated by tools within the context of culture, social rules, and of sharing of workload. None of these elements exist in isolation and a change in any one element will have an impact on the others. Thus, the introduction of new tools may affect, for example, the way that work is shared amongst the participants in the activity system. On the other hand, a change in participants may require a new kind of **mediational tool**. We consider these matters in later chapters; for example, in Chapter 2, we look at new cultural practices that stem from the introduction of new communications tools and in Chapter 7, we consider the impact of new types of students on academic practices.

Tutor, tutee, tool …?

An old but still useful model of the roles that technology can play in learning was offered by Taylor in 1980: he argued that the computer could play one of three principal roles in learning – tutor, tutee, or tool. In the 'tutor' role, the computer teaches the learner; typical examples are adaptive tutoring systems (discussed in Chapter 9) or drill-and-practice applications. The principle is that the knowledge resides in the machine, from where it is delivered to the learner in small chunks with frequent reinforcement. The underlying learning theory is the behaviourist paradigm which originates in the work of psychologists such as Skinner (see Skinner 1974 and Child 2004).

Although we now understand that there is more to learning a language than simply knowing vocabulary and the rules of grammar, drill-and-practice programs still have a place; for example, learners can use drill-and-practice programs for independent revision and learners often feel secure and reassured by drill-and-practice activities. When these types of software are available for mobile use (for example as smartphone apps), learners can use them independently in short blocks of time, for example when waiting for a bus. As we will explain in later chapters, there are several authoring programs which teachers (and learners) can use to create interactive exercises of various kinds, including multiple-choice, short answer questions, gap-filling, and so on. **Authoring software** allows teachers to create a bank of activities which learners can access either from home or in study centres. The activities are reusable and do not need to be stored or reproduced in physical form. Some can provide rapid formative feedback to the tutor. In some cases, a tutoring system can be designed so that it enables personalized differentiation between learners thereby allowing each learner to follow an individualized learning pathway. In addition, some authoring tools are suitable for students to use to create activities and this, whilst providing resources for later 'computer as tutor' tasks, starts to move the technology into the role of 'tutee'.

In the 'tutee' role, the learner teaches the computer. The principle is that the learner constructs knowledge, often through trial and error, by teaching the computer. This is based on the constructivist paradigm which stems from the work of Piaget, who argued that learners have to construct knowledge themselves through experience and through a process of accommodation and assimilation. Papert (1993) developed this theory, arguing that the learning experience is strongest when learners are involved in *making*. Papert's view is that knowledge is constructed more effectively when learners are forced to articulate their knowledge. This might be achieved by creating a product or it might come about through learners being asked to teach or explain to others.

This paradigm of learning fits in well with theories of language learning through interaction. Indeed, when Papert proposed using a programming language called 'Logo' to help children learn geometry, he did so by comparing the learning of maths to learning language. He argued that if children were, in effect, placed in a world called 'Mathland' in which the only way to talk to the local inhabitant (a physical **device** called a 'turtle' or an onscreen character representing the turtle) was through its own language (Logo), they would be forced to learn the language through the communication. When programming turtles with Logo, children have to use the language to teach the turtle to draw shapes and this forces them to think about, build, and articulate their knowledge of geometry.

Although Papert argued for children learning to program computers, this is not the only way in which technology can provide opportunities for learners to make, build, and articulate. Authoring software of the type described above need not be used only by teachers; it can be far more powerful when used by learners to create activities for each other. Furthermore, learners can make videos or audio material and can publish their work through the internet, where they can reach a wider audience than their own classrooms, as we show in Chapter 6. Similarly, learners can use other web-based media, such as blogs, to articulate and publish their work. Presentations, animations, and slideshows made by learners can also be published online. This is perhaps one of the strongest arguments for using technology; it makes it easy for learners to make, build, and articulate – developing their knowledge in the process.

Taylor's third role is computer as 'tool'. This is a broad role that applies to any context in which technology is the means by which a task is achieved. There is no assumption either that the computer will teach or that the computer needs to be taught. Examples of technology used in the role of 'tool' include using a word-processing program to write an essay or editing-software to create a video. It is the act of writing or editing that facilitates the learning rather than the use of technology. However, since Taylor developed his theory of roles, the internet and smartphones have arrived and the role of tool has been extended into one that mediates communication and interactions between people. This leads on to '**social-constructivism**', a theory of learning that has obvious parallels with and benefits for language teaching. This comes primarily from the work of Vygotsky (1978) who argued that learning is constructed first through social interaction and then on the individual plane. Vygotsky further argued that learning takes place within the '**zone of proximal development**' (ZPD), i.e. the gap between what a learner already knows or can do and what the learner can achieve when working in collaboration with someone who is a little more capable (**more able peer**). Vygotsky reasoned that collaboration that allows learning to take place within the ZPD provides a structure that supports the learner whilst the knowledge is being built. Wood et al. (1976) coined the useful term 'scaffolding' to describe this process. Papert argued, by the way, that the Logo turtle is, in effect, a form of scaffolding through collaboration with the turtle. In this case, the child who is programming is the 'more able peer'. This demonstrates that collaboration benefits both partners: the more able peer gains through externalizing and articulating knowledge, whilst the other party gains from the support that the more able peer provides.

Bruner (1978) noted a similar **scaffolding** effect in the talk of mothers and children and he called it the 'communicative ratchet'. This is when the adult carer rephrases the child's words in a way that models more complex language and in so doing supports the child's linguistic development. For children, language develops primarily through social interaction with, as Bruner noted, support from more able speakers. Social-constructivism can also be seen as the foundation of communicative approaches to language learning which rely on learners engaging in activities which force them to talk to each other. Lightbown and Spada (2013) discuss social-constructivist theory in relation to language learning theories, such as Krashen's concept of 'i+1' (Krashen 1997). This theory claims that language learners need to receive **input** (language that they hear or read) at a slightly higher level than they can produce (as in Bruner's 'communicative ratchet') and this appears very similar to the notion of ZPD. Lightbown and Spada explain, however, that the ZPD is a way of looking at the (psychological) readiness to learn whereas **i+1** is about the environment in which the learning takes place.

'Environment' is one of two further roles suggested by Stevenson (2008), the other being technology as 'resource'. As we explain in Chapter 2, digital technologies have created new contexts in which people can engage in shared activity and build community. Two concepts of community are useful here: '**communities of practice**' (CoPs) and 'discourse communities'. Communities of practice come from the work of Lave and Wenger (1991) who looked at learning that is situated in practice, for example, tailors or midwives. When people first become members of a CoP, they learn by observing from the periphery and gradually their participation in the community increases as they develop expertise. In a conventional classroom, there is no true CoP, as Gee (2005) points out, because there is no body of expert members at the heart of the learner community in the classroom. However, digital networks (internet communities, social networks, online games) offer genuine CoPs to which learners may become 'apprentices' and learn through 'lurking' on the fringes of discourse, gradually becoming active participants as their confidence and expertise develop. A CoP is also likely to be a 'discourse community' (Swales, 1990) as shared language – both lexis and **genre** – is one of the factors that holds the community together. However, a CoP will also have some elements of common practice that go beyond discourse. An example of this might be online game players where there is both shared discourse and also shared knowledge of the rules and conventions of the game. Over time, a new player will learn how players behave, develop skill in the tactics of the game, and will also become familiar with the specific linguistic aspects of the game and the player community. It might also be argued that **social networking** sites are also types of CoP, but it is probably more accurate to see these as what Gee (2005) calls **'affinity spaces'** – physical or virtual places in which people develop relationships and discourse communities based on shared interests. In Chapter 2, we expand on language and learning in digital communities.

Socio-cultural theories of learning argue that learning occurs more effectively when people are working together. A more recent development is **'connectivism'** (Siemens, 2005), which is described as 'a learning theory for the digital age' To some extent, connectivism brings together the technological roles that Taylor described in 1980. Siemens argues that learning occurs through engagement with a diversity of ideas and opinions and that knowledge may reside in machines. In some ways, this can be related to Taylor's 'computer as tutor' role, in which the machine teaches the learner, but Siemens is also referring to the ways in which people use machines to store knowledge. The internet provides a vast repository of knowledge (albeit of variable quality) and tends to be the first resort of twenty-first century information seekers. Even academics nowadays are likely to begin work on a literature review by searching electronic databases. This is an example of technology as resource. Stevenson provides other examples of technology as resource, such as teachers using PowerPoint or interactive whiteboards for teaching.

Machines also, as Siemens points out, provide mechanisms for humans to share and generate knowledge. Connectivist theory also draws on the concept of **'rhizomatic knowledge'** (Cormier 2008, Deleuze and Guatarri 1987), which argues that knowledge is not something which exists in its own right, independent of people (platonic knowledge), but is rather located in the minds of many individuals and that new ideas are constructed through shared thinking and conversations. This resonates with the concept of language as a socio-cognitive construct. A living language is not fixed (despite the best efforts of bodies such as the *Académie Française*), but is in a constant state of change. New lexical and grammatical constructs appear all the time and distribute themselves through the population in the same way as a rhizomatic plant moves through the soil. Technology assists with this process, as writers such as Crystal (2010) demonstrate. Not only does technology lead to the need for and development of new words, for example, **'blog'**, 'internet', **'laptop'** but it also facilitates the rapid spread of new language. Increasingly, technology mediates human interactions (not all, obviously) and these interactions make use of different language forms, depending on the media. Crystal (2010) cites examples of **instant messaging** and of mobile phone **text messaging**. These make use of abbreviations and lexical items that incorporate letters, numbers, and punctuation (for example, 'l8' meaning 'late' in English, or 'a2' meaning *adios* in Spanish). These new language forms are both created by and spread, rhizomatically, through the use of technology. We consider this further in Chapter 2.

Communicative and digital competence

As so much of our communication and interaction now occur within digital environments, learners need not only to be able to use language appropriately, but also to manage the technology. Simpson (2005) talked about 'electronic communicative competence' whilst Walker (2007), taking a view that technology is not only about communication, proposed a model of 'ICT competence' which we now prefer to consider 'digital competence'.

Both stem from the model of communicative competence, shown in Figure 1.1 and created by Canale and Swain (1980). The model consists of four elements:

- Linguistic competence means knowing how the language works, being able to fit together sounds to make words, and putting words into grammatical sentences
- Sociolinguistic competence is about understanding how language is used in context – knowing what words and phrases are appropriate in any particular setting to achieve a desired communicative purpose
- Discourse competence is the ability to create and use larger pieces of language to create texts or conduct conversations
- Strategic competence is the ability to manage and navigate communication to repair communication breakdowns, and work around unfamiliar areas of language.

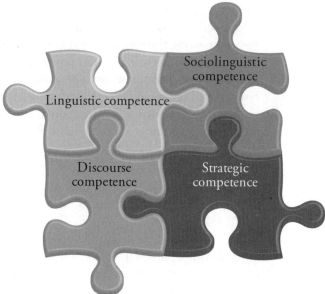

Figure 1.1 Communicative competence

We believe that there is a parallel digital competence which is shown in Figure 1.2.

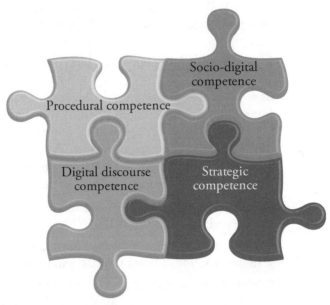

Figure 1. 2 Digital competence

The model of digital competence also consists of four elements:

- Procedural competence: the ability to manipulate the technology in terms of both **hardware** and applications. In other words, procedural competence is about knowing how to use the technology – how to switch it on, which buttons to click, and so on. This could be seen as the 'basic skill' of digital competence and it is certainly the case that many IT training courses focus on this aspect of competence. This is similar to the traditional view that to know a language means knowing the grammar and vocabulary and that these can be taught through methods such as **grammar-translation**. However, just as we now recognize that communicative competence requires more than knowledge of the syntactic, phonological, and lexical 'nuts and bolts', we also need to understand that digital competence requires understanding of how, when, and why to use technologies and how to compensate for gaps in knowledge and skills.

- **Socio-digital competence:** understanding what is appropriate to use in different social contexts and knowledge domains, in terms of both technology and language. An example of socio-digital competence is deciding whether it is appropriate to use **social media**, such as Facebook, for business communication and if so, how it should be used. There is no one-size-fits-all answer to that question; it depends on the nature of the business, the relationships with the other parties in the communication event, and the purpose of the communication. Furthermore, where procedural competence includes knowing what needs to be done in order to control **privacy settings**, socio-digital competence includes knowing what settings are appropriate to business contexts and applying them appropriately. The definition of socio-digital competence shows how technological competence and communicative competence overlap.

An important aspect of socio-digital competence is the understanding of how technology impacts upon language, including the possible creation of new genres, and what types of language are appropriate to use for different audiences in various digital contexts (for example, Crystal 2006).

- Digital discourse competence: the ability to manage an extended task, possibly using several applications and/or types of equipment. An example of digital discourse competence would be the ability to record, edit, and publish a video or to write a blog post with photographs. The task will require a range of skills and technical knowledge. Although digital discourse competence refers to the use of technology for extended tasks, these tasks will invariably require communicative discourse competence as well. When writing the text of this book, for example, we needed digital discourse competence in order to edit the text, make headings, and to create and insert images and diagrams, but we also needed communicative discourse competence in order to structure the text, create paragraphs, and sequence and link ideas using appropriate language forms for each section.

- Strategic competence: the ability to repair problems and work around the gaps in technological knowledge and skills. This does not mean possession of advanced **ICT** skills, but rather the ability to think of alternative routes and options. In order to complete tasks and to communicate effectively using technology, people need to be able to repair both communicative and digital problems. In the digital dimension, this would include being able to switch channels, contacting someone by email or social networking if he or she is not answering the phone, rescuing a deleted document, or knowing how to deal with disruptive online interactions such as **'flaming'** (heated exchanges in online settings, such as email groups or social networks).

For language teachers who want to make use of technology for and with learners, an understanding of digital competence is important because it provides a mechanism for diagnosing, understanding, and repairing the digital needs of learners. Learners who may be procedurally competent may lack the socio-digital competence necessary to choose appropriate tools and language for communicating in digital contexts.

From CALL to TELL

Drawing together the models and theories in this chapter, we feel that Warschauer's model can be combined with others to show how technology has been and is being used to support language learning. We see a move from computer-assisted language learning to 'technology enhanced language learning' (TELL) and also prefer to use Bax's notion of 'approach', rather than 'phase', because we understand that approaches may co-exist, even though the tools may change. One of the main differences between CALL and TELL is that we see technology not as assisting language learning, but as part of the environment in which language exists and is used. As we will go on to explain in Chapter 2, technology provides new contexts as well as new tools for communication. TELL, of course, includes a wider range of devices than 'computer', in particular, phones, game **consoles**, and tablets. We feel that, in many ways, the devices we might want to use in TELL are largely normalized in daily life, albeit not in the language classroom, although there is always the potential for something new, surprising, and exciting to come along.

The table below provides an overview of the different phases of CALL and TELL and how they relate to different approaches to learning and to language psychology.

Approach	Structural/ restricted CALL	Communicative CALL Open CALL	Integrative CALL	TELL
Technology	From mainframe to mobile	PCs	Multimedia, internet	Mobile devices, tablets, multiplayer games, virtual worlds
English-teaching paradigm	Grammar-translation and **audio-lingual**	Communicative language teaching	Content-based ESP/EAP	Communication, interaction
View of language	Structural (a formal structural system)	Cognitive (a mentally constructed system)	Socio-cognitive (developed in social interaction)	Structural, cognitive, socio-cognitive, adaptable
Principal use of technology	Drill and practice	Communicative exercises	Authentic discourse	Normalized
Principal objective	Accuracy	Fluency	Agency	Autonomy within community
View of learning	Behaviourism	Constructivism	Social constructivism/ situated learning	Connectivism
Role of technology	Tutor	Tutee	Mediational tool	Environment, resource

Table 1.1 From CALL to TELL

Summary

In this chapter, we have considered a range of theories about how learning takes place in relation to the roles that technology can play in supporting learning. We have also considered how the role of computers and technology in language learning has changed, whilst noting that 'old' approaches still have validity. Indeed, as the cycles of 'techno-fashion' change, older approaches may take on new roles just as 'drill and practice' applications have moved from the mainframe in the classroom to the mobile phone at the bus stop. However, in the 21st century, technology is inextricably linked with communication and so, in the next chapter, we look more deeply at the role and impact of technology in communication.

Further reading

Ellis, R. 2008. *The study of second language acquisition.* Oxford: Oxford University Press.

Holmes, B. and **J. Gardner.** 2006. *e-Learning: concepts and practice.* London: Sage.

Lightbown, P.M. and **N. Spada.** 2013. *How Languages are Learned* (4th edn.). Oxford: Oxford University Press.

2

COMMUNICATION

Talk is by far the most accessible of pleasures. It costs nothing in money,
it is all profit, it completes our education, founds and fosters our friendships,
and can be enjoyed at any age and in almost any state of health.
ROBERT LOUIS STEVENSON, writer

Aims

In this chapter, we will try to give you some answers to the following questions:

- How do digital technologies create new spaces and purposes for communication?
- What are the effects of digital communications on language?
- How do new types of hardware affect our understanding and use of communications technology?
- What might the implications be for language learning?

Introduction

In Chapter 1, we discussed the different ways in which the complex relationship between technology, learning, and language learning has been viewed. We demonstrated how that relationship is continually evolving as beliefs about learning and language learning change, and the possibilities of technology expand. The authors hope that our enthusiasm for technology was evident as a background to that discussion, because we believe that using technology in ways which genuinely support language learning enables learners to become more independent, collaborative, and engaged.

So if Chapter 1 focused on *how* technology can support and enhance language learning, Chapter 2 focuses on *what* language can be learnt, that is, the kinds of language which can be learnt through using technology in its various forms. This is an important question to consider, because although technology enables us to communicate with each other in many of the traditional **genres** we were accustomed to before the internet, such as reading newspapers online, or talking to family members via Skype, it has also created new types of communication such as **tweeting** about a television programme whilst watching it. We can communicate not only in new ways, but also with different people, people that we would never have encountered in the pre-digital world. These new ways of communicating are still developing, and the language use connected with them is often unstable. Crystal (2010) prefers not to call them 'genres' for this very reason, and instead refers to examples of language use on the internet as **'outputs'**. We will be discussing some of the particular effects of new technological possibilities on the language which students need to produce and understand in later chapters, but in this chapter we would like to take a more general view of the ways in which technology both constrains and facilitates communication.

The first part of this chapter explores the ideas of communication and of context. We consider reasons for communication and how purpose, together with context, decide exactly how communication will take place. The next section looks more closely at digital contexts for communication. We discuss the 'traditional' world-wide web (sometimes known as **Web 1.0**) and the contributory web (**Web 2.0**) in which content is created by users rather than providers. We then go on to consider the question of 'digital natives' versus 'digital immigrants' before thinking about the difference that recent changes in **hardware** (from desk/laptop computers to phones and tablets) might make to our understanding and use of communications technologies. The chapter concludes with some implications for teachers and for learning and teaching.

Communication and context

Although some people may learn languages simply for love of or interest in the language itself, (for example, Gilbert 2006) most of us learn languages (or are made to learn them at school) with the ultimate goal of being able to communicate with other speakers or readers of that language. Communication always has a purpose; generally it starts with something that we want to say or that we want to know. Reasons for communication include exchanging information, ideas, meeting needs, and self-expression. Sometimes communication is also forced upon us, as, for example, being required to write or speak about something as part of a course of study or for an examination. Furthermore, any act of communication involves (at least) two parties: speaker or writer and listener or reader. The audience may be known or unknown, but there has to be one in order for communication to have a purpose. On occasions, as with a personal diary, the writer and reader may be the same person; in these cases the communication is purely to oneself, to one's future self, or to an imaginary audience. Anne Frank's diary, for example, was not written for a public audience. It was a private communication and yet she started all entries as to a fictitious friend, 'Kitty'.

It may appear that there is something new in the fact that internet communication is often received by a wide and unknown audience, but communicating to an 'imagined' audience has gone on for centuries using other media, particularly print. The difference with new technology is that publication is now available to everyone and does not have to be moderated by an editor, whereas in the pre-internet age, publication of communications was available to only a small minority of people and usually subject to an approval process before being made public. Nowadays, anyone can produce a blog, or even publish an **ebook** which they might then sell through an online distributor such as iTunes or Amazon.

Communication involves more than simply language. Bishop (1998) and Norbury et al. (2004) provide a useful outline in the 'children's communication checklist' (CCC), intended for describing the communicative abilities of children. The CCC is widely used for assessing children with language or communication disorders as it allows professionals to evaluate even the most basic forms of communication. It has two main domains: language (consisting of speech, **syntax**, **semantics**, and **coherence**) and **pragmatics** (initiation, stereotypical language context, nonverbal communication, social relations, and interests). The language elements of the CCC are familiar to language teachers: the ability to produce speech with appropriate and understandable sounds; the ability to generate grammatically correct and meaningful utterances; and the ability to string ideas together in a way that makes sense (rather than items which have no connection to each other). Some of the pragmatic elements are probably not so relevant here. For example 'initiation' refers to the ability to instigate communication appropriately, something which can be difficult for people with autism, whilst 'interests' refers to having a very narrow but focused range of interests which again, is a symptom of autism. However, non-verbal communication, social relations, and context are all important when thinking about the impact of digital technologies on language because they may take rather different forms in digital communication from what we are used to in some older kinds of communication.

Communication is always situated: that means that it occurs within a cultural framework and that the users (speakers/listeners/writers/readers) have identifiable roles, relationships, beliefs, aims, and intentions. Saville-Troike (1982) said that a 'communicative event' involved a number of features: a type of event (such as a joke or a lecture); a topic and purpose; a setting (which included location, time, season, and physical aspects of the location); participants (including their age, status, and relationship to each other); message form and content; and rules for interaction with norms of interpretation. All these features determine how we understand and take part in communicative events. We can also see how they might need to be adapted when talking about digital communication, which has new event types where we often can't see any physical setting or have much idea about who the other participants are. These factors, for example, make online dating a risky business: the young, handsome doctor from London (with photo) may not be who he is pretending to be. But the other participants in the **communicative event** (whether known or unknown) and other features of the event which we assume to be the case will still determine our choice of language in digital communication, whether it be for **lexis**, structural complexity, formality, or speed of delivery of spoken language, etc.

However, when new technologies become part of our range of communications options, additional dimensions become significant. For example, digital communication often includes multimodal elements, such as images or sound, even in informal communication events, such as text messages or social network posts. Moreover, a conversation may begin using one medium and continue in another. For example, this morning a colleague asked one of us 'How is your washing machine?' a response to a post made on Facebook about a domestic disaster. Kenning (2006) argues that features of modern communication include changes in the role of space – participants may be geographically separated from each other (perhaps in another room but possibly another continent); time – there may be an extended delay between something being said (or written) and heard (or read); 'range of symbolic cues', for example, face-to-face conversation includes gestures and facial expression whereas these are absent in text chats (but replaced by emoticons); interactivity – the extent to which hearers/readers can respond even with 'I'm listening' signals such as 'hmm'; and 'action orientation', the extent to which communication is addressed to a specific (known) or general (imagined) audience. For example, a blog may be written for a general, unknown readership or it may be written for an audience that is primarily composed of family and friends. These features do not exist solely in digitally mediated communication; they are all a part of all modern communication events.

In the digital age, the concept of 'setting' needs to be extended because technology has created 'virtual' settings that do not exist in the physical world. We do not merely inhabit places, we construct them; no setting, even a physical one, exists without our giving it meaning and significance. Even an environment which might be perceived as wholly natural depends, in its significance for communication, on the meanings attached to it by human beings. These meanings will vary according to culture and according to the activities that take place in the environment. Gee (2006) talks about **'semiotic social spaces'**, by which he means places (real or virtual) where people interact (social) and to which people ascribe meaning (semiotic). Gee points out that these spaces may be real, in the physical sense, or they may be virtual. Many types of virtual social semiotic spaces are detailed later in the chapter and the book but they include social networking sites such as Facebook; online role playing games such as World of Warcraft; virtual learning environments such as Moodle; **web forums** and discussion boards, and also chat rooms. All of these are online spaces in which people meet, create meaning, and develop relationships, and although they are not physical settings, they affect the language which is used within them.

Emotion

One aspect of the human condition which is important in communication but which is often ignored is emotion. The emotional state of the parties engaged in a communicative event affects how communication is both delivered and received. Some forms of communication are 'supposed' to be emotion free, for example, academic writing (Gee and Hayes 2011), and the way that we interpret such texts is coloured by the assumption that the communicator is objective and does not have personal feelings or beliefs regarding the content. In other forms of communication, emotion is acceptable, or even expected (for example, a declaration of love should always demonstrate emotion), but the manner and extent of expressing emotion in communication is culturally determined. Language teachers tend to ignore this aspect of communication although they may obliquely address it through aspects of cross-cultural communication, such as politeness and semiotic gestures (for example, whether a thumbs-up gesture signifies approval or insult). The emotional/affective aspects of communication are important in digital contexts, as we will explain in the next section.

Digital contexts and communication

Digital technologies not only create new environments in which language use occurs, they also bring together interlocutors who might not otherwise have opportunities to interact. It can also be argued that digital contexts create new communicative purposes; for example, **microblogging** is a communicative act that simply did not exist before the advent of Twitter and Facebook.

Whilst digital interaction provides rich resources for language learners, it also means that new linguistic cultures have developed in terms of both language use and cultural behaviours. There is a level of anonymity in some forms of communication which is new to most people (for example, the nearest 'old technology' equivalent for responding publically to what someone wrote was probably a newspaper letters page). As Gee and Hayes (2011: 36) point out, digital interaction creates 'strong weak ties' between people: relationships in which people engage frequently with each other online and may feel that they 'know' each other well over a very short space of time, although they have never met in person. This type of relationship is found in virtual 'social semiotic spaces', such as message boards and online games, and a sense of closeness can develop extremely rapidly. Whilst there are benefits to these 'strong weak ties' which can lead to 'real-life' assistance in times of need, these relationships can also break down frighteningly quickly. Any message board community or email list of long standing will have experienced 'flame wars' in which participants become extremely angry and hurl insults at each other, possibly leading to a fracturing of the community. These flame wars may begin over a simple misunderstanding of a text-based communication or may be started intentionally; there are some people (commonly known as '**trolls**') who enjoy creating friction in online communities. Whatever the initial cause, once 'flaming' begins, it tends to escalate extremely quickly. One explanation for this is that the mediating computer screen or phone screen between people has a distancing or depersonalising effect so that online participants are not fully aware of each other as real people (Wallace 1999). Another hypothesis is that people engage in flaming in order to generate effect (Alonzo and Aiken 2002). This is not inconsistent with the idea that online participants are not fully aware of each other as individuals who may be hurt. Johnson et al. (2009) suggest that reduced **social cues** may lead to more rapid escalation of anger and aggression. Whatever the root causes of flaming, the phenomenon has been around for as long as people have been communicating via computers – as the age of some of the references demonstrates. What is certainly true is that the simultaneous sense of closeness or intimacy that occurs with online relationships means that insults are particularly hurtful. We also believe that online communication tends to be literally (physically) 'in your face', because it happens on a screen which is close to your body. Online communication occurs within the spaces that Hall (1966) defined as 'intimate distance – far phase' (p111) and 'personal distance – close phase' (p113). This is our intimate personal space; the only 'real-life' people allowed to be as close to us physically as our computer or phone screens are those with whom we have extremely intimate relationships: parents, children, lovers, or spouses. If we are learning or teaching languages through **digital media**, we need to be aware of these emotional aspects of communication and develop (or help our learners to develop) strategies for coping with them.

The voice of Authority (Web 1.0)

A distinction is often drawn between older forms of digital communication, in which the content on the web is created and controlled by a site owner, and newer forms of communication, in which there is no 'authority' and in which communication is peer to peer. The former type of communication is often referred to as 'Web 1.0' and the latter as 'Web 2.0'. The differences between them are often muddier than these name tags would suggest; for instance, many online providers of Web 1.0 type information or services have facilities for instant comments by readers. However, in Web 1.0 contexts, editorial controls are very obviously and firmly in place. The content of the original text cannot be altered. Posts which contravene site rules will be removed by a moderator. On other sites, posts will be reviewed by a moderator before they are published online. The work of a **moderator** contributes to the authority and reliability of a site. Whilst comments are not as reliable, in terms of factual accuracy, as main articles, the moderation ensures that comments will not generally contain abusive language or definite lies.

All this contributes to the trustworthiness of the communication which appears on these websites. If the BBC news website or mobile **app** reports an event, then we believe that the item is true and that the event has really occurred as reported. If we first read a report of the event on a blog or web forum (a Web 2.0 phenomenon), then we may not be sure that the event has really occurred. Similarly, if we see a price and item description listed on the official website or mobile app of a store, we believe that both the price and description are factually correct. In terms of materials for language learning, teachers and learners can (more or less) rely on the accuracy of the content of such texts.

Traditionally, activities such as reading a newspaper or a travel brochure, or listening to a radio or television programme have been one-way: the content has been provided to the reader or listener, and the receiver has only limited possibilities to reply. In language classrooms, learners have studied the texts teachers have presented them with, and done the associated tasks they were given. It is worth noting that even Web 1.0, which some might think of as putting traditional forms of communication 'in new bottles', is actually more democratic than previous modes of communication and allows responses from the less powerful or knowledgeable which would not have been possible before.

Multiple voices (Web 2.0)

As we have mentioned above, 'Web 2.0' is a term commonly used for websites that consist entirely of user contributions (and users can be anybody, not just those with authority or status conferred on them in the 'real' world). The key difference between these and Web 1.0 sites is that there is no owning authority who posts editorial material, and they are entirely dependent for their existence on user contributions. Without users to build the resource, there would be no content and the site would close. Examples include video **upload** sites, such as YouTube; social networks, such as Facebook; photo-sharing; **wikis**, such as Wikipedia; blogs and '**folksonomies**' or '**social bookmarking**' where users can share, define, and **tag** links to other sites; online slideshows and presentations; and many other resources. Many of these sites are extremely popular with many thousands of users and contributors. For teachers and learners, they provide invaluable resources both for source material, such as videos, reading texts, and listening material, as well as a forum in which students can publish their work. Most of our chapters include activities that make use of Web 2.0 tools. Some of these are traditional types of activity, for example, using blogs to keep diaries, but Web 2.0 tools allow new types of activity – such as the Twitter task in Chapter 5 – and it is in Web 2.0 that learners are most likely to find new types of language. Web 2.0 tools and resources also generally allow high levels of user interactivity, so they do not only allow users to create content, but also to comment on each other's ideas and quality of work. One question which is often raised, however, concerning the communication on Web 2.0, is that there may be a lot of it, but how good, reliable, and accurate is it? Moreover, if digital technologies are producing new language phenomena, as Crystal (2011) indicates, how can users judge which of them are useful and acceptable and which are perhaps bad models, especially given the fact that much communication in English on the internet is between less expert users?

Language choice and language change in digital communication

Although English dominates the internet, most internet users use their own language most of the time. For example, in 2010 although English was the most used language on the internet with over 536 million users, Chinese was not far behind with more than 444 million users (Internet World Stats 2012). Furthermore, different geo-linguistic cultures use different websites and **social networking** tools; for example, Renren in China or Orkut in Brazil, both popular local equivalents of Facebook. However, the dominance of English means that competence in English (or lack of it) is an important aspect of the 'digital divide'. On the day of writing, Wikipedia had more than 3,907,000 articles in English, three times as many as the next most popular language, which was German with 1,383,000 articles. This means that whilst the internet is lauded as a source of knowledge about all things, a considerable part of that knowledge is not accessible to users who lack competence in English. Furthermore, the different groups of people over the internet communicating in English have differing levels of competence in the language, or might use different varieties of **World English**.

However, English itself is only part of the story. The second important language issue is the extent to which the use of digital technologies might be changing language. Simpson and Walker (forthcoming) talk about 'technolects'. The term '**technolect**' was originally coined to mean the language of a particular technical field, for example, engineering or architecture. However, Simpson and Walker argue that the way that language is commonly used in contexts such as online social networking is so distinct that it can be reasonably called a technolect. An earlier term used for online language was 'netspeak' (Crystal 2006) but much digital language is used in contexts other than 'the net' – for example mobile social networking apps or text messaging – and language choices are based on context (who, why, what) rather than medium. We believe, like Simpson and Walker, that digital technolects are now so common that language learners need to be aware of them if they are to engage in effective digital communication.

Crystal (2011) argues that in the past, changes in recorded language usually took a long time. He contends that the traditional pattern in literate cultures was that, some considerable time after appearing in speech, new lexical items would eventually appear in print. Some time after that, they would be collected by lexicographers and it thus took years for a new item to become embedded in the language. Now, according to Crystal, in the age of the internet a new word can have global reach within hours. However, Crystal does not have any answers about the mysterious factor which determines whether or not a new word becomes a 'keeper', one that becomes embedded in the language, rather than a passing fad. Crystal also argues that, given that the internet has speeded up possibilities for language change, there is actually very little actual evidence of lasting change. This, presumably, depends on what is meant by 'change' and the period of time over which this is measured. We suspect that there is a tendency to confuse internet-speak with teenage slang and assume that the way that young people use language online is 'online language'.

Crystal says that the biggest area of apparent change is vocabulary because this is a primary indicator of culture, so is always the first aspect of language to manifest change. However, he makes the case that only a few thousand internet words have come into existence as opposed to tens of thousands of technical and scientific words. Moreover, only a few of these words have penetrated everyday speech; one example cited by Crystal is 'hack' in its new, internet-age meaning of 'find an (unofficial) solution'. Some words are undoubtedly new, such as the verb 'to google', which is used generally to mean 'search on the internet' (not necessarily with the Google search engine) in the same way that 'to hoover' means to use a vacuum cleaner. Change in society creates new meanings leading to change in language, so it is not surprising that digital technologies require new or different words for people to talk about them.

One fairly clear area of language change appears to be **orthography**, but this does depend on who is addressing whom and for what purpose. In casual digital communication, it is common to see features such as abbreviations, simplified (or absent) punctuation, repetition of letters for emphasis, lower-case writing, and emoticons (use of keyboard symbols to create images indicating emotion such as :-) to suggest a smile). These features are characteristic of online orthography – part of what Crystal terms 'netspeak' – but are not found in all online communication. For example, on newspaper websites the main articles are written in what might be termed 'conventional English'. However, in the reader comments section below a main article, the texts may show the features associated with online orthography: emoticons, abbreviations, and so on.

Crystal argues that in the area of grammar, there is not much evidence of change apart from (reduced) sentence length and less subordination. This, he hypothesizes, may be partly due to the fact that certain forms of digital communication have constraints on length (for example, Twitter posts are restricted to 140 characters). We would also argue that much electronic communication is effectively speech in written form and there tends to be little subordination in spoken language. Crystal notes the 'written speech' effect when writing about syntax in blogs. He comments that many blogs have a 'stream of consciousness effect' that is rare in conventionally published texts and believes that it is in this area of direct-to-audience publishing that digital technologies may have an impact on grammar.

To illustrate the impact of digital communications technologies on language use, here are two texts about the UK television programme *Britain's Got Talent*. The first is from the Wikipedia entry and the second comes from the official Facebook page (both downloaded 10th May 2012).

Text 1 (Wikipedia)

The judges are again asked to express their imagination for the audieces *(sic)* amusement. After all acts have performed, phone lines open for a short time, while the public vote for the act they think were the best. After the votes have been counted, the act that has polled the highest number of public votes is automatically placed in the final. The judges then choose between the second and third most popular acts, with the winner of that vote also gaining a place in the final. All other acts are then eliminated from the competition. From series 5, the rules relating to judges' votes in the results show changed from previous series. In the past, the decision as to which act was sent through to the finals was made by the three judges (from which there would always be a majority). Now that there are four judges, if there is a two-way tie, then, just like The X Factor the result the act with the second highest number of votes from the public would be sent through to the finals, otherwise the judges' decision stands.

http://en.wikipedia.org/wiki/Britain's_Got_Talent.

Text 1 is clearly a written text and could be found in any written context, for example, a book, magazine, or newspaper. There is little that identifies it as an online text. Features of written language include the use of subordinate clauses, correct use of punctuation and capitalization, and formal language, including avoidance of contractions. There are some errors in the text including a spelling mistake and confusing lack of title capitalization in 'The X Factor the result'.

These errors mark the text as not having received the proof-reading that would be expected in paper-based publication (but even reputable paper publications may contain spelling mistakes or typos).

Text 2 (Facebook)

'Right result?!?' (initiating post from the show producers)

Amongst the 1,483 replies are the following:

'yawn! its just singers and dancers going through, getting very samey and boring now, they should not let as many through next year, and the magicians should have gone through tonight, now thats talent! there were amazing!'

'No it wasn't!! Poor Maliki shud hav got through :(I cried wen he didn't d poor lad x'

'sally i thought that on magicans also but when u think about it bgt is 4 the winner 2 perform 4 our queen the magicans maybe good i voted 4 them others did the queen isnt the magicans queen' (Note: the magicians were Swedish.)

http://www.facebook.com/BritainsGotTalent

Text 2 demonstrates a number of features that are characteristic of a digital technolect. The individual posts seem to be written speech, but do not read as dialogue (unlike a playscript). Several features of the text, whilst replicating features of spoken language, could only appear in written text. These include: use of multiple punctuation marks for emphasis (for example, ?!?); abbreviations ('u' to mean 'you', 'shud hav'); use of numbers for words; lack of punctuation and capitalization; and words (or symbols) to indicate facial expression, for example, 'yawn'.

One notable feature of digitally-mediated conversations is that **discourse threads** often overlap or appear out of sequence. Herring first identified this in 1999 when she noted features such as '**disrupted turn adjacency**' and 'overlapping threads'. In face-to-face or in **synchronous** audio (for example, telephone) conversations we generally know who is speaking and wait for the speaker to finish before starting the next 'turn' (although there are techniques for interrupting). In text-based **CMC** (computer-mediated communication) or in **asynchronous** audio **CMC**, however, we do not know who is speaking and so the conventional turn-taking rules break down and several conversations will overlap with speakers starting as soon as they have something to say instead of waiting for 'their turn'. Those who use CMC frequently learn to adjust to the lack of conventional coherence in the conversation. However, for novices, it can be disorientating and confusing and this is something that teachers need to bear in mind when introducing activities that make use of online communication.

Most digital communications tools have been in use for fewer than 20 years and many of the most commonly used media, such as Facebook or Twitter, are less than ten years old at the time of writing. This means that, unlike most non-digital contexts, language forms, conventions and norms are emergent and are co-created by the users of the contexts. This is a significant difference from traditional, non-digital contexts where the conventions, are widely understood and transmitted from parents to children and through the processes of formal education. We have a – more or less – common understanding of what it means, for example, to be polite, in our everyday culture in schools, workplaces, shops, homes, and so on. Although these conventions do change over time, this change has tended to be gradual and, in general, parents and teachers have usually been more competent users of the language than children and language learners. With digital technolects, however, digital language users of all kinds are at the forefront of creating the technolect. It is therefore possible that those learners who are confident and competent users of technology may have a better and more up-to-date understanding of language use in digital contexts than do their teachers. So are teachers redundant? In the next section, we argue that none of us, even individuals from the age groups who are more proficient at using technology, can ever know everything associated with language use in digital contexts.

'Digital natives' and 'digital immigrants'

The terms '**digital natives**' and '**digital immigrants**' were coined by Prensky in 2001 and have been repeated extensively, often with an assumption that this dichotomy is a fact and that all children and young people are 'digital natives' who have a natural affinity with technology. Anecdotal experience often seems to confirm this as we see, for example, YouTube videos of toddlers playing with new-on-the-market **tablet** computers, apparently knowing instinctively how to use the devices. However, it is important to remember that learning is what children do and their natural instinct is to learn from their environment through observation and experimentation. Furthermore, they approach everything without preconceptions about the 'proper' way to use things. An adult may be anxious about breaking a new and expensive **device** and so approach with caution, whereas a child will have no such inhibition. This does not indicate that the child is a 'digital native' with an instinctive understanding of technology. It should be noted that there are also YouTube videos of cats using iPads and iPad apps developed for cats but this is not seen as an indication that cats are 'digital natives'.

Prensky's original idea about 'digital natives' was analogous to the concept of 'native speaker'. He argued that generations who have grown up with computers have a fluency with digital devices which older generations do not have. To a certain extent this is true, but only in as much as we are all habituated to particular practices and tools. However, this does not mean that people cannot learn to use new tools and acquire fluency. Prensky argued that so-called 'digital immigrants' always retain traces of outdated practices, just as an adult language learner is likely to have a 'foreign accent'. However, there is no evidence to support this assumption and those who have researched the topic (for example, Bayne and Ross 2007, Bennett et al. 2008, Bennett and Maton 2010) have found that whilst there are definitely people who are more or less confident with new technology, the difference is not simply due to age, but to a combination of interest and need. Prensky also argued that this fluency of the 'digital native' has caused a change in the way that young people's brains work so that they need more visual stimulus, more use of games, and more use of short-term rewards. Whilst other authors (Carr 2010, Greenfield 2003) make similar claims that the use of **digital technology** alters the structure of the brain, they tend to argue that this is an adverse consequence, whereas Prensky argues that this is a beneficial change that should be supported by new teaching approaches. It should be noted, however, that whilst the brain is undoubtedly plastic and can be developed by intensive practice in a particular field such as music, there is no evidence to support the notion that there has been a wholesale change in the brain structure of 21st century young people.

The problem with the 'digital natives vs. digital immigrants' concept is that it leads to an assumption that all modern young people are intrinsically interested in, motivated by, and expert with digital technologies. This assumption is too broad (Brown and Czerniewizc 2010) but there are two important points to bear in mind. The first is that people, young and old, can and do self-educate with regard to tools that are important in their daily lives. People whose social lives revolve around mobile phones and online social networking will be proficient with these tools and many (but not all) young people fall into this category. This does not mean, however, that they will automatically be excited and engaged by the use of these tools for formal learning (Hoare 2007). The second point is that, given the extremely wide range of digital tools that are available and the rapid pace of development in the field, it is pretty much impossible for any individual to be familiar with all the possibilities. This means that learners may sometimes have more expertise with some aspects of technology than teachers do (although this should not be taken for granted) and teachers should be willing to learn from the learners where this is appropriate. When pupils/students bring an exciting new game, app, or website into the classroom the digital-age teacher needs to be agile enough to think of the possibilities for learning and learn from the students how to exploit the tool.

The role of hardware

In earlier parts of this chapter we have used words such as 'online', 'digital' and 'website' more or less interchangeably. Our intention has not been to deliberately ignore the difference between these terms, but modern device convergence means that it is difficult to distinguish between them. The growth of smartphones and smartphone applications (apps) since 2007 has led to many web-based tools and services becoming available as apps. Examples include Facebook, which is now as likely to be accessed through an app as via the website. Other common examples include newspapers and online shops such as Amazon. Tablets, although they are different from phones in important ways, further extend the options for using technology on the move. Smartphone and tablet technologies are also known as 'mobile and ubiquitous computing' because they give people constant and instant access to digital technology whether they are at home, work, school, or elsewhere. These new tools provide many exciting opportunities for language learning.

One early educational use of phones was the 'assessment for learning in practice settings' project (Coulby et al. 2010), which looked at how learning materials and assessments could be delivered securely to medical students on placements. Handheld game **consoles**, such as Gameboy, Sony PSP, and Nintendo DS, etc., have tended to be used mainly by game players, although there have been attempts to reposition them for a wider market (for example, the Nintendo 'Brain Training') and there has also been educational research looking at the potential of the Sony Playstation Pocket (Sony PSP) for classroom work. **Personal media players**, in the early years, were used for, well, playing media and this was an area that education was quick to exploit with podcasts (see Walker 2009); we will expand on podcasts in Chapter 3. However, the introduction of the iPhone and iPod Touch in 2007 revolutionized handheld and mobile computing. The iPhone was aimed firmly at the consumer market and a major feature was the ease of downloading and installing apps over the air (rather than having to connect the phone to a **desktop** computer). Many apps were free or cost almost nothing and this, together with general ease of use, caused the popularity of the iPhone to soar.

Since 2007, a range of other easy-to-use smartphones, with over-the-air app installation, has become available. However, it should be noted that currently the majority of mobile phones sold worldwide are not smartphones. The two other main mobile phone categories are 'featurephones' and what might be called 'dumbphones'. Featurephones include some apps – particularly social networking – tools and provide internet access, although they tend to be much slower than smartphones. Typically, both smartphones and featurephones include photo and video capability. Dumbphones are basic phones for phone calls and **text messaging** alone; they may or may not include cameras. The fact that, at the time of writing, non-smartphones are still the most frequently used means that they should not be neglected when thinking about educational uses of mobile phones.

The final category of 'mobile and ubiquitous' devices is tablet computers. Phones and tablets are often mentioned in the same sentence as though they are the same kind of device. However, there are important differences and so the two should be thought of separately. An easy distinction is to think of phones as pocket-sized devices, whereas a tablet needs to be carried in a bag. In some ways, the alternative to a tablet is a laptop or netbook computer, although the tablet has created its own niche in the market. Tablets (at least, good ones) have large, clear screens, onscreen keyboards, and turn on instantly without needing time to boot (unlike laptops or desktop computers which usually need several minutes to start). There is a large selection of apps available and these can be installed over the air. Tablets are discussed further in Chapters 8 and 12.

The implication of widespread mobile phone ownership is that people now often have constant/instant access to communications tools especially social networking and text messaging. Adami and Kress (2010) talk about smartphones as creating a change in 'habitus', a term used by sociologists to refer to learned ways of being and acting that we take for granted – simply 'how things are done'. For many people, smartphones are simply part of 'how communication is done' and there is often no obvious distinction between different forms of electronic communication. Email, Twitter, Facebook updates, and **SMS** are often presented as a single stream of communication from friends. This means that there is little value in trying to teach learners how to, for example, compose an email as though email were a genre in its own right. To the smartphone user, there is no difference between email and SMS when communicating with friends. A more useful approach for teachers and students is to think about the context in which the communication takes place (for example, business enquiry, job application, letter to newspaper); the features of that 'communicative event' (purpose, relationship of sender and receiver, etc.); and how to use language which is appropriate for that event.

Summary

As this chapter has shown, digital technologies provide new ways for communication to take place, sometimes with new people. Some of these forms of communication are entirely new whilst others involve the transformation of traditional activities (such as booking travel tickets or shopping). This has led to the development of new ways to use language (technolects) and new purposes for language use. The implications for teachers are:

- There are more resources available on the internet and as apps for language learners, both for receptive use (listening, reading) and for productive use (speaking, writing). However, they are mediated in different ways from more traditional forms of communication, and this may alter the ways in which they are used in learning and teaching.

- There are new kinds of 'communicative events' that learners need to use language to interact in. This may include using language in ways that do not fit traditional rules of syntax and/or orthography. The structure of digitally-mediated conversations may be different from the structure of face-to-face conversations.

- There may be areas, in terms of language, resources, or technology, when teachers need to learn from learners, but not all learners will know the same things about technology use.

- Mobile devices create additional change in the ways that we communicate, such as blurring the boundaries between email, SMS, and social network messages. This leads to new challenges for language teaching but also new possibilities.

Further reading

Crystal, D. 2011. *Internet linguistics.* London: Routledge.

Gee, J.P. and **E.R. Hayes.** 2011. *Language and learning in the digital age.* London: Routledge.

3

LISTENING AND SPEAKING SKILLS

Know how to listen, and you will profit
even from those who talk badly.
PLUTARCH, Greek/Roman historian and writer

Aims

In this chapter, we will try to give you some answers to the following questions:

- What skills do students need to develop in order to be able to listen and speak in a second language?
- What types of spoken language can be found on the internet, and how might they influence students' production and reception of spoken language?
- What opportunities and resources are provided by the internet for developing listening and speaking skills?

Introduction

This chapter focuses on using technology to learn and teach second language (L2) listening and speaking skills. It begins by looking at the different kinds of spoken language which can be found on the internet, and the implications for learning oral skills. The following sections first consider the teaching of listening skills and strategies, and then go on to look at speaking skills and strategies, exploring the ways in which, in each case, technology can support their development.

Spoken language on the internet

On the internet, a lot of speaking and listening seems to take place through the medium of writing. Words which we associate with spoken communication, such as '**chat room**', '**discussion board**', '**conferencing**', and '**social networking**' actually describe communication which tends to take place through written texts, even if those written texts seem to contain many features of spoken language. Consider, for example, this written posting on the Facebook fan site page of Adele, a famous (at the time of writing) British female singer:

> Hi adel ur amazing i have ur album i love u – amber - :)

This text contains many features of spoken language, such as contractions ('you're' as in 'ur'), unclear sentence boundaries (for example between 'amazing' and 'I' and 'album' and 'I), and colloquial language ('amazing'). But it is also written language, communicating between two people, the fan and the singer, who are distant in space and time from each other. Even if Adele chose to reply to the fan, there would be a time lag between the fan's comment, and her response. It doesn't have any of the extra linguistic clues, such as body language and intonation, which help us to interpret a spoken message. The writer has added an **emoticon** at the end of the message to show her attitude, and some researchers (Crystal 2006) have argued that these emoticons or 'smileys' act, although in a rather clumsy way, as replacements for intonation and other prosodic features such as tone and loudness, since they are used to signal the writer's feelings towards what she or he is writing. But even if this example seems to display some of the features of spoken language, it displays many features which are not found in speech, or indeed in 'traditional' writing, but which can be found in other internet genres such as wikis and informational websites. The abbreviations 'ur' and 'u', and the misspelling of the singer's name, for example, suggest different conventions for new kinds of writing where the message is rapid and compressed, as in instant messaging and Twitter. And writing it still is, though it displays a number of 'speech-like' characteristics (Crystal 2006: 32). What might be the effect of this written as-if spoken language on students' development of oral skills? For example, if students have been engaged in online written chat in English, such as **texting** or instant messaging, will that give them more confidence to engage in oral communication on the web and in real life; in other words, can text chat be a rehearsal for the real thing? Or is text chat so different from spoken language, that it does not help to be exposed to it because, for example, students have no idea how it is pronounced? Although, as we will see in Chapter 5 on writing skills, Crystal (2006) argues that much language on the internet is closer to written language than spoken language, Baron (2008) suggests that instant messaging, which is a relatively new phenomenon, had not been much analysed before 2006. She argues that it is much closer to spoken language, and that, for instance, the small units it is delivered in resemble intonation units in speech. If that is the case, Twitter and IM (instant messaging) may well be useful for practising the conceptualization and formulation stages of spoken language, which we describe in more detail in the speaking skills section of this chapter.

Another problem is that, although the internet and mobile devices provide many opportunities for speaking and listening, and in the future might provide many more, such as the speech recognition programmes we mention in Task 5, at present, by far the largest proportion of the language on the internet still appears in written form. Even feedback/comments on videos and podcasts tend to be written. There are some who go as far as arguing that the internet has promoted writing once again as the dominant medium of communication after a period in which oral communication was more powerful and favoured:

> One aspect of the internet revolution which is perhaps not sufficiently remarked is the extent to which it undermines McLuhanite ideology and embodies a return in triumph of the written word.
>
> Rollason (2005: 6)

We still believe that the internet provides many examples of spoken language and opportunities for practising second language (L2) speaking and listening skills; it is just that they are perhaps not as immediately obvious as those for written texts.

While some of the writing on the internet does not seem so different from the written genres we are accustomed to from the pre-internet age, and while there have always been examples of written language which has represented spoken language (in plays, films, speeches, and so on), the Adele fan posting seems to combine features of spoken and written language in new ways. Horowitz and Samuels (1987: 15) predicted that the internet would produce a 'secondary orality', one which 'is not a preliterate but a 'postliterate' society's orality', and which would demand new ways of understanding and producing spoken messages. One of the skills, for example, which people using **web-conferencing** software such as Skype or Adobe Connect need to develop, is coping with time lags between saying something and the other person hearing it. The same people are likely to be multitasking while they are having the conversation, perhaps by simultaneously typing and reading comments, or checking a mobile phone for messages. Another example might be listening to the voice on the satnav in your car, while simultaneously watching a map unfold on the screen and keeping your eyes on the road. None of these language producing or receiving skills are new, but the contexts in which they are needed and the ways in which they have to be combined are. Does this mean we will have to help students develop new or additional ways of processing and interpreting spoken messages on the internet, as opposed to contexts in which they are face to face with their interlocutors? Will those be different to the strategies we already teach students for coping with non-reciprocal or non-synchronous listening and speaking in more traditional contexts, such as university lectures, presentations, phone calls, listening to the radio, and so forth? From this section we can conclude:

1 The internet contains examples of both 'real' spoken language and 'speech-like' written communication and learners need to be familiar with both.
2 'Speech-like' communication might be a useful springboard to real spoken language.
3 Teachers might need to search harder for examples of spoken language on the internet.
4 There are new skills, including multitasking skills, involved in digital oral communication.
   The next sections go on to consider how technology can be used to teach listening and speaking skills in turn.

Second language (L2) listening skills

What kinds of listening skills do second language (L2) learners need to develop? The teaching of listening skills in a second language has been historically rather neglected, and in the past, listening tasks in the classroom tended to be used as a means of introducing or reinforcing new language items without really focusing on the development of competence in understanding the second language itself. However, over the past few years, there have been a number of excellent books – for example Buck 2001, Field 2008, Flowerdew and Miller 2005, Lynch 2009, Wilson 2008 – as well as a number of journal articles reporting on innovative research in the area – for example Tsui and Fullilove 1998, Vandergrift 1999, Goh 2000 – which, by focusing on the skills involved in second language listening and how it could be better taught, have considerably raised the profile of listening in language teachers' minds.

These publications have considered listening from two angles: firstly the psycholinguistic processes involved in receiving and making sense of a spoken message, and secondly the social features which enable listeners to understand the effect of the context in which it was produced on the spoken message. The best-known model for describing the psycholinguistic processes involved in decoding a spoken message was developed by Levelt (1993). In this model, speaking processes mirror listening processes, so it will also be a useful model to use when we consider speaking skills later in this chapter. In this model, a mental 'acoustic-phonetic processor' first analyses the speech signal and produces a representation of its sounds. As Lynch (2009) remarks, this is not always an easy job, because such factors as the speed and clarity of what is being said, the amount of background noise, and the speaker's dialect may make it difficult for the listener to do that analysis. These problems are multiplied if you are listening to a second language. The representation of the sounds is then passed to the 'parser', which separates the stream of speech into separate words, using syntactic, phonological, and lexical knowledge of the language in question. Finally, the 'conceptualizer' enables the listener to understand the speaker's intended meaning, by activating and using the listener's knowledge of the situation in which the message was produced, both of the world and of previous experience of discourse.

In Levelt's model, the psycholinguistic aspects of listening are perhaps more stressed in the acoustic-phonetic and parsing stages, and the social aspects of listening are more prominent in the conceptualizing stage. When people write or talk about the teaching of second language listening, they often refer to the psycholinguistic aspects of listening as 'bottom-up' processes and the social aspects of listening as 'top-down' processes. However, Levelt stressed that these processes did not happen one after the other, but in parallel, so that the brain is processing different elements of the message at the same time. Although fashions in teaching second language listening change, sometimes focusing more on bottom-up, psycholinguistic processes, and sometimes more on top-down social processes, most researchers and teachers agree that you need to help students to develop competence in carrying out both processes.

We have drawn up a list of listening skills which learners need to develop based on a combination of our experience in teaching listening (for example, White 1998), research that we and others have carried out, and similar helpful taxonomies produced by others, such as those mentioned in Rost (2011:119–121). We would like to emphasize that these skills operate in conjunction with each other rather than separately, and that they are all needed in order to successfully understand and respond to a spoken message:

Skill	Examples
Perception	Recognizing individual sounds Discriminating between sounds Identifying reduced sounds in connected speech (elision, assimilation, weak forms, such as 'schwa') Identifying stressed syllables Identifying changes in intonation
Matching sounds to language items in an effort to move towards understanding meaning	Identifying individual word boundaries Identifying words Activating grammatical and semantic information about the words to build an idea about how they might be connected in syntactic units Identifying 'key' words which give an idea about the topic (proposition) of the message Identifying discourse markers which organize and show attitudes towards what is being said Inferring the meaning of unknown words
Interpreting meaning using knowledge of the world	Using knowledge of the topic to guess what the speaker might be saying about it (content schemata) Connecting groups of words to non-linguistic features in the context, such as expressions, gestures, and objects (where these can be seen) Using knowledge about the patterns that particular oral interactions typically take (formal schemata)
Dealing with information	Understanding the overall idea of what you hear (gist) Understanding the main points Understanding details Inferring information which is not explicitly stated, or which the listener has missed
Interacting with the speaker	Coping with variations among speakers, e.g. in speed or accent Recognizing the speaker's intention Identifying the speaker's mood/attitude Predicting what the speaker will say next If the speaker expects a reply, recognizing turn-taking signals Formulating a response to what the speaker has said (whether this is expressed verbally or not)

Table 3.1 Skills involved in second language (L2) listening

Listening strategies

What is the difference between listening skills and listening strategies? We intend to use Field's (2000) distinction between skills, as described in Table 3.1 and strategies. He defines strategies as efforts to compensate for lack of skills, so that second language listeners, who do not know the language, are more likely to need them than first language (L1) listeners. Listening strategies are efforts to overcome problems and uncertainties in understanding a spoken message, and they include actions such as making inferences, predicting, and asking for clarification. They are communication strategies rather than strategies for language learning in general (Field 2008: 294–295). Students probably need to use these strategies less and less as they get more familiar with the language and more competent at listening skills in the second language, although even very proficient native speakers of the language will need to rely on them occasionally, if, for example, their concentration has slipped, or they are listening to someone who is speaking about an unfamiliar topic. We are going to be cautious when we discuss the ways in which listening strategies can be taught, as research does not at present show much positive evidence that training learners to use listening strategies actually works very efficiently. Probably the best approach, as Lynch (2009: 87) points out, is to find out which strategies your students seem to be under-using or not using at all, and model the strategies, afterwards providing practice in them. Some examples of listening strategies are the following:

Strategy	Examples
Inferring	Guessing the meaning of words the listener is uncertain about, or has missed, from clues in the linguistic or non-linguistic context.
Seeking clarification	Getting the speaker to repeat something which the listener has missed. (This could include, for example, replaying a video or audio file.)
Predicting	Rehearsing in your mind what speakers are likely to be going to say, in order to help you to understand better when they actually start speaking.
Focusing	Concentrating and persevering despite problems with understanding. Trying to get the main idea and not worrying about understanding every word.

Table 3.2 Some strategies involved in second language (L2) listening

Using technology to teach listening skills

Listening has often been taught badly in the past. Teachers tended to expose students to listening material, in the form of audio tapes or DVDs, which the students hadn't chosen, and which ignored the possibility of face to face listening, either between students, or student(s) and teacher. Teachers tended to control where, when, and how much listening was done, and also the kinds of comprehension tasks students did in connection with the listening. There was an overconcentration on listening for information, whereas we also listen for interactional reasons, to relate to people, and to understand *why* they are saying something as well as *what* is being said. Perhaps because it was easier to find examples to use in class, there seemed to be an overconcentration on non-reciprocal listening, where listeners are at a distance in time and space from speakers, with no opportunity to interact with them.

It would be a pity to see these disadvantages repeated when using technology to learn and teach second language (L2) listening. One of us suggested in an earlier book (White 1998: 7) that listening could be better learnt and taught if learners were given the opportunity to:

- choose what they listened to
- control when and how often they listened
- make their own listening texts and tasks
- link listening and speaking where possible (i.e. reciprocal listening as well as non-reciprocal listening)
- become active listeners rather than passive overhearers
- reflect on why and where they were having problems in understanding
- reflect on their listening problems.

The tasks which follow suggest some ways in which those principles can be carried out, as well as ways in which listening skills and strategies can be practised.

YouTube is a rich resource for video clips featuring L1 and L2 speakers of numerous languages, including English. These clips include language lessons, 'how to do it' advice, film trailers and excerpts from TV shows. One great advantage of these clips is that individual students can replay or pause them as often as they like. Another big advantage is that while colloquial examples of spoken language occur in clips like this, because they are intended for broadcast, they tend to be scripted or rehearsed in advance. This means that that they tend to be audible, and without the excess of background noise, speaker overlap, or false starts, which make examples of 'real' spoken language which are recorded or listened to in less-than-ideal circumstances, so hard for second language learners to understand. There are some examples of commercial websites which do a good job in designing questions around such clips, and we have cited some examples on our accompanying website www.oup.com/elt/teacher/tell. The problem with such websites is that they do all the work for the students! The teacher/web designers choose the clips, listen to them, and then set tasks. In many ways, they 'steal' opportunities to learn away from students by doing so, as the students could practise a lot of the listening skills and strategies mentioned above, as well as speaking skills, by finding their own clips on YouTube, listening to and discussing them, and then creating tasks for other students to do.

Task 1

Designing your own video listening tasks

You can do this task as a reflective one on your own, or with students. Access YouTube and choose a suitable two-to-three-minute video clip for your students, perhaps one of the types mentioned above.

- Ask your students to watch the clip several times and to design some good questions to accompany it, which will help other students to understand what is said. A site such as Quizlet (see our accompanying website for references) is good for making the questions.
- Ask your students to make a basic web page with an online drag-and-drop website editor (please see our website for suggestions).
- Students can embed both the video and the questions in the webpage. If you are not sure how to do this, please see our website.
- Students can post the webpage link to each other using a class website, a VLE, Facebook, or email, or even write the address on a poster in the classroom so that they can do each other's tasks.

After you or the students have finished the activity, it is useful to reflect on it (and this will produce an interesting discussion about the skills and strategies needed to understand spoken language). You might find the following questions helpful:

- Why did you choose the clip (interest? language?)
- What kinds of difficulties did you experience in listening to the video and understanding what was said? What listening skills from Table 3.1 above did you feel you lacked? How did you try to overcome any difficulties in understanding? Did you use any of the strategies listed in Table 3.2 above?
- Why did you design those particular listening tasks? Did you copy the stages in which listening is often taught in class (getting the main idea, then details?) Or did you focus on ideas or language which you had found interesting? Was designing your own tasks better than doing ones set by other people? If so, why/why not?

You will probably find, whether you do this activity yourself or get your students to do it, that it makes you aware of problems with listening, and the strategies you use to overcome them. Often these things are neglected in lessons aiming to teach listening skills because the emphasis is usually on getting the right answers to comprehension questions, rather than reflecting on the listening process. An interesting variant on this activity is to divide students into groups and ask them to work with the same video clip. This tends to demonstrate very clearly that there are many ways of understanding and interpreting the same message, and that different people may focus on different parts of the message. In a traditional, paper-based class, doing listening activities, everyone has to listen to the same text in the same way.

There is a wealth of listening material available on the internet, such as podcasts on every topic under the sun, and a wide range of radio stations. Teachers still need to make the listening text personal to the students, and to stage the listening activities so that students are guided to understanding the parts of the message that correspond to their aim in listening, for instance to get the main points of the news, or the details of the weather report just for the part of the country they are interested in. Task 2 is an example of how teachers can mediate listening material which is available on the internet and model how it can be used for individual practice outside the classroom:

Task 2

Lean on me – Using lyrics and music

There are a number of internet sites which give access to song lyrics, and there are also videos on sites such as YouTube which show the lyrics as the song is performed. Unfortunately, sites for song lyrics change frequently, but any search for a song title should bring up several results. In this task, we use the song *Lean on Me* by Bill Withers (this is quite useful from a language perspective too, as it expresses the future in a number of different ways, but here we are focusing on listening and speaking skills rather than teaching language items). You can, of course, use any song you wish. We suggest you follow these steps:

- If there isn't a copy of the song available, find it on YouTube (without or without lyrics).
- On the internet, search for 'Lean on Me lyrics'.
- Tell your students the title of the song and ask what they know about it, or people who have sung it. Ask what they think the song might be about, and if they can predict any of the 'content' words they think are likely to be in the song.
- Play the song and ask the students to listen and see if any of the words they predicted appear in the song. Give a prize for the person who predicted most words correctly.
- Play the song again and ask students to write down as many words as they can of the lyrics (pause the song after each verse).
- Display the lyrics for the students to see and get them to compare in pairs who has written the most words down correctly.
- Discuss the meaning of the song.
- As a follow-up, students can create role-plays where one friend supports another – these can be recorded to make movies.

After doing the activity, think about these questions:

- How is listening to a song different from other types of listening?
- What kinds of listening skills and strategies were students practising?
- How easy was it to find the song and the lyrics?
- Would your students be able to do this type of activity on their own?

When teaching listening in class, teachers often focus on listening for information at the expense of other reasons why we as human beings listen, such as for pleasure and entertainment. Listening to a song for pleasure therefore goes some way to redressing the balance. Students will be practising a number of the skills listed in Table 3.1, in particular focusing on recognizing key words and identifying individual word boundaries when they listen for the first time. Of course, students can easily do this kind of activity outside the classroom, but by first doing it in class, the teacher will have modelled a way of doing it effectively.

Just a word of warning: internet lyrics sites and YouTube videos often post lyrics without the approval of the copyright holder. You may simply display a webpage to your class, but you should never copy/paste lyrics to a website of your own or to a YouTube video without permission from the copyright holder.

Students can, of course, create their own listening materials for posting to the internet, by using a program such as Audacity (see our accompanying website). Audacity is a free program for creating and editing audio files. It is powerful, but easy to use and there are a number of tutorial videos available on YouTube; we have linked to some of them on our website. You will need to **download** and install Audacity for this task and also the Lame MP3 encoder (see our website for download links). You will also need a microphone for recording. For this activity, you (or your students) are going to make a brief audio file.

Task 3	**Making listening materials using Audacity**

- Think about what you want to talk about. We suggest that you tell us about something that is important to you – your favourite leisure activity, something about your country, or something about your work. You will probably find it easier if you write a script or, at least, notes, to speak from.
- Record your talk. Your recording should be no more than five minutes long (even five minutes is a long time to talk so you may want your first recording to be shorter).
- Add a music introduction and ending if you wish. There are many sites where you can find royalty-free music for use in podcasts or movies.
- Export your file as an MP3.
- The MP3 file can be uploaded to a VLE, website or blog if you wish to share it.

Now think about these questions.

* How could you use Audacity to make materials for classroom use?
* How could your students make use of Audacity for recording?

Once you have practised with Audacity, you will find that it is not difficult to edit audio files, which will mean that students will be able to produce 'radio' programmes they can distribute on the internet. These might be plays, news reports, documentaries, interviews, or any other genre that you can think of. Using royalty-free music for introductions, conclusions, and transitions can give a professional feel to the work.

You may have noticed that Task 3 was just as much about learning and practising speaking skills as about creating material for other students to practise their listening skills. Speaking and listening are closely related in real life, and should also be connected in language learning. We now move on to considering more specifically what second language (L2) speaking skills and strategies students need to develop, and how technology can support them in doing so.

Speaking skills

As we mentioned earlier, it might be useful to consider the processes involved in speaking as being similar to those involved in Levelt's model for listening, but in reverse with the soon-to-be speaker firstly conceptualizing what he or she is going to say in terms of topic, purpose, and type, or 'genre' of talk, then formulating the spoken message by producing the sounds associated with those words out loud, together with the appropriate stress and intonation. Hedge (2000) points to the criteria for English language speaking tests for second language speakers, such as the Cambridge ESOL exams, as providing useful summaries of some of the main skills which L2 speakers need:

1 being accurate and appropriate in their use of English, which involves intelligible pronunciation, grammatical and lexical correctness, and using language which fits the context and purpose for speaking
2 being fluent, which involves the ability to keep talk flowing smoothly without undue hesitations, and in a coherent fashion, so that the listener can follow the train of thought.

Goh and Burns (2012: 49–66) point out that L2 speakers need to combine knowledge about the target language with an ability to use it effectively. They refer to the notion of communicative competence; competent speakers should have the ability to produce accurate language which is easy for listeners to process and which is appropriate to the context. They describe four 'core' categories of speaking skills which we have paraphrased in the table below:

Core skill	Examples
Pronunciation	Pronouncing vowels, consonants, and blended sounds clearly Using different intonation patterns to communicate old and new information
Performing speech acts	Knowing how to make requests Knowing how to give opinions
Managing interaction	Initiating, maintaining, and ending conversations Turn taking Clarifying meaning
Organizing discourse	Using discourse markers and intonation to signpost changes of topic Being able to structure discourse for different communicative purposes such as stories or instructions

Table 3.3 Second language (L2) speaking skills

They also discuss speaking strategies which they define as ways of coping with the time pressure of expressing yourself in a second language which you do not have complete command of. There are ways of using the resources, linguistic and otherwise, which the learner already possesses, in order to keep communication going. Goh and Burns divide these strategies into cognitive, metacognitive, and interaction strategies. The table below gives examples of each kind of strategy:

Speaking strategy	Example
Cognitive (or psycholinguistic) strategies	Finding ways round a lack of vocabulary through paraphrase, substitution, coining new words, etc.
Metacognitive strategies	Planning or rehearsing what you are going to say Monitoring your language use while you are speaking
Interaction strategies	Asking for help Checking understanding Requesting clarification

Table 3.4 Second language (L2) speaking strategies

Being accurate, appropriate, and fluent are all difficult for L2 speakers, but in our experience it is the fluency aspect which worries learners most. Being placed in a position where they are 'on the spot', and where they have to produce spoken language under time pressure is very stressful, especially as they often do not have native-speaker strategies for gaining time to think and plan, such as using hesitation devices, or using what Thornbury (2005: 23) calls 'prefabricated chunks' such as 'by the way', 'to cut a long story short'. Harmer (2007: 345–346) suggests that one really useful strategy for students is to plan and rehearse what they are going to say before they actually say it, by going over it in their head, or recording it and asking someone else, for example, the teacher or fellow students, to comment on it before they have to do it for real. The internet provides some good opportunities for rehearsing spoken language, but these do raise some of the issues about written-to-be-spoken language which we mentioned at the beginning of this chapter, as we will see in Task 4 below.

Task 4

ChatBots

There are a number of robot-like characters, known as 'chatbots' which are available free on the internet, or to download onto mobile devices, which will have a conversation with you. At the moment, the interaction is rather limited because it involves the user typing in a written question (on the latest version of mobile phones, the user can ask the question orally) and the chatbot giving an answer in spoken and written form.

- Access a chatbot (see the accompanying website for links).
- Type in some questions you would like to ask the chatbot. Also try using the back arrow, which will make the chatbot repeat the replies. Then reflect on the question below:
- What are the advantages and disadvantages for learners of using 'chatbots' to practise speaking and listening skills?

The advantages seem to be that learners can interact on an individual basis with an infinitely patient robot, who will wait as long as it takes for them to compose the language they want to use. The chatbot, in his or her reply, gives a model for pronunciation which the learners can repeat as many times as they wish. The drawback is that the chatbot responses are often in language one would associate more with 'traditional' genres of written language, avoiding, for instance, colloquialisms or incomplete sentences. At present, chatbots allow learners to practice orality in terms of interaction between speaker and listener, and they give them practice in responding appropriately in one of the fixed routines (question, answer, sometimes also feedback) which is commonly found in spoken language. However, they do not allow them to rehearse many of the features of spoken language apart from pronunciation. This will probably change in the future, so it is worth keeping an eye on developments in this area. One interesting possibility at the time of writing, for example, makes use of **webcams**. Teachers record and leave a question for students in a kind of video booth and students video themselves answering it. They can do this from home at a time which suits them, and rehearse their answer first. This kind of interaction is likely to contain many more features of spoken language. It is also worth noting that opportunities already exist for learners to contact each other and exchange languages in real time by Skype and text chat, using sites such as the Language Exchange Community (see our accompanying website) but that they will probably need to be more confident users of the language to do so.

In addition to giving learners opportunities to plan and rehearse spoken language, Harmer also suggests three other ways in which students can develop speaking skills: by repetition, by practising speaking in smaller groups before moving on to larger groups, and by making sure that everybody in the class takes part in speaking activities, something he calls 'mandatory participation'. Technology provides a lot of opportunities for doing these things. Harmer points out that repetition is useful because 'each new encounter with a word or phrase helps fix it in the student's memory' (2007: 346). Students can try to improve on the spoken language the next time round, and they are not having to go through the processes of conceptualizing and formulating the language again, so they can concentrate on articulation. The repetition works best, however, if students get a chance to analyse and evaluate how successful they have been. This feedback could come from the teacher or classmates (and we will see in Task 6 how that works with Vokis used with secondary school students) or it could be the computer which provides the feedback, as in Task 5 below.

Task 5

ecnglish·com.

Speech to text

There are a number of voice-recognition programs which allow you to dictate spoken language and see it converted into written words. One of these is Dragon Naturally Speaking, which is quite expensive, and usually bought by people who have difficulties using keyboards because of injury or disability. However, the same company has also produced apps for mobile and tablet devices, for example Dragon Dictation, which (at the time of writing) is free for iPhone and iPad. Windows has, for some time, included **speech-recognition** software which can be switched on using the control panel (on older PCs this may be in the region and language options). This can be used instead of a keyboard to enter text into programs such as Microsoft Word. Normally, a user needs to 'train' a speech recognition program so that it will be more accurate. However, it can also be used by learners trying to improve pronunciation.

- If you have access to a Windows computer, activate speech recognition. Alternatively, if you have an iPhone or iPad, install the Dragon Dictation app.
- Open either Word or Dragon Dictation and speak a word into the microphone on your computer. If the computer displays it correctly in written form, award yourself a point. Delete the word and try again if the computer does not get the word right, or try saying a new word.
- What do you think are the advantages for learners of using this kind of software?
- What happens if you repeat the word without first deleting the word you have said?

This type of activity allows students to repeat and experiment with modifying their pronunciation until the program represents accurately what they are trying to say. It is psychologically rather pleasing, too, as it appears to be the computer's fault that it 'does not understand' what the student is trying to say, rather than the student's. Students can practise pronunciation privately and as often as they want. The teacher can suggest particular words and phrases or longer stretches of spoken language as homework which could be practised in this way. However, because the programs are designed to make sense of spoken text, they will try to 'guess' a sentence if you say several words. This is why, to use speech recognition, you need to delete each word (or phrase) before speaking the next. One drawback, however, is that this kind of activity focuses on pronunciation rather than stress and intonation. There are programs available (such as the CAN-8 Virtual Laboratory) which allow students to see the intonation and stress patterns of a native speaker on screen and try to copy them. Unfortunately, this is not available for free, but is worth considering if you are setting up computer facilities for your language learners. There are also programs such as Pronunciation Power or apps such as English File Pronunciation that allow you to record yourself and compare your sound to a 'native speaker'.

One difficulty in teaching speaking skills is to make sure that all the students in the class get a chance to speak. Some students will try to avoid speaking because they feel shy about speaking in public, others because they are happy to sit back and let the others do the work! One way of making sure everyone speaks is to ask students to create an **avatar**, and then add a recording of their voice, speaking about any topic they like. They can then post the recording to a blog or a class website. One piece of freely available software (at the time of writing) to do this is the 'Voki' (see our accompanying website). In the next task, we will discuss how one teacher exploited this software to provide both speaking and listening practice for his class, and also the opportunity for peer feedback on speaking.

Task 6	**A Voki webpage for learning to speak Spanish**

A widely-read education blogger, José Picardo, used Vokis with his Year 9 (age 13–14) learners of Spanish. The learners created weird and wonderful avatars of aliens, clowns and so on, using the Voki software, and then recorded a short description of themselves. The Vokis and the personal introductions were posted on a website and other learners commented on them. You will find a link to José's website and can read more about the steps which Jose and his students took to create the website on our own accompanying website.

- Either alone, with colleagues or with students, experiment with creating your own Voki. What is the effect of being able to create another personality for yourself?
- What kinds of speaking and listening skills are being practised by using Vokis in the ways in which José Picardo did?

The notion of gaining confidence by assuming another personality goes as far back in our collective memories as Suggestopedia, a method of learning languages which was developed in the 1970s. In Suggestopedia, students took on different names and identities, and this was felt to remove the stress from producing language, since it was another self who was making the errors. The pictures of the avatars act like masks and allow the students to express sides of their personality which are often hidden (for example the clown). The same goes for avatars in virtual worlds such as Second Life, where adults could also practise speaking (we would not recommend this for teenagers or younger children, however, because of security issues). One of us, for example, found it very liberating to create an avatar for herself that represented her as a purple 'cyberpunk'; she then travelled around in Second Life having conversations in Italian in this persona.

In order to comment on the recordings made by other students, learners on the website have to listen carefully. They will also learn a lot about how, in order to be intelligible to listeners, speakers need to speak clearly and at an appropriate pace, and use intonation, pitch, and stress to sound interesting. Activities like this show learners that listening is closely connected with speaking, and that what speakers say and the way they say it can make listening easy or difficult. Students also benefited from being able to rehearse what they wanted to say within a small supportive group of classmates, before they had to try out talking about these personal details in the real world of an exchange visit to Spain.

So far in this section, we have tended to focus on particular speaking skills, for example pronunciation and performing **speech acts**, such as asking questions, or describing oneself. We have also discussed quite short bursts of spoken language. The final activity in this chapter considers longer stretches of discourse and the kinds of speaking strategies which students might need for interacting with each other synchronously, with all the pressures of having to produce spoken language in 'real time' without much preparation.

Task 7	**Speaking and listening practice in a virtual space**

Either explore one of the options for online classrooms which are currently available, such as WizIQ (please see our website for suggestions) or think about how you could use Skype to connect students who are separated from each other geographically.

- What kinds of speaking activity could students do in such a 'virtual space'?
- What opportunities for speaking and listening does it offer which a conventional classroom does not?
- Which of the speaking skills and strategies in Tables 3.3 and 3.4 will students practise?

In online classrooms, students can talk to each other at a distance using audio and video, so this is ideal if teachers want to twin their class with one elsewhere in the world. The online classroom lends itself to discussions on particular topics, presentations by groups of learners, problem-solving activities, communication-gap tasks, and so on; in short all the activities you might do in a 'traditional' classroom. The added bonus is that students are being exposed to different accents, and because they are conversing with people who are not as familiar as their classmates, it is likely that there will be a greater pressure to use the shared target language rather than lapsing into a shared first language. As they are speaking to unfamiliar people at a distance, and have not had the opportunity to totally prepare and rehearse what they are going to say, they are more likely to make use of the cognitive and interaction strategies we mentioned in Table 3.1. Some teachers have made use of Skype for pair-work between students in two schools in different countries, in which they have exchanged information on different topics, or done a communication-gap activity. The students can see each other on a webcam, and have really enjoyed the experience of getting to know another learner from a different part of the world. Online classrooms also have a facility for recording the class so that students can replay and watch or listen to it again.

Summary

In the first part of this chapter, we discussed the fact that the internet provides examples of 'real' spoken language and also new genres of 'speech-like' written communication. We suggested that producing 'written-as-if spoken' language in the form of text messaging or online chat can sometimes scaffold students to then move on to real life speaking. Technology provides exciting opportunities for students to interact with spoken language in ways which allow them to replay, rehearse, and repeat oral language in non-threatening and supportive contexts. It also provides them with opportunities to create their own listening materials, as well as take advantage of the wealth of audio material available online. **Virtual classrooms** give learners the opportunity to take part in synchronous real-time discussions with other students elsewhere in the world.

Further reading

Lynch, T. 2009. *Teaching second language listening*. Oxford: Oxford University Press.

Nah, K. C., P. White and **R. Sussex.** 2008. 'The potential of using a mobile phone to access the internet for learning EFL listening skills within a Korean context'. *ReCALL* 20: 331–347.

Xuan, T. D. 2012. 'Using internet resources to teach listening and speaking'. Presentation at the ICT in Education Victoria Conference 2012, 26th May 2012. Retrieved 13 September 2012, from http://ictev.vic.edu.au/proposal/2358/using-internet-resources-teach-listening-and-speaking.

4 READING SKILLS

You don't have to burn books to destroy a culture.
Just get people to stop reading them.
RAY BRADBURY, writer

Aims

In this chapter, we will try to give you some answers to the following questions:
- What skills and strategies are involved in reading in a second language?
- How can technology motivate and support second language reading?
- What kinds of second language reading resources can technology provide?

Introduction

The first part of this chapter outlines some of the skills involved in second language (L2) reading. It also considers the opportunities and challenges presented by the emergence of new kinds of online 'reading communities' and digital texts for reading. (Some of the visual aspects of these texts will be further discussed in Chapter 6). The second part of the chapter looks at the ways in which technology can be used to support the development of reading skills in general. Reading for academic purposes is addressed in Chapter 7.

Reading in a first language (L1) and second language (L2)

Learning to read in a first language (L1) is a hard-won skill. Even if we do not remember incidents in our own journey in learning to read, we have probably seen children we know go through the slow and painful process of matching orthography to sounds, sounding out words bit by bit, learning how to read some whole words by sight alone, and using context (sentence structure, the pictures in the book, the story so far, knowledge of the world, hints given by adults reading with you) to develop the ability to read. The whole process of achieving a minimal ability to read can typically take children learning to read English as a first language as long as a year. Grabe (2009) says that learning to read in different first languages requires different deployment of the same universal reading skills, such as matching sounds to orthography, or using syntactic clues. For instance, children learning to read in English or French, which are written in alphabetical orthographies in which there are less predictable sound to letter correspondences than in, say, Italian or Turkish, need to develop sight recognition of very frequently occurring words and parts of words early on. Chinese children, dealing with a non-alphabetical orthography, will take longer to process a single word, because it contains more information in the characters which make up the word than do English letters.

This suggests that when we start to read in a second language, we may need to develop different processing strategies at word level. Learners whose first language is written in an orthography like that of Spanish or Greek, for example, both of which tend to have closer correspondences between sounds and letters than English does, need to adjust their word-processing strategies when reading English as a second language in order to recognize frequently occurring words and parts of words by sight (Grabe 2009: 127). The good news for L2 teachers is that they can make use of a wealth of material available on line for L1 readers of English to help with these particular strategies. There are a number of online quizzes and games available which practise sight reading of words and the rhyme parts of word endings so that readers can make analogies between spelling patterns they have learnt and new words. These sites also provide practice in matching orthography with sounds. You can find these sites by googling terms such as 'ICT reading games', or 'sight word reading games'. You can find examples on the website which accompanies this book. Students need to be a little tolerant of the fact these sites are designed for children, but they are often quite fun.

It will probably not have occurred to many L2 teachers of English that they could, in the area of word processing for beginning L2 readers at least, make use of learning material designed for first language readers. In fact, the whole question of what we need to learn to do differently when we start reading in a second language, and how it resembles and differs from learning to read in a first language is a complex one. It covers many other levels of processing besides that of words. When learners start reading in a second language, they have usually had considerable experience of reading in their first language, and as well as language-processing skills, they will also have developed higher order reading abilities concerned with dealing with information, such as identifying main ideas and evaluating information. They will also have gained familiarity with reading particular genres in their first language, So we need to consider how an already established ability to read in a first language may interact with learning to read in a second language. When does experience in reading in first language facilitate L2 reading, and when does it hinder it? And how can technology help with some of the difficulties?

How is reading in a second language different?

We tend to start reading in a second language in very different circumstances from those in which we started reading in our first language. When we first learnt to read in our first language, we already knew at least 5,000 words orally (Cunningham 2005), whereas we are usually plunged into reading a second language at an early stage, when we know very little of the language. Readers in an L2 are constantly confronted with vocabulary they do not know, and syntactic patterns they are unfamiliar with, even if they are reading texts which have been simplified. They are perpetually having to monitor how well they have understood, identify problems in understanding, and try to find solutions. Perfetti (1991) noted that students who had lower levels of proficiency in the second language gave most of their effort to processing individual words in an effort to build up small scale units of meaning (or 'propositions'), which gave them no spare capacity in working memory for constructing larger scale understanding and critical interpretation of the whole text. They simply didn't yet have the automatic recognition of function words, morphemes, and vocabulary to enable them to attend to these other things and become more fluent readers. In terms of exposure to reading texts, it used to be the case that readers had limited access to reading texts in the second language, compared to their first language, and that most of those texts were given to them in the classroom.

Technology potentially makes millions of texts available online in the second language, but learners have to be motivated to seek them out, and some of those texts will be better written than others. Second language readers may be encountering written genres they are unfamiliar with in their first language. Alternatively, they may be reading a genre which is familiar from their first language, but which organizes information in different ways. Second language readers may also have difficulty with unfamiliar cultural references in texts. Quite often, students will read quite different things in their first language than they do in a second language; Wallace (1988) and McKay (1993) have noted that first language reading tends to relate more to our 'private' roles, such as enjoying poetry and literature, whilst second language reading relates to the more public roles we play in a society, such as work or study. Finally, attitudes to the printed word may be different in the first language culture. It can be difficult for students coming from a culture in which the written word carries the weight of unquestioned authority to critically evaluate or compare texts, which they are often required to do when reading in English as a second language. All these differences between first language and second language reading experiences suggest a number of conscious reading strategies which students need to learn when trying to understand texts in a second language.

The next section considers the skills involved in reading in both first language and second language. People who write about 'skills' and 'strategies' in second language reading seem to use the two terms more interchangeably than do those who write about listening, but for our purposes here, we are defining reading strategies as techniques which readers use consciously to fulfil their reasons for reading, such as predicting, inferring, re-reading, and making connections between different parts of the text, whereas skills are more like the unconscious processes we discuss in the paragraph which follows. We realize, as Grabe and Stoller (2002:15) point out, that the distinction between the two may not, in fact, be very clear cut, as fluent readers may use some strategies automatically. Nevertheless, by the end of the next section, we hope to have built up an overall picture of the skills/strategies which second language readers need to develop.

Skills and strategies in second language (L2) reading

A number of models of the skills involved in reading have been proposed over the years, and, as for listening in Chapter 3, the psycholinguistic models tend to focus on so called 'bottom-up' and 'top-down' processes of reading and the ways in which these interact with each other. Bottom-up processes are concerned with matching the written symbols on the page (letters or logographs) with sounds, identifying words, using syntactic information to help construct meaning, and using working memory to assist these operations. Top-down processing involves using expectations about the likely content, organization, and language of the text to predict, infer, and confirm individual words in the text and build up an understanding of the text. Top-down processing makes use of knowledge of the world and of how particular kinds of text are structured, as well as the language use which is typical of particular kinds of text. Most theorists would suggest that these two levels of process are interwoven, although they might disagree about exactly how (Hudson, 2007). Our reasons for reading the text will also influence the processes.

It is fair to say that these psycholinguistic models focus on the relationship between readers and texts, and the ways in which readers 'extract' or 'mine' meaning from texts. However, the things we read are produced within a particular culture, and we read them for a reason. Reading cannot be understood as a psycholinguistic process only; it has social dimensions too. Writers write in order to communicate their ideas to readers and each reader will react differently. A good illustration of this fact are the very different reactions to the same novel which individual members of reading groups may have. 'New literacy' approaches to reading (for example, Street 1993) emphasize the relationship between readers and writers, and they also consider how, why, and where the reading is done, and how social context may influence reading processes and comprehension of written texts.

Building on what we have said above, it seems that the following skills and strategies might be needed by L2 readers, although we do not suggest that this is a definitive list:

Type of skill/strategy	Examples
Identifying letters	Realizing that 'a' and 'A' are the same letter.
Matching sounds to orthography	Working out that the letter combination 'ough' may represent more than one set of sounds.
Dealing with unknown words	Using syntactic or morphological information or knowledge about the topic of the text in order to deduce the meaning of the word 'muddy'; using a dictionary (could be an online one, or a **hyperlink** to a gloss or translation of the word). Developing a 'sight' recognition of frequently occurring words such as 'the'. 'of', 'and' etc.
Using morphological and syntactic clues to interpret the meaning of sentences and form propositions	Knowing that 'a' and 'the' come before nouns. Knowing that the morpheme 'ed' attached to a verb stem signals a past tense.
Using knowledge of the world to predict or infer information	Predicting that a text in a newspaper or magazine about a famous band is likely to contain news about upcoming 'gigs'.
Using knowledge about the typical structure and language of particular genres	Knowing that articles about academic research, as well as advertisements, are likely to follow an SPSE (situation-problem-solution-evaluation) organization. Knowing that fairy stories in English often start 'Once upon a time …'.
Setting appropriate goals for comprehension	Deciding whether you need to get just the main ideas,(skimming) or specific information (scanning), or reading to get an in depth idea of the information contained in the whole text. Successfully interpreting what the writer wanted the reader to get from the text.
Evaluating/appreciating the information given in the text	Enjoying a story. Deciding which news report of the same event is the best.

Table 4.1 Skills and strategies needed by second language (L2) readers

We can see that second language readers might need support in developing all of these skills, given that they are reading in a language they do not know well, and reading texts produced in another culture. These skills apply to all kinds of reading, including the academic reading mentioned in Chapter 7, although different kinds of reading purpose may emphasize certain skills, such as 'evaluating information' in the case of academic texts.

How technology has changed the ways in which we read

The 'new literacy' approaches we mentioned in the previous section are helpful for analysing the effects of technology on how reading is done, and the ways in which relationships between readers and writers are changing. As we note elsewhere in this book, for example in Chapter 5 on writing skills, technology has had the effect of 'democratizing' reading and writing, so that not only 'expert' writers can be read by large numbers of people: anyone can be read widely on the web through blogging, Wikipedia, posts on social networking sites, and so forth. Readers can write back to the original producer of the text, and add to or amend texts, so that the same group of people may often be involved in both reading and writing the same text. The internet has also created new kinds of reading and writing communities who are connected to each other by common interests, such as bloggers who read, quote, and link to each other's blogs.

Task 1

New reading communities

Read about the three 'reading communities' below, and then reflect on the questions which follow.

Reading Community 1

In 2008, a private language school in Portugal set up a blog on which EFL students posted reviews of books they had enjoyed. The unsimplified books, chosen by the students, could be either in English or Portuguese. All the reviews were in English. Students could comment on the reviews. The blog seems to have been very active between 2008 and 2010, but after that time does not seem to have had any posts. However the Facebook page for the school now features a section called 'Tiny texts' in which students are able to read and listen to short texts produced by an international site for EFL materials on matters of interest such as 'yarn bombing' (about knitting) and 'wrap rage' (about over-packaging products). The texts have some words which are highlighted and explained, students can listen to the text being read by a native speaker, and there is also a voluntary follow-up comprehension test. Students can also access the texts directly in Facebook.

Reading Community 2

Jean-Paul DuQuette set up an EFL reading circle in Second Life, a virtual world. He explains how he did this in DuQuette (2011). He asked for six volunteers and they read *Bookworms Club Bronze: Stories for Reading Circle*, published by Oxford University Press which is a collection of short, graded stories designed for a group of learners who each take roles in the circle. The roles are: 'Discussion Leader' (responsible for asking basic warm-up questions and keeping the conversation going if it falters); 'Summarizer' (responsible for summarizing the story), 'Word Master' (responsible for choosing five words that are important to the story); 'Culture Collector' (responsible for drawing parallels between the culture in the stories and the learners' own cultures); 'Passage Person' (responsible for choosing three passages to discuss that are important to the story); and 'Connector' (responsible for making connections to the learners' real lives). The participants read a story, and then had a discussion on it in a visual reading space constructed in Second Life, a Victorian-style room with a fireplace and couches.

The discussion was conducted on headphones, so everyone could hear each other's contributions, and they could also see each other's avatars. The discussion was led by an instructor. One notable feature of the interaction in the reading circle was that members shared hyperlinks in order to help each other understand. One example was when some learners did not know what a 'crane' was when it was mentioned in a story; another member uploaded and shared a picture of the bird with everyone in the circle. Members of the original circle, as well as the instructor, created other reading circles which are still taking place at the time of writing.

Reading Community 3

Melania Paduraru, a teacher in Romania, set up a Google site as a platform for her students to be able to post homework and also read each other's homework attempts before the date on which it would be graded. She explains how she did this in Paduraru (2011). The teacher assigned online reading, often based on short stories or excerpts from plays, but also suggesting other texts, such as news items and videos, which linked to the theme of the story. Students were given writing tasks based on their reading. She says that the students often read more than the initial texts which had been assigned to them, clicking on other links they found. They always read their classmates' answers before posting their own work, either to get ideas, to satisfy their curiosity, or to avoid repeating what others had said. She points out that students do not usually have access to what their classmates have written for homework, and that they may not realize that they are unconsciously evaluating what they are reading, and comparing it with their own efforts. The site was still active at the time of writing.

- Which reading skills and strategies were being practised in each of the three reading communities?
- Why do you think some communities lasted longer than others?

Reading Community 1 practised 'setting appropriate goals for comprehension' because the people who posted reviews had to extract and remember the main points of the story. It also focused on 'evaluating/appreciating the information given in the text'. Of course, other reading skills were practised too. Perhaps this community did not survive because it was a shifting one – in private language schools people tend to dip in and out of classes and may not know each other outside class. It seems to have depended on student contributions alone to keep the momentum going, and the fact that the students knew each other in 'real life' might have been an important factor in motivating interaction on the website, which stopped once they no longer met together in a real life classroom. Transferring the activity to Facebook in a different form seems to have made it more teacher directed and individual; we would argue that it has created a different kind of 'reading community' (or perhaps not even a 'community' at all, but a set of unconnected individuals) with different motivations for reading.

Reading Community 2 was highly structured and seems, by assigning roles, to have deliberately set out to focus on a wide variety of reading skills such as 'dealing with unknown words' (the 'Word Master'), 'using knowledge of the world to predict or infer information' (the 'Culture Collector' and the 'Connector') and 'setting appropriate goals for comprehension' (the 'Summarizer'). DuQuette was initially worried that students who were used to very casual and spontaneous learning experiences in Second Life would react badly to such tight rules and organization, but they seemed to like them once they had got used to them. Unlike Reading Community 1, the participants did not know each other at all in real life and were taking part from places all over the world. We could speculate that it was the 'rules' and a shared interest in learning English through reading which bound this community together. But were they a 'community' in the same sense as 'Reading Community 1' or more like the 'affinity spaces' we mentioned in Chapter 1?

Reading Community 3 seemed to have focused particularly on 'setting appropriate goals for comprehension' when students were reading the texts they were given initially by the teacher. When reading other students' work, however, the focus was more on 'evaluating/appreciating the information given in the text'. Other lower level reading skills would also have been practised, as in Reading Communities 1 and 2. Reading Community 3 knew each other in real life, like Reading Community 1, although over a longer period of time if they were in the same class for six or seven years. They were also directed by a leader, the teacher, and structured by rules, like Reading Community 2. Moreover, this community was a writing community as well as a reading community, and bound together by institutional practices and teacher assessment. Yet individuals still had some freedom to choose some of the things they read, and what they wrote. All these factors probably combined to ensure that this was a long-lived and highly-motivated community.

Reading, motivation, and 'community'

The three examples in Task 1 have illustrated something very interesting about the ways in which technology may have changed how reading is done socially. In the nineteenth century, it was common for a group of people to listen while something was being read aloud to them; they formed a community who were very interested in the content of what was being read to them, even if they were not doing the actual reading. A typical situation in the UK might be mother or father reading aloud from a Dickens or Trollope novel by the fireside. Then in the twentieth century, reading seemed to become a solitary occupation, something people did in private. The only time it was shared was when children were learning to read in their first language. If you did reading in the L2 classroom, students usually read individually to themselves, and then did comprehension questions together. They usually could not choose what they read, or what follow-up comprehension tasks they did. The three reading communities in Task 1 seem to illustrate ways in which technology is now once again enabling the process of reading to being shared as well as the product, and in a closer, more collaborative, and student-directed way. In some ways these communities seem be part of the recent social phenomena of first language reading groups which have become so popular worldwide. Reading Community 2, with its Victorian room, almost seems to be going back to fireside reading. Students taking academic courses online and commenting to each other on texts they have read are also forming one of these reading communities. Grabe (2009: 191–192) says that there is a dearth of research on L2 reading motivation, but cites research on motivation for reading in a first language which points to the following as important for developing reading skills:

1 success in learning something through reading

2 student choice and autonomy

3 social collaboration for reading tasks

4 support and **scaffolding** for reading strategies

5 interesting texts

6 opportunities for extended reading

7 evaluation and feedback that support learning.

We can see some of these features in all the three reading communities we examined in Task 1, but would suggest that the more long-lived communities display more of the features. They were, of course, different kinds of community, some of whom knew each other in 'real life' and some of whom did not, but they all shared reading processes and outcomes with each other. We could say that these types of community, which technology makes possible, increase motivation to read.

Another interesting shared feature of all the three reading communities in Task 1 was that they were all based on reading works of fiction. We noted earlier that a lot of second language reading is factual, for academic or work purposes, and it is good to see that these students are getting experience of the more personal kinds of reading as they might do in a first language. Reading literature exposes readers to creative uses of the second language, and ensures that some reading in the second language is done for entertainment and enjoyment as well as for learning information.

Using technology to learn and teach reading skills

In conventional language classrooms, a well-established way of helping second language readers to understand a text is to divide a lesson into three stages, pre-, during- and post-reading (Hedge 2000), and to encourage students to engage top-down and bottom-up levels of processing in an interactive way:

> Without a good understanding of a reasonable proportion of the details gained or proposed through some bottom-up processing, we may find it difficult to come to a clear general picture of what a text is about. But without some global understanding of the topic that is written about, even an understanding of the details may not be enough.

(Harmer 2007: 270)

In devising reading tasks themselves or using those from a coursebook, teachers are scaffolding their students' developing ability to understand a particular second language (L2) text. During the pre-reading phase they often discuss the topic of the text, or use the title or pictures accompanying the text to get an overall idea of what the text might be about. They activate their existing cultural knowledge about the topic, and perhaps get some **input** from the teacher about the second language culture. They establish what kind of text it might be, how that genre of text might be structured, and establish a reason for reading the text. Perhaps they are also introduced to some useful key words to prepare them for some of the new language they will meet in the text. During the phase of the lesson in which they are actually reading the text, learners are given tasks which encourage them to read actively, and to use reading strategies such as predicting what will come next, or guessing the meaning of unknown words. They might be encouraged to take notes, or to react to the opinions expressed in the text, or fill in charts and answer questions to help them identify the important pieces of information. They may also be asked to notice how the information in the text is organized, for example by spotting discourse markers. Post-reading activities typically ask the students to make use of the information and language they have been exposed to in the text in ways which fit in with their purpose for reading the text. Perhaps they will use their notes for a writing activity, or discuss some of the issues raised in the text.

When 'during-reading activities' are done in traditional language classrooms, it is the teacher who decides what tasks should be done in what order, but they are left with very little idea of how students carry out those tasks, or what their individual difficulties with reading the text might be. There is usually some kind of group feedback in class, but usually only a few students get the chance to give their answers. Technology provides a way of students doing these 'during-reading' activities at their own pace, and the teacher and other students being able to access and share evidence of comprehension.

Task 2	**Scrible**

Scrible is a **browser plug-in** which you can activate when you have found an online text that you think will interest your students. It enables you to highlight text and post virtual 'sticky notes', then save the text and share it with your students. Go to the site (see our website at www.oup.com/elt/teacher/tell for details). Take the tour on the website, sign up, and experiment with using the tool on a text.

• How could you use this tool to scaffold second language reading comprehension for students?
• What advantages would such a tool have over reading tasks in print coursebooks?

The tool allows you to post reading tasks for your students using 'sticky notes'. You could also ask students to highlight parts of the text, such as discourse markers, important points, vocabulary, or syntactic features. Students could reply to the teacher and other students by setting their own reading tasks for the others to carry out. The teacher will be able to see how each student works with the text, and can adjust tasks to suit different students. Students will be able to work directly online with the text outside the classroom, either alone or collaboratively. All these features make the reading experience more personalized, interactive and flexible than a print coursebook would be able to do. You will also have introduced students to a useful tool which they can use for other research and academic purposes beyond the language classroom (see Chapter 7 on study skills).

Using digital texts for second language (L2) reading

The kinds of texts which were used for reading by the communities in Task 1 were paper books and student writing posted on a website (Community 1), simplified readers available in digital form (Community 2), and student writing posted onto a website (Community 3). Technology has provided vast resources of texts which are easily available to readers in digital form, such as online newspapers, magazines and journals, online courses, e-books, websites, and digital and **interactive fiction**. Second language readers can access 'simplified readers' electronically from **ELT** publishers or free websites. Texts, including graphic novels which contain images which support second language comprehension, can be downloaded onto mobile devices. Many of these texts have either existed first in paper form, or are available in both paper and digital form. As we note in Chapter 6 on visual learning digital texts use images, embedded video and sound files, and links to other websites, in ways which encourage readers to interact with the text on the screen, and to move on to other texts, drawing these texts together in a single reading event. This is very different from the linear and sustained reading of one text which continues to be typical of the way second language reading skills are taught in many classrooms and coursebooks.

There are also an increasing number of texts which are 'born digital', that is, they have only ever existed in digital form and were created for viewing on the screen of a computer or handheld device from the very beginning. These texts typically combine text, music, sound effects, and interaction with the reader, who may be required to perform actions, such as answering questions, completing puzzles or surveys, and taking part in games. In the case of **digital fiction**, the reader can also continue the story on their own. It is likely that these kinds of texts will increase in number in the future, so it is good to expose second language readers to them. The majority of texts being produced currently are fiction rather than factual texts, but this bias may change. There may be some issues about whether the multimodal nature of these texts makes them easier or more difficult to understand for second language readers.

Task 3

Inanimate Alice – **Using digital fiction**

Search for an example of digital fiction on the internet by typing in the search terms 'digital fiction', or 'digital non-fiction', or search some digital authors, such as Kate Pullinger or Tim Wright's *Kidnapped* or *In Search of Oldton*. One example of digital fiction which was being used for second language (L2) reading at the time of writing was *Inanimate Alice*, a story which recounts the adventures of the main character, Alice, as she travels the world.

Figure 4.1 Screenshot of a digital fiction story

The screen shows what the students read, 'My friends dared me to climb to the top of the building'. There is also some other text to read: 'Keep Clear'. The physical setting displayed in the visual image makes the meaning clearer. The students decide on an appropriate action to drive the story forward, based on what they have read on the screen.

Explore one of these digital texts.

- Would it be useful for second language (L2) reading?
- What support would you need to provide as a teacher?

Such digital texts give the reader lots of choice about what they read, when and where, especially as they can read the text on mobile devices. Teachers can make use of the visuals in the text to get students to make predictions about what will happen next, if it is a digital story, or what information they will be given next, if it is a factual text. The text can be used for spin-off discussions and projects. Teachers can also ask students to evaluate how well they think the author of the text combines words, images, and sounds to build up tension, or to explain something. However, some teachers have commented that their students have found the sounds and images distracting, and that, in their opinion, these elements have sometimes made it more difficult for students to understand the written text. It may be that images which directly support comprehension of the written text are helpful, but others are not, and may impede rather than support the reading process.

Digital fiction has links with an older tradition of 'interactive fiction'. This sprang out of early game playing on computers and it makes use of straight text without visuals. The story usually starts with some screens of text, giving background on who the reader is in the game, where they are, and their objectives. The reader has to read the text and then write a simple command in order to move on to the next part of the story. So if the text tells you are standing in a library, and there is an important and mysterious closed book on the table in front of you, you might type 'take the book' or 'open the book' or even 'examine the book'. If the command is correct, the game moves on to the next stage. If not, the screen will tell you that you need to choose another action. If you get stuck, you can type the command 'help'. In many ways, these games copy what print reading mazes such as Bere and Rinvolucri (1981) did, with the bonus that rather than reading and choosing an option which has already been provided, the readers are involved in creating and writing down their own options. Task 4 illustrates one story which has been used for teaching English as a second language. You can read more about how this was done on Joe Pereira's blog (refer to our website for more details).

Task 4	**Interactive fiction**

Try googling an example of 'interactive fiction', or go to the interactive story, entitled '9:05', by Adam Cadre, which can be found on our website. Then answer the following questions:

- What do the students have to do?
- What second language (L2) reading skills might this be useful for teaching?

- What support might the teacher have to provide ?
- What sort of relationship is being created between reading and writing in the second language (L2)?

The students have to read the text onscreen very carefully, and then decide what to type in to move on to the next stage of the story, discussing possibilities with each other. This kind of interaction encourages the development of lower-level word-processing skills, since the students will need to read and understand all the details of the scene, and all the words in the text. The teacher will need to encourage students to access online dictionaries for the meaning and pronunciation of unknown words, or to enter the text in a site which will highlight all the words (see our website for suggestions) – students can then click on the words they need explained or translated. This environment does not contain images, so many 'gamers' will actually draw sketches of the rooms in the story, and this is something students can be encouraged to do. The connection between reading and writing is mutually helpful because the reading text provides many of the words which students will need to reuse when they type in commands. This kind of 'interactive fiction' is very similar to video games which involve reading; Gee (2007) has pointed to some of the advantages for first language reading of using such games, and Nevill et al. (2009) and others have investigated their use in improving second language (L2) reading skills; the gains seem to be particularly in the area of vocabulary learning.

Connections between second language (L2) reading and writing

There are many ways in which technology enables L2 reading texts to be combined with listening, speaking, and writing skills. In the case of listening and speaking, the 'Tiny texts' example in Task 1, Reading Community 1, allowed students to read a second language text and listen to it at the same time if they wanted to. In Reading Community 2, the students spoke to each other using headsets as they discussed the reading text in Second Life. Students can watch films and read subtitles or access the film script and read at the same time as listening. Nik Peachey suggests using a program called CuePrompt for reading aloud in class. This program allows the user to paste text into a screen, which then scrolls the text like a teleprompter at a speed you and the students choose. He explains how to use it on his blog (see our website for more details). Reading and writing are particularly closely associated in some kinds of second language reading, such as reading (and writing) for academic purposes. Hudson (2007) says that while the processes of reading and writing have differences, they also have many similarities, as both readers and writers are involved in 'creating an internal text', building up propositions and connecting them with previous knowledge. Readers and writers are engaged in a kind of dialogue with each other mediated through the text, as readers try to link their own experiences with the linguistic cues the writer is providing in order to understand a text, and writers try to convey their meaning in a manner which is considerate of readers. There have been a number of studies on the ways in which reading helps people to become good writers. Some of these studies have focused on the ways in which first language and second language readers recognize the ways of organizing information which are typical of particular genres, and use those discourse patterns when they write themselves, for example, Lenski and Johns (1997) with reports, and Crowhurst (1991) with reading and writing persuasive texts. Task 5 looks at ways in which technology can help students and teachers to use 'graphic organizers' to discover how the information in a text is structured.

Task 5	### Using graphic organizers

Graphic organizers are visual ways of organising the information which writers convey to readers. They have also been called 'mind maps' or 'entity relationship charts'. They can be used to show different kinds of relationship between the information, such as different characters or events in a narrative, descriptions, comparing and contrasting, classifying, cause and effect, and so on. Teachers have used mind maps for many years as a way of encouraging students to extract information from texts, to generate ideas, and to see new possible connections between different kinds of information. Technology permits learners and teachers to download and create all kinds of possible mind-map designs from fairly conservative visuals such as Venn diagrams, spiderwebs, wheels, and trees, to more elaborate and decorative items, such as ice-cream cones and butterflies. Students can add photos and drawings to the mind map. You can find websites which will help you do this by googling 'graphic organizers educational use'. Currently, EnchantedLearning has a number of suggestions for types and uses of organizers, and Inspiration and Kidspiration have free trials of software. Students can complete an organizer alone or collaboratively on screen. You can find these and other suggestions on our accompanying website.

- Try using one of the organizers as a way of jotting down some themes from this chapter, together with your own ideas and thoughts about using technology for teaching reading skills.
- Did you find this a better way of representing your understanding of the chapter than just writing a series of notes in bullet form? Why/why not?
- Could you think of other graphics requiring you to associate a number of themes with a single central topic which you could use for organizing this kind of information?

You may have found this method made your mind work more creatively. Making images in this way allows students, by transposing ideas from a text which they have read into a different form, to see them from a new perspective, which can give rise to new thinking and learning. They are useful for visual learners, and whilst do not make as many demands for producing language on learners as writing a summary would do, they effectively demonstrate whether or not learners have understood what they have read. Graphic organizer websites suggest spidergrams, clouds, and clocks for generating summaries and overviews, whereas flowcharts or Venn diagrams are useful for narratives and comparisons. When students have written information in the graphic organizer, they are then prepared for a further writing task which can, in turn, lead to new perspectives on the information in the text, more than a student would gain from simply rereading the text (Fitzgerald and Shanahan 2000: 43)

Summary

This chapter has considered some of the skills and strategies which second language (L2) readers need to develop, and some of the differences that may exist between reading in a second language and a first language. We suggested that new reading habits and new kinds of **digital text** may be changing the way in which reading is done. Students have a wealth of reading material readily available to them on the Internet, including simplified readers, e-books, and online newspapers, as well as texts which have been 'born digital'. The tasks in this chapter have illustrated some of the types of reading texts which are available to students. There may need to be fresh approaches to reading instruction which do not assume that reading is done in a solitary, linear way within the confines of the classroom. Reading could be done in a more motivating way in collaboration with others online, or interactively with a digital text. Some examples have been given for using technology for 'during-reading' activities which allow students to set tasks for each other, and other activities which link the teaching of reading with writing, listening, and speaking skills.

Further reading

Chapelle, C. and **J. Jamieson,** 2008. *Tips for teaching with CALL: practical approaches to computer assisted language learning.* Harlow: Pearson Longman.

DuQuette, J-P. 2011. 'Buckling down: initiating an EFL reading circle in a casual online learning group'. *JALTCALL Journal* 7.1: 79–92.
Paduraru, M. 2011. 'Online homework'. *IATEFL Voices* 222, September–October 2011: 4–5.

5

WRITING SKILLS

I write entirely to find out what I'm thinking, what I'm looking at, what I see and what it means.
JOAN DIDION, writer

You never have to change anything you got up in the middle of the night to write.
SAUL BELLOW, writer

Aims

In this chapter, we try to give you some answers to the following questions:

- What skills do students need to learn when writing in a second language (L2)?
- How can technology support the learning of writing skills?
- How has technology altered the nature of writing – how it is done, how it is read by an audience, and how it is shaped?

Introduction

Technology has provided us with new opportunities and challenges for learning the skills of writing; at the same time it has altered the ways in which we conceive of and perform many writing tasks. The first section of this chapter considers some of the skills involved in second language writing and the teaching approaches which are currently used. The second part looks at how technology can support those approaches and the final sections consider the various new written genres which are emerging through digital communication with the difficulties and advantages these present for learning how to write.

What skills do second language (L2) writers need to learn?

Writing is an important skill for both first language (L1) and second language (L2) learners. Written examinations, letters of application, curriculum vitae, and so forth act as important means of entry to education and jobs: if you cannot write proficiently, the sad fact is that you will probably be 'excluded from a wide range of social roles' (Tribble 1996).

Task 1

How second language (L2) writers feel

A group of proficient L2 writers who were just about to embark on an MA in TESOL were asked how they felt about the large amount of 'high stakes' writing in English which they would be required to do over the next year. Read their comments (given in their own words and spelling) and consider the questions which follow:

1 'I feel afraid and anxious especially about my grammar.'
2 'I do not exactly know how to write in an academic tone. I cannot tell which words are academic, and which words are spoken words.'
3 'I feel worried about the writing system that the School of Education is expecting for us to use.'
4 'I want to explore some writing skills including western logical thinking and organization.'
5 'How much reading is enough for an assignment?'
6 'Am I going to have enough information to get close to the word count required?'
7 'I'm afraid to do plagerism (not sure of the spelling) without intention.'

What kinds of problems with writing do these comments reveal? Do they apply to L1 writers as well as L2 writers?

The quotations introduce a number of the problems we might associate with writing in both a first language, as well as a second language. In comments 1 and 2, the writers feel that their knowledge of various aspects of the language (grammar, vocabulary) may not be adequate. In comments three and seven, they are worried about not knowing the rules of a genre which is new to them (academic assignments). Comment four seems to express the idea that genres may be organized differently in a second language culture. Comments five and six are about content – getting the ideas to write about, and being able to keep on writing. None of our proficient writers mentioned problems with a new script, but beginning second language writers would probably have done so in similar circumstances. It was interesting that, while these writers recognized their problems with writing, they had plans for dealing with them independently out of class as well as in class, and they were very positive about their ability to do so. Without any prompting, they mentioned ways in which technology could help them, such as using the internet to look up and translate words, or using grammar and spell checkers. The student comments are about the perceived requirements of academic writing, but they echo the general second language writing skills defined by experts in the field such as Hyland (2009), Swales (1990), Tribble (1996), and White and Arndt (1991). We have also found it useful to refer to Schellekens (2007), who discusses the writing skills needed by newly arrived immigrants, and Cameron (2001) who considers children learning to write in a second language. The table below shows a number of the skills which are involved in second language writing:

Skills involved in second language (L2) writing
Writing in a new script
Understanding the links between sounds and spelling (no easy task if the language is English!)
Using the L2 language system to express ideas accurately and clearly
Connecting ideas to create a coherent structure, using discourse markers and linking words
Arranging ideas into rhetorical patterns – for example, problem-solution, which will be recognizable and interpretable by the reader
Using the language and organizational structure appropriate to a particular genre
Planning, reviewing, revising, and editing drafts of a piece of writing so as to get closer to the meaning the writer wishes to express
Picturing an intended audience and goal, and shaping a piece of writing in a way that communicates most effectively with that audience and achieves that goal
Obeying the rules of a particular discourse community, while also expressing the writer's own individual voice

Table 5.1 *Skills involved in second language (L2) writing*

Current approaches to the teaching of writing

Traditionally, approaches to L2 writing have focused on three main areas (Hyland 2009). The first is the actual piece of writing produced by the learner (often called the 'product' approach, which concentrates on the language and organization of written texts), the second focuses on the writer and what she/he does to produce a text (the 'process' approach, which acknowledges, for example, that writers may produce and edit a number of drafts before the final version), and the third focuses on the reader and the ways in which the writer engages with an audience in a social context, i.e. writing as a 'social practice'. Current methodology tends to combine these approaches, since both research into second language writing and teachers' and students' experience in learning and using writing skills in the 'real world' suggest that text, writer, and reader are inextricably bound up with each other and cannot be artificially separated. Learners need to draw on all three approaches in order to become proficient writers. If we go back to the second language writing skills which we described in the previous section, we can see that different skills may lend themselves to different approaches, but that the approaches also tend to overlap.

Writing skill	Approach
Writing in a new script	Product – usually involves copying examples
Understanding the links between sounds and spelling (no easy task if the language is English!)	Product – but readers expect correct spelling; incorrect spelling may hamper intelligibility
Using the L2 language system to express ideas accurately and clearly	Product – but also entails the fact that the ideas are being communicated to an audience
Connecting ideas to create a coherent structure, using discourse markers and linking words	Product – but also entails the fact that the ideas are being communicated to an audience
Arranging ideas into rhetorical patterns – for example, problem-solution, which will be recognizable and interpretable by the reader	Product – but also involves reader expectations
Using language and organizational structure appropriate to a particular genre	Product – but also involves reader expectations
Planning, reviewing, revising and editing drafts of their writing to get closer to the meaning the writer wishes to express	Process – but is often done together with others who read and comment as an audience
Picturing an intended audience and goal, shaping a piece of writing in a way that communicates most effectively with that audience and achieves that goal	Social practice
Obeying the rules of a particular discourse community, while also expressing the writer's own individual voice	Social practice – but also involves linguistic knowledge of genres

Table 5.2 Writing skills and teaching approaches

In the classroom, the three approaches we mentioned above have been associated with particular methods of teaching writing (Badger and White 2000, Harmer 2007). Product approaches, for example, often involve students in analysing the language and organization of model texts, or reproducing part of a text but with variations to make it more personal. Process approaches get students to brainstorm ideas, draft texts, then ask others to read and comment, and – as a result – edit for content and language, and redraft. The editing and drafting process is repeated until the writer is happy with the final draft. Social practice approaches focus on analysing genres but also try to give students a sense of the expectations of readers in a particular context (for example, a university department, a sports club, a small business). Teaching techniques for the social practice approach can involve students in ethnographic research of a particular discourse community, in which, for example, they choose a particular 'field site' – a class they are taking, a workplace, a professional organization – and find out what texts are produced in that setting, as well as interviewing the people who produce and receive them (Johns, Hyland et al. 2006). Technology can be used to support all three approaches.

Product approaches

Task 2

OWLs

Online Writing Labs (OWLs) have been around for almost as long as the internet. One of the oldest and best known is the Purdue University OWL which has been in existence since 1995. OWLs provide a wide range of resources for writers including grammar advice, guidance on referencing, tips on getting started, avoiding writer's block, and so on. Although OWLs are generally intended for students at the home university, many – including the Purdue OWL – have sections for visitors.

Exploring the OWL

Go to the Purdue University OWL (see our accompanying website at www.oup.com/elt/teacher/tell for details) and access the area of the site that is available to non-members of the university.

- What kinds of resources are available?
- What is the target audience for these resources?
- Would any of the resources be useful for your learners? Which ones? Why?

Using the OWL

Choose a resource or group of resources that you might use in a lesson with your learners. Why have you chosen this resource?

- Where in the lesson would you use this resource?
- How will you introduce it to your learners?
- What will you ask your learners to do with the resource?
- How would this fit with your overall approach to teaching writing?

OWL resources are generally intended for learners to use as reference material when they are struggling with writing outside the classroom. Some of the useful material which is provided includes exercises on spelling, punctuation, sentence structure, vocabulary, and summarizing small sections of text. There are also frameworks which help the learner with the organization of genres such as business letters. These are the kinds of activities which we would associate with a product approach. One way of introducing the OWLS facilities to a class might be to get them to explore and evaluate the resources. Pairs or groups of students could make notes about one of the resources and then present it to the class, adding their own evaluative comments about how useful they think the resource is.

Process approaches

Technology has made the process approach much easier to carry out in classrooms. If we think of writing as involving cyclical processes of idea generation, planning, drafting, composing, editing, and revising (White and Arndt 1991), there are many technological tools which are currently available for second language (L2) writers to do these things, and there are likely to be even more in the future. Here is a representative, but probably not exhaustive, list:

Idea generation and researching the genre:
mind mapping, scrapbooking, digital storytelling, online encyclopaedias, Wikipedia, web quests.

Planning/finding the language:
online dictionaries, concordances, genre analysing from the internet, Word/ PowerPoint outlining, writing model tools such as Easywriter, WriteFix, English-Zone, My Access.

Drafting (involves small amounts of text):
word processors, sticky notes, fast switching between applications so notes are alongside text, programs which predict and read out text as you type it, such as WordQ.

Composing:
Etherpad and wikish for collaborative composition, word processing, inserting pictures, music, weblinks, online writing labs such as DIWE 7.

Editing for content and language:
word processing.

Revision:
wikis, Googledocs, conferencing, feedback from tutor using 'comment' facility.

Task 3

Maps and plans

This task focuses on helping students to plan their writing. You will need a mind mapping program or website (see our website for suggestions) for the first part of this activity and then some presentation software (for example, PowerPoint). The activity asks you to plan a report about how technology can help students to learn writing skills.

- Using your mind-mapping program, make a mind map about the main ideas that you have taken from this chapter and any other ideas that you can add.
- Use the mind map to group and structure your ideas into themes for the report.
- Once the mind map is complete, you have the option to present your ideas to others. A PowerPoint presentation will help you to further organize your ideas.
- Export your mind map as an image file and insert the image into a PowerPoint presentation.
- Using one slide for each planned section of your report, outline your main points and subheadings.

- If possible, present your report outline to your colleagues and use their feedback to improve your report.

Mind mapping on paper is a commonly used technique for planning a piece of writing. The advantage of mind-mapping software is that the final map can be exported and saved. With most mind-mapping software, it is possible to add extensive text notes to the branches of a map, which means that quite a lot of the document can be written at this stage of the process. Mind-mapping software also makes it easy to move map branches and to rearrange the hierarchy of the branches. Mind-mapping tools also facilitate collaboration. Some of the online mind-mapping tools allow users to collaborate in real time, even when they are not in the same physical location, but any mind map can be emailed to collaborative writing partners for comments.

Presentation software can also be useful for planning writing, especially of extended texts such as reports. Presentations are naturally broken into slides and this allows writers to think about how to structure the content for each individual section – or even paragraph. This can be particularly useful for writers who are struggling to construct paragraphs. The slide heading should always contain the main point that the slide is making (equivalent to the key sentence of a paragraph) with the evidence and supporting points as bulleted items. Whilst creating presentations with flipchart paper or overhead transparencies is possible without technology, there is no doubt that it is software such as PowerPoint that has really brought presentations into the classroom. However, there have been accusations (for example, Gabriel 2008) that such software is often overused by teachers and others in powerful positions, which means that activities which put presentation software in the hands of learners can be especially valuable.

Word-processing tools such as the review and comment facilities in Word, dictionaries, spelling and grammar checkers etc., all allow for feedback on writing in progress. The next task shows how feedback can be given in a dynamic and collaborative way between tutor and student using a collaborative word-processing tool which helps the student to draft, edit, and revise.

Task 4	**Writing tutorial**

Because EtherPad is a collaborative word processor, this task really requires two people. If this is not possible then you can 'pretend' to be two people by opening and switching between two browser programs (for example, Internet Explorer and Firefox). You can use one browser to create the pad and then copy/paste the share link into the address bar or the other browser.

One partner will take the role of tutor and the other will take the role of student. We recommend that you use EtherPad, which is an online collaborative word processor, for this activity, but if that is no longer available then you could use a virtual classroom to share an ordinary word-processing program (see Chapter 3 for more about using virtual classrooms).

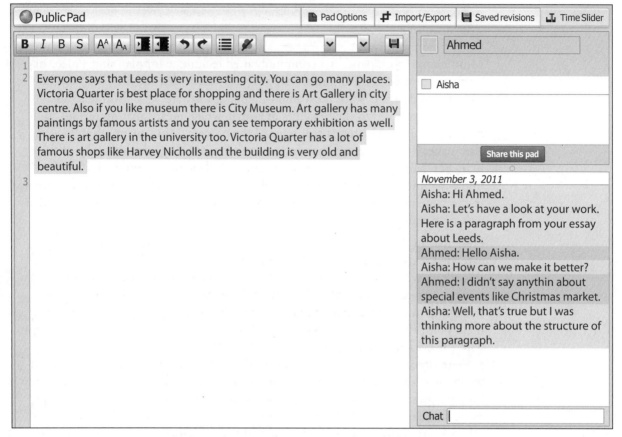

Figure 5.1 Screenshot of a collaborative word processor

- Go to one of the EtherPad sites listed on our website and open a new pad.
- Paste or upload some text from a second language (L2) writer into the pad (you could use the prepared text on our website or your own text).
- Using the **chat facility**, the tutor should explain to the student how the text can be improved. The student can, of course, ask questions. The students then edit the text following tutor instruction. If you like, you can choose to focus on a particular difficulty. If the student tends to write unstructured paragraphs, you could revise one paragraph so that it has a key sentence followed by evidence/examples. The student would then revise another paragraph in the same way.

Usually, feedback given to students about their writing is static. Even in a face-to-face tutorial, the feedback tends to be about text that does not change. However, if you are using a shared word processor, both tutor and learner can edit the document in real time. The tutor can model good writing and the student can, immediately, follow the model. As the student is writing, the tutor can comment on the process. This allows the student to benefit from working with, in Vygotskian terms, a '**more able peer**' (Vygotsky 1978).

Using the text chat window for discussion means that the learner can practise ideas in writing before adding them to the main text. The text chat does not have to be in the same language as the main text, so at least part of the discussion could be in the first language (L1). Even where the target language is used in the chat it does not need to be in the same genre as the main text; learners understand that text chat allows informality, 'txt spk' and emoticons where the main document does not (Tikkirou and Walker, in preparation).

Social practice approach

At the time of writing, Twitter is a popular **microblogging** site. The site allows users to post messages of up to 140 characters, either typed into the site or sent via text message. Users can also 'retweet' messages that they have read, and send them on to other people whom they think might be interested. Several websites (such as newspapers) allow articles to be '**tweeted**' from the website. Users can opt to 'follow' other users and the use of 'hashtags' enables users to tag items and to search for themed posts. Twitter can be seen as a community, as a way to keep up with news or as a way to update friends and followers with personal news. This kind of activity is called 'microblogging'. There have been several major political events, especially in the Middle East, where Twitter has played an important role by enabling ordinary people to broadcast news (globally) as it developed. Facebook 'status updates' provide another microblogging service. There are also alternative micro blogging services for education (see our website) which may be more appropriate to your context.

Task 5 shows how microblogging can be used to help L2 students practise summary skills when communicating with a virtual audience.

Task 5

News tweetment

This is designed as an activity for a group or class. You can undertake this activity on your own, but this may not give you the opportunity to experience the social aspects of Twitter. You will each need a Twitter account (or an account with an alternative microblogging service).

Make sure that you are 'following' other members of the group on Twitter.

Every day, for at least a week, choose a news item that interests you and post a tweet that expresses the main point of the headline and your opinion of it. Don't use the 'tweet' buttons that are included on many news websites; the tweet must be in your own words. You can, however, use a 'tweet' button in order to find a shortened link for a webpage as long as you use your own words instead of the news headline.

At the end of the week consider:

- How easy or difficult was it to summarize the articles and your opinions in 140 characters?
- What effect did the demands of a 140-character post have on your writing, thinking, and language?
- If you worked with colleagues, did the replies of other tweeters help you?
- What other ways can you think of to use Twitter for writing activities in your classroom?

One of the skills which learners need for academic writing in a second language is knowing when and how to summarize in their own words. The 140-character limit on Twitter means that in order to communicate their ideas, writers need to think clearly and choose the words which will communicate their idea most effectively. The possibility of instant feedback will let them know if they have done so. Microblogging can be used to learn both writing and reading skills simultaneously, and because tweets are only 140 characters long, they are not too daunting for second language learners to produce or absorb. Some of our teacher trainees came up with the following suggestions for using microblogging for language and content learning:

- Follow an **ESOL** or language 'guru' such as Stephen Fry, Stephen Krashen, or Scott Thornbury and learn from their tweets (language as well as content).

- Send a word or an idiom a day to other 'followers' in the same class, or post a new word, which the others have to guess the meaning of.

- Tell a story, with each person taking it in turn to add a line of the story. The students can choose the best tweets to summarize into a final story, which is posted as a blog.

- Tweeting 'in character'. This method has been used by the Royal Shakespeare company in the UK to tweet the play *Romeo and Juliet* with six actors playing different roles in the play and linking their followers to, for example, videos of Juliet's room and her songs. You could also tweet as a historical character, which others have to guess, or pretend you are commenting on a historical event you are all present at.

- Use Twitter to start discussions, such as 'What does pollution mean to you?' or 'How can we solve the economic crisis?' which can then be followed by a classroom discussion or by collating the opinions into a website.

- Tweet about the learning process as you work on a written assignment – sharing good resources, tips, and difficulties.

New challenges for teaching second language (L2) writing

The exponential increase in written digital communication poses some new challenges for teachers of second language writing skills. Firstly, new written genres are emerging which are still relatively unstable, and so it becomes more difficult to predict their language and organization. Sometimes it seems that communicating the message is more important than linguistic correctness, (it is not considered polite to correct someone's spelling in an email or an SMS message, for example). It is calculated that currently two thirds of the texts in English on the internet are written by second language speakers, which again has consequences for the notion of correctness. All these factors present difficulties for the product approach and exactly what language to teach, although on the other hand, technology has made it much easier to show students sample texts or 'products' in a particular genre by accessing them on the internet. Similarly, the audience for written texts on the internet has become wider and more unpredictable, which poses some questions for the social practice approach, which has tended to view the audience as more specific and local.

There are other challenges that teachers face when using technology to teach second language writing. One has to do with **plagiarism**. One of the ways in which writers become more proficient is to imitate the language of those who are already skilled in a particular genre. Second language writers find it very helpful to reproduce or modify 'correct' examples of language as a means of learning grammatical and rhetorical structures and vocabulary, and this is why it is one of the features of the product approach. Yet such practices, if done at the wrong time and place, or in the wrong way, can be considered plagiarism. Word processing and the internet together create new possibilities for plagiarism because it is so easy to copy and paste, and a lot of internet communication involves reusing other people's texts, such as when we 'retweet' a message, or forward an email. The audience for internet texts is wide and anonymous. Once a text has been produced by the original writer and sent to the original recipient, it is easy for anyone to reproduce the text and to disseminate it in ways which the original writer could never have envisaged. Celebrities and politicians have found this out to their cost! This has radically altered notions of authorship and ownership of written texts, and it is something which students need to be aware of when they launch a text into **cyberspace**. Task 6 will ask you to consider some of these issues related to the copying of internet texts, copyright and plagiarism.

| Task 6 | ### Why I sent Oxford a rejection letter |

The following text, which is overleaf on page 70, appeared in the online edition of The Guardian on January 19th, 2012. Read it and then consider the questions below:

- Who was the intended audience for the email?
- Who was the actual audience?
- Would the writer have written differently, do you think, if she had known her email would **go viral**?
- Do you think the girl's friend was right to post her email on Facebook?
- Was posting the email on Facebook an act of plagiarism by the friend?
- The newspaper article invites you to 'share'. If you did so, would it involve you in doing any writing?
- What are the implications of this story for students who wish to publish their writing on the web?

| News | Paralympics | Sport | Comment | Culture | Business | Money | Life & style | Travel | Environment |

Comment is free

Why I sent Oxford a rejection letter

Withdrawing my application to the university makes perfect sense – it's a symbol of unfairness in our education system

Share 1722

Comments 1011

'I sent the email after returning from my interview at Oxford, to prove to a couple of my friends that Oxbridge did not need to be held in awe.'

A little over a month ago, I sent Oxford a rejection email that parodied the thousands that they send each year. Much to my surprise, it has become a bit of an internet hit, and has provoked reactions of both horror and amusement.

In it, I wrote: "I have now considered your establishment as a place to read Law (Jurisprudence). I very much regret to inform you that I will be withdrawing my application. I realise you may be disappointed by this decision, but you were in competition with many fantastic universities and following your interview I am afraid you do not quite meet the standard of the universities I will be considering."
I sent the email after returning from my interview at Magdalen College, Oxford, to prove to a couple of my friends that Oxbridge did not need to be held in awe. One of them subsequently shared it on Facebook because he found it funny.

I certainly did not expect the email to spread as far as it has. Varying between offers of TV interviews and hundreds of enthusiastic Facebook messages (including, rather bizarrely, dozens from Peru), it has certainly been far-reaching. I find this hard to explain – but perhaps it's because there is little light-hearted mockery of Oxbridge around. Many of my friends and undoubtedly many strangers were unable to comprehend that I'd sent such an email to this bastion of prestige and privilege. Why was I not afraid of damaging my future prospects as a lawyer? Didn't I think this might hurt my chances with other universities?

For me, such questions paint a picture of a very cynical society. I do not want to study law because I want to be rich, or wear an uncomfortable wig and cloak. Perhaps optimistically, I want to study law because I am interested in justice.

To me, withdrawing my application to an institution that is a symbol of unfairness in both our education and the legal system (which is so dominated by Oxbridge graduates) makes perfect sense, and I am reluctant to be part of a system so heavily dominated by such a narrow group of self-selecting elites. It seems tragic that people often seem to believe that individuals should compromise their beliefs in favour of improving their ambiguous "future prospects".

So, why did I apply in the first place? If you're achieving high grades at A-level (or equivalent) you can feel quite a lot of pressure to "prove yourself" by getting an Oxbridge offer. Coupled with the fact that I grew up on benefits in council estates throughout Bristol – not a type of heritage often associated with Oxbridge interview – I decided to give it a try.

It was only at interview that I started to question what exactly I was trying to prove. I was well aware that fantastic candidates are often turned down, and I did not believe that this was a true reflection of their academic potential. It no longer made any sense to me to subject myself to their judgment, and so I withdrew my application.

As to my opinions on the future of Oxbridge, I share many of the views put forward by Owen Jones . Although I take issue with his concern that not going to Oxbridge gives you a "chip on your shoulder", which seemingly makes your opinion less valid. I did not write to Oxford to avoid the risk of being labelled as an "Oxbridge reject": I already am one. Last year I made an (admittedly weak) application to Cambridge and was inevitably rejected post-interview. I am proud of the so-called "chip on my shoulder" and I do not believe anyone's opinion should be invalidated simply because they did not attend Oxbridge.

A year ago, I was in awe of the beautiful buildings of Oxbridge, but today I am in awe of the sheer number of people who, like me, have managed to not take it so seriously. Ultimately, I am not harming Oxford by laughing at it, and it is an amazing feeling to realise that so many people are enjoying my email. I hope that at a time when youth unemployment has hit an astounding 22.3%, my inconsequential mockery of this venerable institution provides a little light-hearted humour.

Figure 5.2 Why I sent Oxford a rejection letter

The intended audience were a couple of friends and some tutors at Oxford University, but the actual audience extended into thousands, as it was posted by one of the friends on Facebook, and then picked up by the press and news media. It seems that, in this case, the original writer was quite happy for the email to be read by a wide audience, although it is interesting that some of the comments she received on Facebook were quite insulting, calling her silly and stupid for turning down a possible place at a very prestigious university. There have been other cases in which the original writer did not expect, or was unhappy with their emails or tweets being widely circulated. The morality of forwarding emails or other written texts only intended for the recipient is debatable, but it was not plagiarism because the original recipient, and following recipients, probably 'framed' the original email with their own comments, making it clear it was not their own text. New writing practices contain a lot of this framing. When people get into trouble, it is for not framing or otherwise making it clear that they have not themselves written the text they have copied. Another moral of this story is that students and their teachers need to be careful what they say and where they publish texts on the internet because they can take on a life of their own in ways the original writer could not have imagined.

Another challenge is connected to the more general problem of how L2 writers can develop their own individual 'voice' and express individual identity. Johns, Hyland et al. note that:

> One reason that second language writers find academic genres so daunting is that they are frequently told, by textbooks, style gurus, and sometimes by teachers, to abandon their personalities and write in an 'objective', neutral way. All writing, however, is an act of identity in which people take positions, engage their readers, and express themselves in different ways.

(Johns, Hyland et al. 2006: 237)

They have a number of suggestions about how individual writer 'stance' or position can be expressed linguistically. Expressing individual attitude while conforming to the rules of a particular genre remains a problem for both L1 and L2 writers. Part of asserting identity or voice is in relation to the audience we are addressing, and that becomes more difficult if it is a wide and unpredictable audience on the internet. It is often suggested that L2 writers may benefit from practising their writing at first in a 'sheltered' environment in cyberspace, for a specific and known audience, which can be done by controlling access so that users need a username and password to read or comment on the work. Some commentators, however, believe that writers on the internet do have a clear sense of audience and context (Myers 2010). In some ways, the receivers of written messages on the internet may be more real, because they can respond, than those traditionally evoked in classroom writing tasks: 'Audiences in cyberspace may not always be as 'imaginary' as they often seem to be in traditional composition classes.' (Bloch 2008: 118). Bloch tracks the comments of his students, showing that they picture their imaginary audiences in some detail as they design websites (2008: 118–121) and have a real sense of who they are writing for.

How technology is changing the way we write

We have alluded earlier in this chapter, and also in Chapter 3, to the emergence of new written genres on the internet which have their own, highly individual ways of using language and structuring ideas. We have considered one example of these new genres, Twitter. In this section, we consider two further examples, wikis and blogs, in terms of the kinds of writing skills they develop and the opportunities they provide for language learning.

Wikis

Wikis have already been used by teachers for teaching reading and writing skills, although there has been relatively little actual research into wiki-based writing outside the higher education sector. One primary-school example is Doult and Walker (in preparation) who used wikis to develop non-chronological report writing, as shown in the screenshot below.

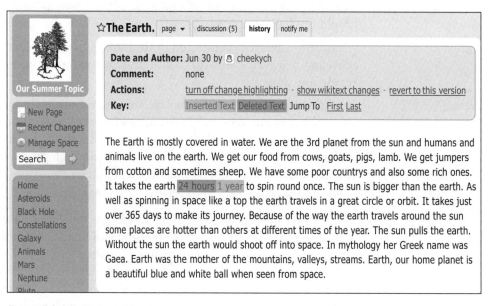

Figure 5.3 Screenshot of a wiki

Sze (2008) has some interesting suggestions for many ways in which wikis can be used with secondary school ESL students. These include collaborative poetry or story writing; student-made quizzes and worksheets; using wikis to plan class activities, such as a party; and question/response type activities, such as an 'agony aunt' website. One of us makes extensive use of wikis for annotated class lists where students add photographs and personal descriptions. Another colleague uses them so that students can continue class discussions and prepare assignments together. Warschauer suggests that wikis and blogs may develop different writing skills. Writing a wiki helps with:

exploring identity, expressing one's voice, airing diverse views and developing community ...Wikis are ... an especially powerful digital tool for collaborative writing and collective knowledge development

(Warschauer 2010: 4–5)

Blogs and wikis are often mentioned in the same breath as though they are interchangeable. However, there are important differences which need to be considered when deciding which tool to use for a particular task. In general, even when a blog has multiple authors, most individual blog posts are written by a single author. Although most blogging platforms allow published posts to be edited, it is rare for a published post to undergo substantial changes and so a blog post can be considered as a 'finished' piece of writing. Wikis, on the other hand, are designed for multi-author writing and any individual wiki page is likely to have been written and edited by several people. It is not uncommon for wiki pages to be edited several times after publication, and the edits may be substantial, so a wiki page is always a work in progress. Wikis contain a history feature which shows how the page has been edited, when, and by whom, and allows the page to be reverted to an earlier version. This is why Wikipedia can allow editing of all but the most contentious pages; frivolous or malicious edits can be undone in seconds. Wiki histories, by the way, can be extremely useful for teachers assessing group projects as the history shows exactly what each group member has contributed.

Task 7	**Public wikis or Wikipedia**

Look at a page in a public wiki such as Wikipedia, which is available at: http://en.wikipedia.org/. You might like to choose a topic which you are an expert on, such as a type of music or a sport. Read both the main article page and the discussion page (you can find tabs for the discussion page at the top of the main page). Then try to answer the following questions:

- How are the main article and the discussion page different?
- Who do you think is the audience for each page?
- How are the texts arranged?
- Is each page a single text or multiple texts?
- Did either page include material other than words? For what purpose?
- How many voices can you 'hear' on each page?
- How does the language use in the two pages differ?
- Is the main article 'finished'? How can you tell?

This activity demonstrates two genres of internet writing which appear in the same 'space'. The formal wiki article is intended to provide objective information to an unknown, public audience and to do so in a way that conveys authority. Although there are multiple authors, as can be seen by viewing the page history, the article is written with the aim that a single voice be heard. It looks rather like an entry in a print encyclopaedia, with images and a list of references at the end. It may also contain audio or video files. The discussion page is different. It is an informal conversation between peers about how the main page could be improved –

although some may feel they have more authority than others and try to convince the others that they know what they are talking about. But the language is much closer to spoken language, the language of chat. In the Wikipedia entry on 'folk music', for example, people write things like 'All right guys, this has gotten out of control', and 'Thanks, I'm quite happy with that'. The authors use pseudonyms and may or may not know each other in real life – the likelihood is that they do not and that their shared enterprise and conversations are entirely within the wiki. Both the main page and the discussion page show that authors require considerable skill to negotiate joint authorship (coincidentally, this is a skill which students develop when they are exposed to the process approach to writing). Both pages also demonstrate that internet texts are often dynamic and continually a 'work in progress'. Although a Wikipedia article may seem complete, users are engaged in a continuous process of editing and updating. The community of editors is not fixed; new editors may join at any time and each new participant will bring his or her own ideas to the text. There is never a point when the article can be considered finished.

The Wikipedia pages we considered in Task 7 demonstrate a number of features of internet texts in general. For instance, a wiki does not seem to comfortably belong to a single genre of 'traditional' writing. There is a lot of latitude in traditional genres; writers such as Swales (1990) have noted that examples of a genre can range considerably from those that are most typical of the genre to those that are less so. However, for the first time we are experiencing the emergence of a large number of relatively unstable and rapidly evolving written genres such as email, texting, chat, blogging, tweeting, **instant messaging**, and social networking. Crystal (2011) has questioned whether they can be called single genres, since each contains such a wide variety of purposes, topics, and addressees. Only the widest of generalizations can be made about the linguistic features of writing on the internet: 'On the whole, internet language is better seen as writing which has been pulled some way in the direction of speech rather than speech which has been written down' (Crystal 2011:21). How do we prepare second language (L2) writers for producing appropriate texts, not just for established genres but also for these new genres, which are unstable, rapidly developing, and blur the distinctions between written and spoken language? Perhaps the answer is that students can only learn through the experience of writing them, with feedback from readers, who can include the teacher.

Blogs

Having an audience who comment on the student's writing can encourage and focus the writing process, and **blogs** have been a very popular means of creating such an audience. Educators have used them for a number of learning purposes with students, to encourage reflection and critical thinking (Chan and Ridgway 2006, Mynard 2007) for content learning, and for developing reading and writing skills and general language learning (Campbell 2003, Johnson 2004, Abu Bakar and Ismail 2009).

| **Task 8** | **Blog for a week** |

Start a blog. You can find sites which will help you set up a blog – currently Google's *Blogger* and *WordPress* are good free sites, and *Blogger* enables you to set up a 'closed group' blogsite. Although there are some sites that offer paid-for versions with enhanced features, you can usually get all that you need from the free versions available. You will need to sign up for an account so that you can log in and post. Look at some examples of 'top' blogs (which Blogger calls 'blogs of note' and Wordpress refers to as 'Freshly Pressed') to get some inspiration and an idea of what the genre consists of if you are new to blogging.

To make a post, click the 'new post' button. You will then see the editing interface, which is where you write your text. Of course, the interface on different blogging sites will vary, but all will have an editing interface. Whichever site you choose will give you a similar range of features. There will always be basic editing tools that allow images to be inserted and links to be created. In addition, there will always be a choice between 'compose' mode, which allows you to type and edit text, and HTML mode, which allows you to edit the underlying code. Make sure you are in 'compose' mode and type your first post.

When you have set up your blog, try to write a new post every day for a week. If you are working on this activity with colleagues, read and comment on posts from other group members. After the end of the week think about these questions:

- Who was the audience for your blog? How did you indicate that in your writing?
- Did you include material other than text? Why?
- How easy/difficult was it to think of blog content each day? Did it become more or less easy/difficult as the week progressed?
- Did your voice change during the week?
- How easy/difficult was it to comment on posts made by other people?
- If you received comments, did that make a difference to your writing? How/Why?
- Will you continue with your blog? Why/Why not?
- Is this a good way for students to learn second language (L2) writing?

One problem that you might have found with this task is that no direction was given regarding the blog content. Some blogs are kept as personal journals, but you can use blogs for other purposes too. Some people may feel too exposed if they are asked to publish their personal activities or thoughts to the internet so it may be better to decide on a theme for your blog. The 'blogosphere' abounds with themed blogs: craft-based blogs, about professional lives, travellers' tales, stories of family life, and so on. Not only does a blog theme provide a focus for your writing, it also gives you entry into a community of writers who share your interest. This will attract an audience who will both read and comment on the blog, creating not only authentic context but adding motivation (and encouraging you to read other blogs on your theme).

People expect blogs to be well written, and they also expect that blogs will look more like websites than books, so they usually contain visual material such as photos, and can also include audio and video material and web references. Blogs may be open to a global audience or they may be restricted so that only invited users (who need passwords) can read the content. Commenting, similarly, can be open to all or may be restricted to logged in users only. You probably found that the comments of others encouraged you to keep writing and made you express your ideas more clearly. As you will notice from your own posts, blogs allow work to be published quickly (and with a professional appearance) and they provide an authentic audience for student writing. Keeping a blog on a regular basis can help students to develop writing discipline and fluency, and to find their own voice in writing. If the audience responds through comments then this can motivate learners to continue writing. However, a drawback of blogging is that, by default, blogs invite comments and if no comments are posted then this can be demotivating as the writer may interpret this as 'nobody is reading my blog'. This can be overcome by disabling comments or by adding a 'page tracker' which provides statistics showing how many people have viewed a page (and often other information such as from which countries the readers originate). Page trackers may be provided by the blog site or by a third party and you will find some examples on our website.

Blogs are ideal for student learning from a number of points of view. Although the blog looks 'published' it is also fluid, and learners can refine, backtrack, and rethink in their next posting. It is a medium in which they are free to explore and reflect. They can see how their writing develops over a period of time by comparing earlier blogs with later ones. Students blogging to each other in a group develop their ideas through interaction with peers and teachers, and construct meaning within the social context of the blog network. Because other people can see the blog, students are more careful about looking up words they need in online dictionaries, and checking grammar and spelling (Abu Bakar and Ismail 2009: 49). In their study of ESL bloggers, they found that students felt they could still be creative even though their English was limited. They felt able to write longer online than on paper, because they were able to take their time and do it when they wanted to, and they could express themselves more freely. Abu Bakar and Ismail found that their students made gains in writing skills: 'their writing progressed tremendously in terms of sentence and paragraph length.' (2009: 49)

Campbell (2003) says that blogs can be used by tutors to create reading for their students, set up tasks, guide self study, and give feedback, and by learners to comment on their learning experience, to develop critical thinking skills by commenting on a piece of reading they have been given or found themselves, as a kind of bulletin board to post ideas related to classroom discussion topics, for projects, and for an international classroom exchange. Teachers could give individual feedback to students on the language and content of their blogs, or choose to do a 'writing feedback' blog for the whole group.

As Task 7 has demonstrated, it is now also possible to ask the question 'when is a text ever finished?' Word processing makes it very easy for writers to make constant changes to a text which they are writing, by deleting and copying and pasting, but they tend not to save previous drafts, so the version they are currently working on is always the 'final' version. Does this make the writing process different from, say, revisions made to a handwritten text where the writer could easily go back and reconsider changes a second or third time? If you see the manuscripts of writers such as Jane Austen or Charles Dickens, you can see how they must have been continually referring to their original text as they made changes, and sometimes going back to their first thoughts. Using word processors has radically altered the way in which we change and edit texts. Texts can be altered by other people as well as the original writer; they can be posted on the Internet and then modified or changed by others. As we have seen in Task 7, wikis are texts built up by a number of authors, and technology provides easy ways of composing a text collaboratively with other people. Web pages are continually being modified by a number of people and are different each time you visit them. We might suggest, in fact, that the management of the writing process has moved from the original writer to the readers, who may become co-authors of the text as they add to or modify the text after reading it; all the more reason for teaching writing and reading skills together rather than artificially separating them. The other question is who decides when a text is 'finished', i.e. ready for 'publication' or evaluation, in the second language (L2) classroom? The teacher? The students?

Summary

In this chapter, we have tried to show how new written genres are being created by the internet, and how technology is creating new possibilities for learning to write in a second language (L2). Technology offers students the chance to write in their own time outside the classroom, to access a range of tools to support their individual writing needs, and to get an immediate response from a wide audience which does not just consist of the teacher. We might speculate that, as a result, students are now getting much more feedback about the content of their writing as well as the language.

Further reading

Johnson, A. 2004. 'Creating a Writing course utilising Class and Student Blogs'. *Internet TESL Journal* 10/8. Accessed 4 November 2011 at http://iteslj.org/ Techniques/Johnson-Blogs.

6

MULTIMODAL LITERACIES: LEARNING THROUGH VISUALS

That's the thing about pictures: they seduce you.
DAVID BYRNE, musician and artist

Of all of our inventions for mass communication, pictures
still speak the most universally understood language.
WALT DISNEY, film producer

Aims

In this chapter, we discuss some possible answers to the following questions:

- How do visual materials, activities, and tools support language learning?
- How can technology provide us with new and exciting opportunities for sourcing and producing visual material for teaching and learning?
- Are we teaching 'new' literacies if **multimodal** texts, in which images and words are combined, are constructed and understood in ways which differ from traditional texts?

Introduction

At the beginning of this chapter, we will give you an overview of some of the issues and opportunities for learning which we believe have been created by the increasingly visual culture in which we live. We consider the different roles which visuals can play in conveying information, and the relationships they may have with words when combined together in multimodal texts. We also discuss the part which teachers may play in helping students to understand and produce multimodal texts. The second part of the chapter considers some of the ways in which visuals (both static and moving images) can be used to support language learning.

The role of visuals in language learning

There are constant worries in the press that the information contained in multimodal texts which combine images and words, and the speed with which these texts are delivered to the receiver, are creating 'information overload'. There are fears that this may result in shortened attention spans and superficial thinking in the future. Wood and Hastings (2009) refer to research which shows that the average person is bombarded with 100,000 words per day, and the majority of this verbal input is accompanied by visuals of some kind. Carr (2010) says that the variety and speed of digital information is affecting our cognitive processes including reading and memory, which suggests that teachers have a vital role in helping students to be selective in what they attend to in these multimodal messages. He provides a lot of anecdotal evidence to show that people have less patience now with text-based material which does not contain visuals, so that the use of images to attract and sustain the receiver's interest becomes even more important.

How do the visuals which now seem to accompany every kind of verbal text actually work in conveying a message? In his 'dual coding theory', Paivio (2006) said that words and images are processed and stored in different ways by the brain, as 'logogens' and 'imagens' respectively, and that images which gave the same message as the words could help learning and memorization by building redundancy into a multimodal message. For instance, children could better recall a story they had heard if they linked it to a mental visual image which showed the climax of the story (Sadoski 1985, cited in Paivio 2006). However, there are different views on this and Mayer (2005), for example, argues that under certain conditions, combining written text with images can actually impede understanding, although images combined with spoken words can be beneficial. So some caution is needed when claiming that all texts which combine image and written words are helpful. However, one positive example is Wall et al. (2005), who asked students how helpful they felt the visuals on Interactive White Boards (IWBs) were for helping them learn. IWBs typically make it very easy for images to be incorporated into lessons in conjunction with verbal texts (such as the teacher's words or coursebooks). The students felt that images helped them to understand the content of a lesson better: 'The visual helps me to understand the complicated things'; 'The more she (the teacher) says what we need to do, I understand it more, but it's better to have visual effects.' The following task allows you to reflect on how visuals might support learning in different ways from words.

Task 1   **Words and pictures**

Form a pair with someone else. One of you should write a short description of the room you are in whilst the other person draws three or four pictures to illustrate the room. Try to convey the feeling and atmosphere of the room as well as its physical layout. Take about five minutes to do this. When you have finished, compare the two descriptions.

- How do they differ from/resemble each other?
- What can images do which words can't, in communicating a message? (and vice versa?)
- If you had to choose either the written text or the pictures to give a more complete description of the room, which would you choose?
- Why might drawing be a useful tool for language learners?

You may have mentioned that the visuals allowed you to see spatial relationships more clearly between people, furniture, room dimensions, and so forth. The visuals may also have showed facial expressions and clothes more clearly, and given some indication of which country the room was in. The person drawing the pictures probably also took less time to do so than the writer, who in turn may have found it harder to decide when their text was complete. On the other hand, atmosphere and feeling were probably more accurately conveyed by the writer (unless the drawer was extremely skilful). You may have decided that you needed both words and pictures to achieve a more complete set of information about what the classroom looked like. The drawers may have enjoyed their task more than the writers. The explanation of the drawing will have probably prompted a lot of communicative language use, so that language learning could be happening incidentally as a product of focusing on a visual image.

As Task 1 suggested, visuals support learning in the following ways (you may think of others):

- Images (and video) meet learner expectations. We now live in a highly visual culture, in which images are a major vehicle for conveying meaning (Callow 2005). For example, it could be argued that images are now an essential component of on-line writing.

- Images and video give information that can only be only be provided visually.

- Images and video allow learners to see a context, body language, facial expressions, and artefacts. This provides learners with the opportunity to learn about other cultures and also to 'hook into' global culture.

- Images and video bring the real world into the classroom (Goldstein 2008). When learners create visual products such as photo diaries or videos which they post onto blogs or video-sharing sites, they can be viewed by and receive comments from people beyond the current classroom context, who provide a genuine audience to communicate with.

- Images and video cater for students who have a more 'visual' learning style, although we have some reservations about learning styles and would suggest that most, if not all, sighted students are now very adept at learning through visual images.

- Images and video provide a quick and economical means of conveying a message; as the adage says, 'a picture is worth a thousand words'.

- Visual materials have an emotional impact; 'if you really want to move people, don't use words, use images' said one of our colleagues. Images can be analysed and explained rationally, but they are also ways of tapping into the unconscious mind and the emotions (Callow 2005). A number of our colleagues also report using visuals for humour, to lighten the mood in the classroom.

- Visual materials can support language learning by creating a void which needs to be filled by language. (Keddie 2009)

- Images and video can create redundancy if the same message is repeated in two modes, visual and verbal.

Which of the roles for images in learning and teaching above would you consider most important for you?

Concerning the last point, research based on Paivio's dual coding theory has shown rather contradictory results with regard to the question of whether more learning occurs if words and images convey messages which are different from each other, or when the images support and repeat the verbal message, or when words and images represent complementary aspects of the same message. Garry et al. (2007) found that the choice of accompanying images can affect a person's memory of what a text is about, and they appeared to work best if they convey complementary rather than completely different messages. However, in everyday life we are more used to processing different messages in words and visuals. In a television sports report, for instance, we might see a miserable-looking football manager sitting on the benches, but hear details of the game. We might even have written text scrolling at the bottom of the screen giving the score of a completely different football match. We seem to have no problem with processing the different messages simultaneously in our L1, but it may be more difficult in an L2.

Computer technology as a resource for visuals

In the second half of this chapter, we will suggest a number of readily available and inexpensive or free sources of visual material using technology, including image banks, slideshow creators, photo editing and cartoon strip tools, animation creators, and video sharing sites. Teachers and students can use this material to create and share their own multimodal texts, and promote learning by making, building, articulating and sharing, as mentioned in Chapter 1.

Task 2 illustrates how activities which involve making or reproducing visual materials can give students opportunities to articulate their knowledge and in doing so, provide a powerful learning experience.

Task 2   **Video dictionary**

A colleague of ours, Carol Wild, wanted her Malaysian students to learn some new vocabulary items in English. She asked them to contribute to a video dictionary project at OneStopEnglish. The students worked in groups. Each group chose a word they wanted to learn, and made a video based on the word. One group chose the word 'apologize'. They illustrated the word in written form, explaining its grammatical form, meaning, and pronunciation.

Then they wrote and acted out a short scene in which the meaning of the word was conveyed visually, especially through facial expression, and was also used in a dialogue (one student had inadvertently borrowed another student's book). At the time of writing, you could view the video they made on YouTube (see our accompanying website, www.oup.com/elt/teacher/tell for references).

- Do you think different messages were being conveyed through the visual and verbal channels?
- Can you suggest any reasons why this was a particularly successful way of learning vocabulary for the students?

It may sometimes be difficult to decide if visual and verbal input are delivering the same, different, or complementary messages. To make it even more complicated, visuals are subject to individual, subjective interpretations, as well as those shared by other members of a culture (Callow 2005), so that two people might get differing messages from the same visual. In Task 2, they seem to be complementary aspects of what is involved in making an apology. In this example, the visual **channel** seems to be helpful in supporting the learning of an abstract concept, 'apologize', through displaying the word visually and acting out the dialogue.

We would suggest that this activity was so successful as a learning opportunity because the students were involved both in creating the images and the verbal text which accompanied them (please see Chapter 1 for more about 'making' and social-constructivist theories of learning). Dubois and Vial (2000) point out that: 'the more educational materials promote connections between the two methods of coding (visual and verbal), the more learning will take place'. The Video Dictionary activity encouraged the learners to make these connections. It also engaged them in the social practice of creating a multimodal text, (containing images, sound, the written word, and movement) helping to develop literacy skills for that genre (a video produced for a language learning site on YouTube). We will have more to say about the advantages of this kind of learning in Activities 8 and 10.

What role do visuals play in the 'new' literacies?

Until recently, we would only have been talking about 'teaching literacy' in relation to helping students to understand and produce texts which consisted solely of words. We are now surrounded at every turn in our daily lives by digital texts which combine images, words, and sounds in ever expanding and innovative ways. Crystal (2006) describes the innovative language use which these new forms of communication are producing, which is of interest not just to L1 speakers but also those who are being exposed to them in an L2. These new forms of communication often challenge traditional ideas concerning the authorship, permanence, and truth of texts. Some of these digital texts may be viewed rather uncomfortably by educational establishments as associated with social interaction rather than learning – how, for example, can 'tweeting' or Facebook updates help learning? Carrington and Robinson (2010) argue that we need to recognize the informal learning networks which could be promoted by these and other digital technologies. They also say that young people need a 'parallel pedagogy' which helps students gain skills in both print and digital text:

> there is no longer a place for a view of literacy that values either skills and practices with static print or those with digital text … it is time our classrooms became places where digital and print literacies come together to allow … opportunities to develop the skills and attitudes (learners) will need to navigate complex urban sites and social forms. (Carrington and Robinson 2010: 3-4)

As teachers of English as a second language (L2), increasingly use digital technologies in their teaching, they become inextricably engaged in teaching these literacies as part of their job. They therefore need to be aware of how images and words combine to create meaning and how such texts may be 'read' and produced by learners. Task 3 invites you to consider the part which images play in conveying meaning and guiding understanding in a relatively new genre, the 'webpage'.

Task 3	**Reading a webpage**

Access a webpage for a well-known retailer, such as, for example, Amazon or IKEA. Read the web page and consider the questions which follow:

- What did you read first? Where did your eyes go?
- Where is the biggest visual and why do you think it is placed there?
- How are the other visuals used?
- Is there repetition of the same information in visuals and words?
- Are there long pieces of information?
- Does 'reading' a web page demand different literacy skills reading a coursebook?

Websites contain a juxtaposition of words and images which demand rather different reading skills from books, newspapers, and magazines. Research by Jakob Neilsen (cited in his 'Alertbox', see our accompanying website for details) shows that people typically scan a website for isolated words and phrases, and that they rarely scroll down to the bottom of a web page, instead they tend to read in an 'F' shape which concentrates on the top of a web page (so you would have probably have read from left to right at the top of the webpage, perhaps also letting your eyes go down the left-hand side, too). Notice that links which the website designers want you to click on are often placed along the top and left-hand side of the page in anticipation that you will read in this shape. Readers usually click on links near the top of the page which will send them to other places in a non-linear fashion. (It can be argued that we don't typically read paper texts in a particularly linear way either). The information is given in small doses, with the most important information at the beginning of a paragraph, and the images in general merely repeat the verbal information in visual form. The images are very skilfully placed on the site to encourage you to scroll down the page, and to read the right-hand side of the page, which you might not otherwise naturally do. The visuals are being used to attract you, and above all, to seduce you into reading the webpage in a certain way (as in the Byrne quote at the beginning of this chapter). The images on websites play a particular role in guiding (but not dictating) how the website is read and in what order. Students and teachers need to be aware of this role when producing multimodal texts such as websites and e-portfolios.

Multimodality and learning

All learning and teaching involves the use of a number of modes, including speaking, writing, images, and movement, which give learners the opportunity to understand and combine information represented in different ways. Presenting information simultaneously through different modes allows for a fuller and deeper understanding of that information. While all learning is multimodal, the special thing about computer technology is that it allows learners and teachers to manipulate the various modes and to break free of the temporal linearity of traditional classroom instruction; to combine modes such as sound, text and image; to easily access visual material such as images and videos which may help clarify information presented in other modes; to control the flow of information by means of pause and rewind buttons; and to disambiguate or extend understanding of information by searching for other modes such, as subtitles for images, or oral pronunciations of words in on-line dictionaries.

The teacher's role in supporting the new 'literacies'

We are now living in an era where multimodal texts combining words, sounds, images, and movement place different demands on the receivers and producers of these texts, requiring a redefinition of what it means to be 'literate'. What might language teachers' roles be in helping students to understand and produce multimodal texts – such as webpages, PowerPoint presentations and videos – which combine images with spoken or written words? Teachers know that it is their students, not them, who now have the expertise in creating multimodal texts and also in being able to effortlessly produce and respond to a number of texts simultaneously: 'It's not unusual for a youngster to be phoning, facebooking, selling something on E-bay and surfing cable TV channels at the same time' (Sutherland 2010). Pre-schoolers as young as three now have the ability to use a wide range of digital tools including cameras, photo-editing, games, instant messaging, and so on. The role of teachers in the future will probably be not so much to teach students how to understand and produce multimodal texts (though there may still be some of that in primary school with younger children). We predict that teachers in the future will be more focused on helping students to critically analyse these texts and to produce ones which communicate meaning effectively and appropriately in a particular social domain. In doing so, they will be teaching literacies in the plural, including **visual literacy**, rather than the traditional interpretation of literacy as confined to reading and writing (Callow 2005, Gee 2003). We will see an example of critical evaluation in Task 4.

Classroom activities

The activities which follow allow you to reflect further on some of the issues we have raised in the first part of the chapter. As with all our activity suggestions, you can work through these activities with fellow teachers and/or you can use them with your own learners. The activities progress from accessing and evaluating material which already exists in cyberspace towards making your own material and achieving the transition between utilizing still and moving images.

Task 4

Finding and being critical about online video

The purpose of this activity is to think about how to search for online video and what you might need to consider when you evaluate it for possible use with a class. Although video sharing sites are full of material which might be useful to you, not all is of good quality and this activity will suggest questions that you can bear in mind when selecting video material.

Go to a video-sharing website such as YouTube and, in the search box, type 'learn Spanish' (or the language of your choice).

- How many results do you get?
- Choose one of the videos at random. Who made it? What is its purpose? Could you use it in your classroom and, if so, how?

This activity demonstrates the vast number of free tutorials that you can find on video-sharing websites. However, as you will (we hope) have observed they are of varying quality. The creators of online video tutorials typically fall into three groups: Firstly, there are the experts (either professional or amateur) who want to share their passion for the topic and are happy to give their expertise for free. Sometimes these experts also offer either face-to-face or online tuition for payment but even so, their free video tutorials are genuinely useful in their own right Secondly, we have the professionals (either organizations or individuals) who create free video tutorials as 'taster sessions' for paid-for online tuition. In these cases, the video tutorials are of limited use because the main aim is to encourage people to sign up for further tuition Finally, there are amateurs who have enthusiasm for the subject but very little knowledge or expertise. A typical example is a teenager with limited knowledge creating the video tutorial from her or his bedroom.

There is a fourth category of tutorials which have been created for reasons other than genuine interest in teaching – spoofs, political rants, disguises for unsavoury material, and so on. However, these are easy to spot and so can be ignored for our purposes. These questions are useful for judging the value and integrity of an online video tutorial for you or your students:

- How does the tutor demonstrate her or his expertise? Does he or she appear to be using her or his own name? Is there a link to a website with more information about her or his background and qualifications?

- How many comments are there from viewers of the video and what do they typically say about the video? Are they critical or do they say that the tutorial has been useful to them? People making online comments can be extremely blunt and will not generally withhold negative feedback. Whilst this can be uncomfortable for the producer of the material, it can be extremely useful for prospective viewers/users.

- What is your informed opinion about the video? Is the content consistent with what you already know or with what other experts say? Somebody who is acknowledged as a major expert in a field may well propose a new or radical idea but is unlikely to do this in a free online video unless it is from a lecture or conference presentation.

For those working in the area of study skills or language for academic purposes, this activity can be a useful preliminary for students learning to evaluate other online resources such as Wikipedia, blogs, or online journal and newspaper articles. One major concern for academic staff nowadays is students' uncritical use of web material. University tutors will frequently recommend using online journals, but will disapprove of Wikipedia. For students who are planning to progress into further academic study, it is essential that they learn to distinguish between and evaluate different types of online resources. Video can seem less authoritative than text and therefore easier to critique. The additional information provided non-verbally (for example, facial expression or background setting) can also help students to consider whether a presenter seems confident or hesitant about the topic. In **EAP** classes, therefore, a development of this activity would be to choose a selection of online text-based resources and ask students to evaluate them using the similar set of questions to those above.

| Task 5 | **Finding and evaluating images** |

One of the problems that many people experience is finding appropriate images that are not constrained by copyright. This activity explores two different ways of searching for images and looks at the benefits and drawbacks of both.

Imagine that you have to teach a lesson that includes vocabulary related to clothing. Go to Google (www.google.com) and click on 'images'. Search for pictures of clothing items such as shoes or hats.

- Which of the resulting images could you use in your teaching materials? Which ones would you not be able to use? Why?
- Repeat your search using http://search.creativecommons.org/. Which of these images could you use? Why?
- Which search provided the most diverse range of images?

You probably found that the Google website gave you very straightforward images which would match well with the denotative meaning of concrete objects. Many of the images are taken from shopping websites. On the other hand, the Creative Commons website gave you much more unexpected images and was able to provide visuals which illustrated abstract ideas such as 'warmth' and 'kindness'. It also seemed to provide images which were sensory and emotional, and conveyed something about the feelings and values of the person who created the image. Sometimes in learning we need visuals which are factual, and sometimes we need ones which will appeal to our emotions and creativity.

One of the problems which plagues users of visual materials is copyright. Copyright rules vary from country to country (see the UNESCO portal, details on our website, for more information) but in general, a piece of material belongs to the person who created it and nobody else has an automatic right to use it or to modify it. Very often, people will use an ordinary search engine such as Google to find images without realizing that the material shown in the search results is subject to copyright and the owner may not have given permission for other people to use it. One solution to the problem of copyright is the Creative Commons Licence (http://creativecommons.org/). There are various forms of Creative Commons Licence but the basic principle is that they allow the creator's work to be used for non-commercial purposes. All work that is licensed under a Creative Commons Licence states clearly how it may be used.

Task 6	## Making a digital guidebook

The next three activities all make use of images in project work. The aim of these activities, from a learner's point of view, is to create something that will make use of their language and which they can publish to an audience. The reflections at the end of each activity draw out points that the teacher might want to bear in mind when carrying out these types of activity with learners.

- Work with a partner. You are going to make a simple visitor guide to the place where you live or work. You will be using adjectives that describe places. You will also be using past tense verb forms to describe historical events. You do not have to be serious!

- Open some presentation software such as PowerPoint or an online slideshow creator (some examples are listed below). You could also start out by writing your captions on paper or in a Word document and pasting them into the software later.

- Firstly you are going to describe the place as it is now, and this part of the guidebook should be entitled 'Modern times'. You should search for pictures that show buildings, parks, roads and, other recent features of the area or city and paste them into your slideshow. You should then write a caption for each picture saying why the feature is important or interesting.

- The second section describes the place as it once was: 'History'. Write a sequence of simple captions about the (real or imaginary) historical significance of places in your area. Search for images to fit your captions.

- Which is the most effective approach: to write your captions first and then search for pictures to fit, or to start by finding the pictures and then writing appropriate captions?

- Which approach makes most use of the target language?

When presented with an activity like this, many learners will tend to start by searching for images unless they are directed otherwise. However, due to the distracting nature of the internet, this approach is likely to lead to time wasting and lack of focus. A more productive and language-focused approach is to begin with the writing and then find images that relate to the text. In some cases with this kind of activity, humour, and interest can come from images that provide a message that contradicts the text.

Picture-based stories and activities can, of course, also make use of photographs that learners have taken themselves. To do this, learners would need to think about the types of photographs that they wanted to gather and how/where they could take the pictures using digital cameras. The learners can then edit the photographs, using either image-editing programs, such as Photoshop, or the online tools provided by photo-sharing sites such as Picasa. There is a risk that learners will become engrossed in the taking and editing of the photographs and, however motivating these are, the teacher may occasionally need to refocus them on the language-learning elements of the activity. We suggest a number of useful websites for this and other activities in this chapter on the website which accompanies this book. Most online photo storage/sharing services allow albums to be created which can then be displayed as slideshows. Some photo-sharing sites also provide basic editing tools. For the language classroom, the online tools may be more useful than full-featured image-editing software, such as PhotoShop, because less time is needed to learn how to use the simple online tools (assuming that image-editing has not been introduced in other classes) and the lack of features makes the tools less distracting than full programs might be.

| Task 7 | **Comic-strip story (static images)** |

This activity could use images found on the internet or it could be based on images made by the learners. Learners could use photographs of people, places, or objects. The images do not necessarily need to tell the story – they can be illustrations that relate to key points in the story. Alternatively, toys such as Playmobil could be photographed to depict the story. Choose a traditional story, perhaps one from your own country which will not be familiar to other members of the class. You will retell the story in the form of a comic strip using both narrative captions and speech bubbles.

- Look at one of the online comic strip tools mentioned on our website. You can use one of these or you can develop your story using presentation software such as PowerPoint.
- Imagine that you are going to give this activity to a class of children – say, aged 9–10 years. How would you introduce the activity? At what point should the children start working with the comic-strip creation tool? What should they do before they use the digital tools?

As we mention in Chapter 1, Papert and Harel (1991) argue that learning is most effective when it comes about through making. Their view is that learners not only need to 'do', to be active in their learning but also need to articulate their knowledge and make it visible to others: they call this philosophy '**Constructionism**'. Learners need to think about the language used in stories and narrative in order to plan and draft the text for the comic strips. The task enables them to externalize their linguistic knowledge and does so in a way that is entertaining and motivating. Papert and Harel say that it is this process of articulation and making that leads to deep learning. Therefore, whilst watching the comic-strip story will help learners to understand and remember the language, the learner who made the story will have learned much more deeply than those who simply watch the completed product.

| Task 8 | **Animated dialogue (moving images)** |

This activity provides a bridge between the use of still images in earlier tasks and activities where learners use video cameras. For any product with moving images it is probably best to create a storyboard whilst in the planning stage. This allows users to plan exactly what will happen at every stage of the animation or movie and what language should be used.

Many online animations creators include ready-made characters which learners can use for this activity. Alternatively, learners could make or draw their own images. However, as this work would be part of a language lesson rather than an **ICT** lesson, it is probably best to work with ready-made characters.

- Work with a partner. Think of several different ways that you could phrase a request in the target language and several different ways that you might agree or refuse a request. Draft a short dialogue between two people in which one person makes increasingly strange or difficult requests and the other person consistently agrees or refuses (until the final request when the respondent changes position).
- Using an online animation creator, such as GoAnimate, provide animation for your dialogue.
- In which parts of your activity did you and your partner make most use of the target language (including use of the target language to talk about what you were doing)?
- How much thought and effort did you put into writing your dialogues? Did you change your writing when you were creating the animation? How and why?
- Writing dialogues is a popular activity in the language classroom. What value is added by the animation creator tools?

José Picardo, a widely-read education blogger, is a keen user of animations in his work as a secondary school language teacher. He finds that making animations excites the students and motivates them to write in the foreign language. The screenshot below is an example of some work produced by one of José's 12-year-old learners. The complete video can be seen on José's website (see our accompanying website for details).

Figure 6.1 Screenshot of a student's animated story

The children feel as though they are writing for real characters rather than simply doing a classroom exercise. Furthermore, many children (and adults) feel anxious about writing in a foreign language and the animation tool allows the emotional focus to be taken away from the writing. With some online animation creators, it is possible to create a soundtrack as well as, or instead of, written text. This can help learners who are nervous about speaking aloud because the spoken language is distanced from the learner and put in the mouth of a cartoon character.

Making a cartoon strip is a traditional classroom activity and can, of course, be done in ways that do not include technology. The advantages of creating an animated cartoon are, firstly, the professional appearance (which is likely to be motivating to learners) and, secondly, that the animation can be published online and this adds to the authenticity of the task. Animated stories can be created with dedicated tools such as those below. However, it is also possible to use games or virtual environments such as Second Life. Gee and Hayes (2010) cite examples of people using games such as The Sims to create animated movies which can be posted online to illustrate extended written text. Both Second Life and The Sims include 'video camera' tools, but screen-capture software could also be used for this purpose.

Task 9	**House-racing video**

In this activity learners 'shoot' their own video. The hardware can be very simple. You do not need a dedicated video camera; most digital cameras will be adequate, as will a good-quality mobile phone. The activity aims to demonstrate what is involved in planning, preparing, and creating a video. The finished product can be as 'rough' or as polished as you wish. It is possible to plan, shoot, and upload the video without any editing. However, as learners gain experience, they may prefer to edit the video for a more professional product.

- For this activity you will need to work in groups of four. The main language focus is continuous verb forms, but the activity will also provide an opportunity to practice temporal linkers and the present perfect. The televisual genre is sports commentary.
- Two people will be 'actors', the third will operate the camera, and the fourth person will be the commentator. You can either record the commentary at the same time as the video or record a soundtrack separately and add it later.
- Think about some household chores that contain a range of smaller tasks (for example, cooking a meal or cleaning a room). If you are in an educational institution, they could include tidying the classroom, preparing a meal in the student cafeteria, cleaning the secretary's office, sweeping the corridor, etc.
- Your two actors must imagine that they are taking part in a race against each other to complete the tasks. The commentator will describe, in the manner of a sports commentator, what the actors are doing. For example:
- 'Maryam is washing the glasses … that's very good, she's moving on to the knives … Oh no! It looks as though she's dropped and broken a glass, hard luck Maryam! Georg is catching up with her … he's already stacked the plates.'

Show the video in class and get the students to vote on the best performance of the task. Before showing the video you could ask students to predict who will be first in the race. If you have several videos, you could use them to compare different ways of approaching the task. This is another activity where the learning comes through the process of making. Learners have to articulate their linguistic knowledge through planning and narrating the video. There will also be a lot of discussion around the planning and making of the video and, whilst we hope this will make use of the target language, with mono-lingual groups this discussion is likely to take place in the local language.

Completed videos can be uploaded to video-sharing sites such as YouTube. This enables them to be seen by a wider audience and to receive comments. This increases the authenticity of the task and can be motivating for learners. However, there is a lot of concern nowadays about video material that includes children, caused by fear that the material could be misappropriated or could put children at risk. Because of this, some schools may be reluctant to allow children to take part in videos or they may not allow the videos to be placed online. This does not mean that children cannot participate in video-making activities, however. Possible solutions include using puppets or for child actors to wear masks (which can add to the humour of the video).

Once you have tried making simple videos, you can experiment with editing using a program such as MovieMaker (free with Microsoft Windows) or iMovie (the Mac OS equivalent). These programs are simple to use and there is a wide range of tutorials available on video sharing sites such as YouTube (offering an opportunity to use your video-evaluation skills). Editing might include cutting the video, splicing clips together in a different order, mixing two videos into one; adding credits or other text, and adding music. The 'House-racing' task is ideal for editing practice as you can make two videos and then mix them together so that you are cutting from one person to the other, or you could have a split screen to show both people doing the race at the same time. When working with video cameras, it is important to create a storyboard before the 'shoot' so that everyone knows where they should be and how to set up the scenes. Storyboarding is similar in process to the planning stages of writing and so a task involving storyboards can be useful in helping learners to understand how they might move from their initial ideas to the creation of text.

Summary

In this chapter we have tried to show that visual images, rather than being servants or adjuncts of the written word, are actual powerful ways of conveying meaning in their own right. Images play a vital role in creating meaning in multimodal texts, and both teachers and language learners need to be capable of interpreting and producing texts which contain both visuals and words. We argued that this involved teaching a new kind of 'literacy', and that the teacher's role might especially be that of promoting critical analysis of such texts. In the second half of the chapter, we gave examples of some multimodal texts in which the visual element supports language learning in a number of ways.

Further reading

Callow, J. (2005). 'Literacy and the Visual: Broadening our Vision.' *English Teaching: Practice and Critique.* 4/1: 6–19.

Keddie, J. (2009). *Images.* Oxford: Oxford University Press.

Wall, K., S. Higgins and **H. Smith** et al. (2005). '"The visual helps me understand the complicated things": pupil views of teaching and learning with interactive whiteboards'. *The British Journal of Educational Technology* 36/5: 851–867.

7

STUDY SKILLS AND EAP

There are more men ennobled by study than by nature.
MARCUS TULLIUS CICERO, Roman philosopher and ovator

Study lends a kind of enchantment to all our surroundings.
HONORÉ DE BALZAC, French writer

Aims

In this chapter, we will try to give you some answers to the following questions:

- How has technology changed the way that we study (particularly in higher education)?
- What do students need to know or be able to do in order to study in digitally-mediated environments?

Introduction

English for academic purposes is about providing the language, skills, and understandings that are necessary for higher study through the medium of English. Although English for academic purposes (EAP) and study skills are not synonymous, many EAP courses include study techniques and the practice of academic skills; for example, the teaching of reading for academic purposes has always included not only general reading strategies such as skimming, and scanning, but also critical reading and techniques for effective note taking, recognizing that academic reading is often the precursor to academic writing. Technology has not greatly affected academic language, but has made a considerable impact on academic skills. Because of this, wherever EAP teachers use academic practice activities, it is helpful to incorporate digital tools of the kind that students might expect to use in their future studies.

This chapter is about skills and tools in relation to academic study. Earlier chapters in this book deal with **language skills** and processes more generally and so for more information about how to teach those skills, even in EAP contexts, you should look at Chapter 3 for listening and speaking, Chapter 4 for reading, and Chapter 5 for writing. The first part of this chapter looks at some of the ways that technology has changed study. The chapter then moves on to consider what students need to know, starting with **VLEs** as these often tend, nowadays, to act as containers for study tools and materials. We then think about academic reading – going from the reading process to writing and looking at some of the issues that are particular to academic writing. The next two sections are about listening and speaking (particularly group work), and the final section talks briefly about using technology to support language production.

How has technology changed the way we study?

As we saw in chapters 1 and 2, activity is mediated by tools and takes place within the context of community, rules, and sharing workload. Changing any of the elements in an activity system has an impact on the other elements and on the nature of the activity itself. In the case of academic study, the mediational tools have changed with the introduction of technology but also, over the last two or three decades, the 'subjects' of the activity system (particularly students) have also changed. More students travel overseas to universities, particularly to English-speaking countries, so the number of international students has grown considerably (to say nothing of international campuses which teach courses in English in non-English-speaking countries). In addition to this, the number of 'home' students has also grown, especially in the UK which remains a popular destination for international students. The increase in 'home' students means that universities are recruiting more 'non-traditional' students and all of these changes in the student population means that higher education institutions have looked for new ways of teaching and new tools (therefore technology) to mediate and support learning and teaching. This has led to some new study practices which involve different ways of sharing the workload of learning. For example, student collaboration is now used widely because it enables students to scaffold and support each other's learning. This does not mean that students teach each other, but because students are more active in their learning they have to do more of the 'work'. Another example is the use of online tests, particularly multiple-choice and other tests with right/wrong answers, this passes some of the work of exam marking to a computer. Online submission of assignments means that the work of collecting assignments passes from administrative staff to the computer system. When teaching materials are placed online, perhaps through a virtual learning environment, the responsibility for making sure that students have the materials is passed from tutors to students. Online databases, catalogues, journals, and ebooks make resources more accessible to students, but also pass some of the work of locating materials to students instead of library staff. This means that students are expected to be more independent and self-reliant than ever before. In addition, students are expected to take part in a wide range of individual and group tasks, many of which make use of digital tools.

The 21st century university is heavily reliant on technology; in fact, higher education was the first education sector to adopt mass use of technology. Although the specific tools vary between institutions and subjects, students are expected to use virtual learning environments; word processing, online library services, online journals, ebooks, online registration and course management, presentation software, email, blogs and/or e-portfolios, plagiarism checkers, and perhaps also specialist software. In addition, there are many useful tools for students such as **mind-mapping** and **reference-management** software which are beneficial but not required. Back in the 1990s, when one of us was teaching English for academic purposes (EAP) in a UK university, the first stage of our academic writing course (taught in a computer cluster) was to teach students how to log on to the computer. Nowadays, it tends to be assumed that students know how to use the most common software and so they will only be given tuition for software or tools that are specific to the subject or to the institution.

Our experience is that that, although students do know how to use software such as word processing, they often have not learned the techniques which are most useful for study (such as proper use of headings). Moreover, as we mentioned in Chapter 5 (Writing), the combination of the internet and word processing has led to an increase in cases of plagiarism, as it is so easy to copy and paste text from a website into an assignment that many students may be tempted to cheat, especially when working under pressure. However, it is also very easy to copy and paste text from an electronic document into working notes, which then become part of an assignment, thus leading to inadvertent plagiarism. Our experience, working with international students, is that most plagiarism is accidental and referencing/ plagiarism is the aspect of academic writing that causes most stress to students.

Technology has not only had an impact on 'traditional' study, but has also allowed the development of new or different forms or assessment and ways of working. These include **multimedia** presentations, collaborative writing on wikis, participation on discussion boards, (including group or individual blogs), e-portfolios, **learning journals**, video, interactive lectures, assessment or supplementary activities in Second Life, use of social networking, and more. In some cases, students might be expected to use mobile or tablet technologies; for instance, at Leeds University in the UK, medical students are provided with smartphones for learning and assessment whilst on placement (Coulby et al. 2010).

Student collaboration and group work are now common in higher education. In part, this is for pedagogic reasons drawing on the work of people such as Vygotsky (1978), who argued that learning is a social process and that people who are provided with opportunities to learn together and discuss their ideas can 'scaffold' each other's learning. Digital tools can provide very effective facilitation of collaborative learning and this may be another reason for its growth in popularity. It is now very easy for tutors to set up collaborative online spaces and activities and this means that tutors are more likely to make use of these tools. Certainly, one of the biggest technology-based changes in higher education has been a shift towards more collaborative working for students. For learners who have grown up within a strongly teacher-based education system the emphasis on collaboration can be disorientating. It can therefore be helpful to give students opportunities to engage in technology-supported collaboration during study skills or EAP courses.

What do learners need to know?

Virtual Learning Environments (VLEs)

The VLE is a common feature of English medium universities – in fact, of many universities across the world. They are commonly used to organize student work, to provide space for student collaboration; as a repository for materials such as lecture notes and readings lists and for student assessment. The use of VLEs from the teacher's perspective is explained in more detail in Chapter 10, but if an EAP course is preparing students for English-medium higher education then it is important to include use of a VLE. Our anecdotal experience is that many students, even those coming through the UK school system where VLEs are commonplace, do not make adequate use of the VLE. From a tutor's point of view, it is very frustrating if a student complains that they have received no information about the assignment when a list of essay titles has been in the VLE from the beginning of term. Even if your institution does not have a VLE, you could set up a course website that contains all the information students need so that they can get the habit of using your VLE or website as the first place to look for any information about their studies. For those students who do not have previous experience of VLEs this will help considerably when they go on to further study as it is likely that a VLE will be one of their basic study tools.

Reading

The first challenge with regard to reading is locating and choosing appropriate texts. Although tutors usually provide reading lists detailing essential and recommended books, chapters, and papers, students are also expected to 'read around' the subject and find texts that are not on the reading lists. This increases in importance at higher levels of study. Furthermore, as all international academic journals are now available electronically, the range of texts that students can be expected to explore has increased. Students are no longer expected to confine themselves to their own subject shelves in the campus library; almost the entire academic world is at their command. Even articles in journals to which the institution does not subscribe may be ordered through the inter-library loan system.

Students taking higher degrees, such as a PhD, will be expected to undertake a systematic review of literature and will do this with the support of an experienced supervisor. EAP tutors are not usually expected to teach students how to undertake a systematic literature review of the type required for doctoral study, but the academic reading component of an EAP course might include sessions on searching for articles. Ingenta Connect is an important online database for academic journals and is a valuable reference tool for academics because it can search across an extensive range of academic journals quickly and easily. It is an equally valuable resource for EAP teachers who have to deal with a broad range of major subject areas in the class. One classroom, for example, may contain students studying engineering, business, dentistry, politics, education, and English literature. Somehow, the EAP teacher has to provide materials that will address the needs of these different students without being impenetrable to the others: the range of abstracts available via Ingenta Connect and other databases can be very helpful with this. The database provides authentic academic material from across the spectrum of academic areas. This means that whatever a student is studying, it should be possible to find abstracts from her or his own field. As far as possible, students can be placed in interest teams to find and work with the abstracts.

| Task 1 | **Ingenta Connect** |

This task is intended to work through with a colleague if possible. If you are working alone, you can still do the search and create questions.

- Go to the Ingenta Connect website (see our accompanying website for details) and search for 'Academic English'.
- Choose three of the results and read the abstracts; this may require clicking through to the journal webpage. You should not have to pay to read an abstract so if the abstract is not available then choose an alternative.
- Write ten comprehension questions about the three abstracts; some questions may be about individual abstracts whilst others may require reading across all three.
- Swap texts and questions with a colleague. Answer each other's questions

This is an excellent activity for students and is best if they work in teams of two or three to write (and answer) the questions. We are indebted to Sheelagh Deller's *Lessons from the Learner* (1990) for the inspiration for this type of activity.

In addition to traditional academic texts, such as journals or books, and **'grey literature'** (documents that have some official status such as charitable/government reports, newspapers, and magazines, but do not have the academic control that is provided by the peer review process used by journals), students also have access to a very wide range of online texts. These include blogs, news sites, opinion sites and, of course, Wikipedia. The problem for students is how to evaluate these different electronic resources and decide which are appropriate for their studies. The most clearly reputable academic texts, of course, are in peer-reviewed journals and students can feel safe with those from publishers such as Elsevier, Sage, and Wiley. However, at the time of writing, there is controversy over the high cost of these journals and the way that cost makes knowledge inaccessible to those who do not have access to an institutional subscription. This has led to the development of online open-access journals, such as PlosOne (an interactive **open-access journal** for peer-reviewed scientific and medical research). Whilst this is a positive initiative for researchers, for students it adds to the confusion about which texts are regarded as reputable sources.

Blogs fall into a grey area and can be difficult for students to evaluate. Some blogs are posted on sites that have, reputation of their own (for example, *The Guardian* or *Huffington Post*) whilst some are posted on sites that might be assumed to be reputable such as university websites. However, whilst *The Guardian* exercises some editorial control over its blogs, universities generally do no more than remove sites which contravene basic rules, such as the JANET Acceptable Use Policy (JANET

2011). Therefore, whilst it might be assumed that a webpage with a URL ending '.ac.uk' can be trusted as an academic source, in reality it may be no more than the individual opinion of the writer.

There are well-known and highly regarded academics who keep blogs. This is where they post updates on their work and comment on news items relevant to their work. They may also post material related to their personal lives and interests. A good example is Professor Mark Warschauer, who is a respected academic researcher in the fields of digital literacies and technology enhanced language learning. This means that anything he writes on these topics carries a certain amount of authority. Like many academics, Professor Warschauer uses **social media** (blogs, Twitter, Facebook, etc.) to discuss news topics related to his work, research in progress, emerging ideas, and so on. Generally speaking, social media posts have not been tested by research (although they may be about other people's published research). Furthermore, the writer has complete control over what they post on social media. It does not have to be evaluated by other researchers so there is no objective assessment of quality.

Task 2	### Mark Warschauer and Papyrus News

Go to Mark Warschauer's professional blog (see our accompanying website at www.oup.com/elt/teacher/tell for details) and read the first academic post. Then look at the following online article – *Digital Literacies: Laptops and Inspired Writing*, Warschauer, M., K. Arada, and B. Zheng, 2010. You can also find the details of how to access this on our website. Read both texts and think about these questions:

- How are these texts different?
- Are there differences in the author's voice?
- Who do you think is the main audience?
- Is one text more reliable than the other? Why?
- One is in a **peer-reviewed journal** whilst the other is a blog. Does this influence your opinion of the texts?
- Do these texts have different purposes? If so, what are they?

Unlike the blog post, the academic paper by Warschauer et al. (2010) has been published in a peer-reviewed journal; the literature, methodology, results and conclusions have been evaluated by other academics who have given feedback, and this has been taken into account before revising the article for final publication. This means that, even if you have never heard of the authors, you can trust that the article is robust. With the blog posts, on the other hand, we have to base our judgement on what we know of the author's reputation. As experienced academics, we know that Professor Warschauer has an excellent reputation and therefore can trust that his opinions are based on research. Inexperienced students, however, will not have that background knowledge of the field and so this kind of exercise can help them to understand the difference between academic publication via social media, and academic publication through peer-reviewed journals. Whilst material from peer-reviewed journal publications can be cited with confidence, students need to be far more cautious when citing blogs and other social media documents, even when they have been written by known and respected professors.

Another challenge for 21ˢᵗ century students is evaluating the reliability of wiki documents, including Wikipedia. It can be argued that Wikipedia is now so well known and has so many contributors (including university academics) that it can be considered a reliable source. Some pages are locked so that only registered and approved editors can change them, but these pages are in the minority and generally relate to high-profile political figures. Other pages can be edited by anyone; a Wikipedia account is not necessary. The editing process is not entirely anonymous; the **IP address** of the editing computer is displayed in the history page so malicious or libellous editors could be tracked if necessary, but this is a series of numbers – for example, 31.185.200.156 – and so is not helpful to the casual reader. Wikipedia now includes tools that help readers to gauge reliability. One of these is flagging articles that need support or citations: the flag appears at the top of the article to which it applies so that readers can see immediately if there are known shortcomings (see Figure 7.1, below).

Figure 7.1 Wikipedia flag

There is also a rating system (Figure 7.2) in which readers are invited to judge the quality of an article with a chart to show the ratings received so far. Whilst there is an argument that a very large number of people together, will produce an accurate evaluation (Surowiecki 2005), it should be noted that, unlike the academic peer-reviewing system, Wikipedia does not have any objective evaluation of its raters' expertise.

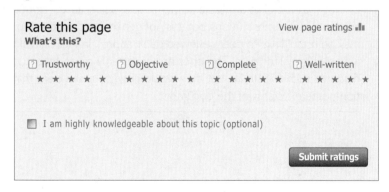

Figure 7.2 Wikipedia rating system

One academic evaluation of Wikipedia, conducted by university librarians, West and Williamson (2009: 268) concluded that in general, articles are 'highly objective, reasonably accurate, clearly presented, and reasonably complete' and is therefore a useful information source, at least with regard to popular culture. They found relatively little vandalism but, in some cases, there were important gaps in the information presented. However, in their evaluation, West and Williamson were only able to use their own knowledge of the subjects covered and some of the details they disregarded might have been important to a reader seeking specialist information.

Wikipedia is not, however, the only wiki-based information source. There are many others, such as Wiktionary (http://www.wiktionary.org/), which students may stumble across when searching online. Many of these are about a single specialist area.

Task 3   **Saltwiki**

Saltwiki is an academic wiki. To access it, go to the Saltwiki home page (see our accompanying website for details) and look at the information and the discussion page. Think about these questions:

- What is the purpose of Saltwiki?
- Who can contribute to the wiki?
- How are academic quality and robustness maintained?
- Would this be an authoritative and reliable source for students in this area? Why or why not? How would the students know?

As with other social media, academics may use wikis as way of reporting or discussing work in progress. Wikis can be particularly useful for sharing ideas during a research project and for a research team to develop work for publication. They can also be used for early dissemination of research findings or for researchers in specific areas to discuss their work and develop new projects. Researchers may develop a wiki or a blog as a way of bringing together a range of resources in their field, for example in order to create an authoritative 'one-stop shop' for the field. The problem for students is that a project wiki or blog may look like a reliable academic source because it contains the names of known academic staff or institutions, but it is not generally considered to be one (although there may be useful links to peer-reviewed publications). In fact, Saltwiki could be considered a type of 'grey literature'. This does not necessarily mean that students could not cite a resource such as Saltwiki, but they would need to make clear that they understand the non-academic status of the document.

From reading to writing

As mentioned above, one of the biggest worries of our students is referencing/plagiarism. Plagiarism is a growing problem and so the penalties can be severe, even when the plagiarism is accidental. Furthermore, tutors often issue draconian warnings – with good intentions – but the effect can be to induce panic in students. However, much accidental plagiarism can be avoided by efficient management of references and there are good tools available for this. Many universities include reference-management software, such as Endnote, on campus systems. Reference managers allow users to store bibliographic information and, on request, will format this information as a reference that complies with whichever system (for example, **Harvard** or **APA**) is needed. The software also contains space to write information such as abstracts and comments about the book or article. There are also free web-based reference managers such as CiteULike. CiteULike is particularly useful because it is supported by some major academic publishers who include a CiteULike button on their journal webpages. This allows users to send references directly to a CiteULike library without needing to find the bibliographic information for themselves. Of course, it is also possible to enter bibliographic details manually so that users can record references which are not automatically linked to CiteULike.

Task 4

(CiteULike)

Go to CiteULike and create an account. Then go to the *Journal of English for Academic Purposes* (for details see our accompanying website). Browse the journal and choose a paper that looks interesting to you.

- Once you have selected a paper, click the CiteULike button in the 'Share' box.
- Review the information in CiteULike and copy the article to your library.
- Click 'export' and choose a format. Unless you use a citation manager, we suggest you choose 'RTF' or 'Formatted Text'.
- Select a citation format; for example this book uses 'Oxford', but our students in the universities where we teach are expected to use 'Harvard'. Then click 'export'. You will be asked to open a document which contains a perfectly formatted reference that you can copy and paste into a word processor document.
- Return to the CiteULike homepage and you may notice that it recommends other articles that are related to the contents of your personal CiteULike library.

At the time of writing, CiteULike is only available on the web, but there are other reference-management systems (such as Delicious) that are also available as apps for phones or tablets. One thing that all these systems have in common (as well as easy formatting) is that they are social. Users can make their libraries available to other people. Furthermore, the system makes recommendations based on what other users who have read/stored the same articles as you have in their own libraries. Users can 'tag' items that they store in their libraries so that if, for example, a student who is collecting references for a module called (say) 'TELL 101' can tag all the articles related to that module with 'TELL101', which will allow her or him to search for them later when writing the assignment.

Keeping track of bibliographic information is, of course, only one aspect of avoiding plagiarism but it is the one where technology can provide most support. Students still need to learn techniques for paraphrasing, citing, and quoting source texts and there are a number of excellent books that can help with this. We particularly like Mary Deane's *Inside Track to Academic Research, Writing & Referencing* (Longman 2010). Many university library websites also contain comprehensive guides to the referencing systems in use at the institution. It should be remembered that different subject areas and different institutions use different systems, so tutors on generic academic skills courses cannot provide answers to all questions about referencing. However, students who know where they will undertake further study can look at the library websites to see what will be expected of them. Students should always be discouraged from copying and pasting text, even into a reference management system; it is too easy to forget quotation marks and this can lead to accidental plagiarism. Although we cover mindmapping in Chapter 5 (Writing), it is worth remembering that mindmaps can also be useful for making notes when reading. Transferring information from the source text to a mindmap not only helps readers to process and understand the content, but can also help them to avoid copying and pasting large chunks of text. As we say frequently to students, 'You need to make it your own' and creating a mindmap can be a useful stage in this process. Chapter 4 includes a task which looks in more detail at the use of graphic organizers, including mindmaps, for collecting information when reading.

Writing

Probably the most important digital tool for academic writing is the word processor. Most students nowadays will know how to use software such as Microsoft Word or Apple Pages and are likely to have used it in school. However, as mentioned above, this does not mean that they know how to use the features that are particularly useful for academic writing. Full-featured word-processing software, for example Microsoft Word, typically includes a number of tools that are extremely helpful for writing. It should be pointed out that most of these tools have existed in word processors for many years, yet it seems that students are rarely aware of them. They include:

- Headings – Many students use formatting such as bold, italic, underlining, or different/larger fonts to identify subheadings. However, when the heading styles built into the software are used, the program embeds a code into the text that identifies it as a heading or subheading. This code is not (usually) displayed on screen; the writer simply sees the formatting, for example bold or italic text or different and/or larger font. However the software 'knows' that the code is there and it can then be used to create cross-references within the text both to sections and to page numbers. For example, Microsoft Word has a menu tab or item called 'references'. Within that, there is an option called 'cross-reference'. The cross-reference option presents a drop-down list of items, such as numbered item (which might be a figure or table), heading, or footnote. There is a second drop-down list with items such as item number and page number. Using these two lists, the writer can write a sentence such as 'Task 1 showed us that ...' with Task 1 as the cross-reference. If the text is subsequently rearranged so that Task 1 becomes, for example, Task 8, the internal links can be automatically updated so that all the cross-references are correct. There is no need to work through the document to try and remember how the sections have been moved and where Task 1 has now been located.

It is also possible to create lists of contents and of tables when proper headings and captions have been used. Word-processing software includes functions for creating tables of contents, etc. In Microsoft Word, these are also in the references menu. The software reads the headings and captions and uses these to create the tables, with page numbers. Again, the tables of contents can be automatically updated so that the page numbers are always correct.

Use of headings also allows writers to navigate the document by means of something called the document map. This can be extremely useful when writing large documents such as a dissertation, as it helps the writer to find specific sections easily.

- Captions – word-processing software typically includes a tool called 'insert caption' which will insert captions for a table or figure. As with headings, if this tool is used together with the 'insert cross-reference' tool, it is easy to refer in the text to a figure and update that cross-reference if the sequence of figures is changed. It will also be easy to create and update a list of figures/tables if this is needed.

- Comments – the tool 'insert comment' allows writers to add notes that are not part of the main text (usually the comments look like thought bubbles or sticky notes). In draft work, writers can make comments either for their own reference or as questions to a reader – for example, a tutor reviewing the work. It can be a very useful way of adding reminders such as 'check this reference or 'add something about xxx'. Comments are often used by tutors reading draft work.

- Track changes – the 'track changes' tool marks revisions to a text so that it is possible to see who made the changes and what has been deleted or inserted. This is clearly useful for multi-authored texts because it allows writers to see the contributions of each individual, but it is also helpful for single authors as it means that changes to the text are not lost. Writers who change their mind about a deleted or moved paragraph can easily restore the text if 'track changes' has been used.

In addition to full-featured word-processing programs, there are also programs with a very limited range of features. An example of this is Ommwriter (see our accompany website for details) which allows text entry and deletion with minimal formatting options. Even the small number of options available vanishes unless the cursor is hovering over the bar. Ommwriter is designed to provide a distraction-free environment so that writers are able to concentrate on creating the text rather than making it look pretty. This type of environment can be particularly useful for younger learners and others who struggle to maintain focus on their writing. Since the writing of extended texts (such as essays of 3,000–6,000 words) is often a major part of assessment at university level, especially in the UK, it is important that students preparing for courses that involve extended writing have opportunities to practise the technology skills that they will need to write and manage their essays and reports.

One of the reasons that plagiarism is such a major headache for international students is that many, when they study in an English-medium institution, are entering a different academic culture. In some academic cultures, it is considered good practice to show respect for the words of the 'masters' through repetition. However, in the academic culture of English-speaking (in fact, of all western countries) this is called 'plagiarism' and is an academic offence. As we have said earlier, effective reference management can help to prevent accidental plagiarism, but it does not help those students who have learned that good marks are gained by reproducing 'official wisdom' to understand the process of critical analysis and synthesis of this wisdom that is required in western academic culture. One of the responsibilities of EAP tutors is to help students understand how to adapt to the culture of English academic writing and this includes learning how to paraphrase and incorporate other people's work in a way that is acceptable and does not constitute plagiarism. Many universities nowadays use software such as Turnitin to detect possible plagiarism. To refer to Turnitin as a 'plagiarism detector' is a misnomer. The software compares submitted work against a database of all work that has been submitted and also to internet sources. It then produces a 'similarity report' which shows which parts of the submitted text are similar to other documents. Turnitin does not offer a trial, but if your institution has an account, it can be very interesting to copy and paste a page from Wikipedia. However, a high similarity index does not mean that work has been plagiarized because it can be caused by, for example, repeating an essay title in the page headers or by using quotations in a format that Turnitin does not recognize (such as italicizing quotations; Turnitin only recognizes double inverted commas as indicating quotations). It is, therefore, always necessary for academic staff to check the report. The Turnitin website has a video which demonstrates the process by which reports are produced.

Listening

The traditional lecture is still a major part of university education. Students may also be provided with a range of other audio materials, such as podcasts, recorded lectures, or videos. These can usually be replayed at will and so are easier for students who struggle with listening to spoken English. However, the one-time lecture is still a problem for students whose first language is not English. Now that audio-recording devices are cheap and widely available (for example, on mobile phones) we see an increasing number of students recording lectures, although this should never be done without the permission of the lecturer. However, a significant change with regard to lectures is the use of visual material. Although lecturers have always used visual aids, from the blackboard to the overhead projector, almost all lecturers nowadays use some kind of presentation software, most commonly PowerPoint or an equivalent, to prepare their lectures. It has been argued (Tufte 2003a, 2003b) that PowerPoint is used too widely but often not very well but, like it or not, the electronic slide presentation is now ubiquitous. PowerPoint slides can contain images, text, video/audio context, and 'objects' such as spreadsheet tables. Most commonly they are used for text images or data intended to support the spoken lecture. Some lecturers will hand out paper copies of slides, but this practice is not universal (or necessarily desirable). In institutions which have a VLE, it is a common practice for lecturers to make slides available electronically before or after the lecture. On the surface, it seems that slides should make it easier for students to understand spoken lectures, but this is not necessarily the case. Research into multimodal presentation of information (Mayer 2009) has found that visual materials enhance understanding only when they match the spoken text. When the two sets of information diverge, the visual component becomes a distraction rather than a support. This may seem obvious but, unfortunately, it cannot be assumed that all lecturers are aware of this or that they will design their slides appropriately. However, a recent study, Wecker (2012) shows that students remember less of the information presented orally when it is accompanied by slides (but remember more of the slide-based information). Wecker attributes this to 'dysfunctional attention' and hypothesizes that this is more likely to occur with listeners who attach more importance to slides. This is extremely significant for EAP tutors as students studying in a second language are more likely to rely on slides for information and, by doing so, they can miss essential information presented orally

This means that EAP classes can usefully help to prepare students for slide-assisted lectures by teaching them how to 'tune out' visually distracting slides (or slide-handouts) and focus on essential spoken content. It is worth reminding students that slides will always be available after a lecture (either uploaded to a VLE for all students or by request from the tutor) whereas the oral information is presented only whilst the tutor is speaking.

Task 5	**Slideshare**

Slideshare contains a huge number of uploaded slide presentations, with or without soundtracks. Log on to Slideshare (see our accompanying website for details) and from the video selection, choose a slideshow with a spoken soundtrack.

- Watch the video with the sound muted and note the main points of the presentation.
- Play the video again, this time with the screen turned off or away from you. Note the main points.
- How different are the two sets of points that you have noted? Was most of the information conveyed by the slides or by the spoken text?

As the slides have been uploaded to Slideshare it is possible that they will have been designed to stand apart from the spoken text. However a quick skim through Slideshare will demonstrate that in many presentations, images are chosen for impact rather than information. Using this activity with students will help them to separate the visual from the spoken information channels so that they can understand the need to focus on what is being said, rather than what they have to read during a lecture.

Speaking and group work

Although students are still expected to engage in traditional 'academic speaking' activities such as tutorials and seminars, the modern emphasis on collaborative learning means that students are expected to participate in a lot of group work. Group work might take place face to face, online, or may be 'blended', using a combination of face-to-face and online modes. As we discussed in Chapter 2, the concept of 'talk' is broader in online environments than in the real world, as it can encompass text-based conversations as well as spoken ones. Sometimes computer-mediated communication (**CMC**) conversations can be carried out entirely through textual media; for example by using asynchronous discussion boards. However, other tools, such as virtual classrooms, will allow a mixture of text chat and spoken conversation. Students may also be expected to use asynchronous speech tools, such as **voice boards**, podcasts, or videos. As Chapter 2 explained, including both virtual classrooms and voice boards in CMC can cause discourse turns to overlap and discussion threads to be disrupted, so students need to learn how to participate in these kinds of disjointed conversations. In addition to this, in environments which combine speech and text, such as virtual classrooms, voice boards, or even Skype, the two modes can overlap; so a conversation, or even a single speech 'turn', may begin in one mode and then continue in the other. For example, when conducting doctoral supervisions using a virtual classroom, we frequently find ourselves making speech turns like the following:

Spoken   Deane is a really useful source book for referencing.

Written   Deane, M. (2010). *Academic research, writing and referencing.* Harlow: Longman. You should be able to find it in the library.

Spoken   But it's probably worth buying a copy.

Our experience (Walker 2003) confirms Warschauer's (1996) finding that students whose first language is not English are likely to talk more when using text-based CMC. Although students may find typed conversation clumsy at first, as they become more fluent with their fingers, they realize they are freed from the fear that people will not understand their spoken English. Warschauer also argues, and our experience again agrees with him, that students who for personal or cultural reasons are 'quieter' are more likely to 'speak' when using text-based CMC. Because of this, it might be tempting to make extensive use of text-based CMC in the EAP classroom and, indeed, this can be a useful bridging activity to help students develop confidence about expressing themselves in English. However, students still need practice in speaking, so that when they are later obliged to give presentations to or participate in groups work with competent English speakers then they feel able to do so.

One of the contexts in which students are likely to encounter CMC, both **synchronous** and **asynchronous**, is **distance learning**. Distance learning is not, of course, a new phenomenon but its prevalence has been increased by the availability of technological tools to support long-distance delivery and interaction. Many of the tools that we have mentioned above will be incorporated into distance provision but it is likely that everything will revolve around a VLE, possibly with some virtual classroom or web-conferencing software.

Task 6	**Virtual classroom**

For this task you will need to use a free or trial virtual classroom (see our website for suggestions). Some of these products offer classes or webinars where you can experience the features of the software; for example Adobe Connect has frequent scheduled webinars and you can find a list on the Adobe Connect website. If you are working alone, you can join one of these classes instead of doing the group task.

- Work with partner or in a group of three and sign up for a trial of a virtual classroom.
- In the classroom discuss this question: 'What might be the main benefits and drawbacks of distance learning?' Whilst using the virtual classroom facility, make sure that you use all the facilities – audio/video, text chat, and the whiteboard.
- Consider this question: 'What do learners need to know in order to use this type of environment effectively?'

Virtual classrooms provide excellent opportunities for students to practice synchronous online discourse. In the EAP classroom, an occasional online session can help to prepare students for the demands of conducting a conversation in both text and speech and allow them to practise some of the 'new' conventions of text-based speech (see Chapter 3). If this is used in conjunction with a discussion forum, perhaps in a VLE, then students will also be able to experience the difference between synchronous and asynchronous online discussions.

Productivity

One of the ways in which technology supports students is that it can help them to manage their studies. There is a wide range of note-taking and **productivity software** available for keyboard-based computers, tablets, and mobiles. Whilst this area is not specifically relevant for English language, it is useful for students to explore when they are preparing for higher education. This task is planned as a group project but you can do this on your own without preparing a presentation or writing a report.

| **Task 7** | **Notes and productivity** |

On the web or on your tablet or mobile phone, search for apps in these areas:

| to do list | diary | mindmapping |
| notes | timetable | flashcards |

- Evaluate a selection of apps in each category. How well are they rated by other users? How much do they cost? How easy are they to use? How well do they synchronize with other platforms (for example, from phone to web)? If possible, try out some of the apps.
- In your group, prepare a short presentation recommending a selection of apps study. Give your reasons for each recommendation.
- In your group, use Google Docs, or a similar shared writing environment, to prepare a group report on your findings and recommendations.

This activity is useful for students because it does not matter how diverse the group is (in terms of academic fields). All students need to take notes, manage their timetables, and so on. It gives the students an opportunity to work together to prepare a presentation and a report, thus preparing them for some of the group activities that they may need to undertake in their further study.

Summary

In this chapter, we have shown how digital tools have changed higher education. Students are expected to produce almost all of their work electronically and this may include work in new formats, such as slideshows. Students are also expected to engage in more collaborative learning activities, often mediated electronically, and to produce collaborative outputs. Digital tools can make life easier for students; for example electronic journals and reference managers may make certain aspects of academic study easier to manage. However, there can also be pitfalls, such as accidental plagiarism. It cannot be assumed that students will automatically know how to use digital tools for study, so it can be helpful to incorporate these tools into the EAP classroom and curriculum.

Further reading

Deane, M. 2010. *Academic research, writing and referencing.* Harlow: Longman.

Hyland, K. 2006. *English for Academic Purposes: An Advanced Resource Book.* Abingdon: Routledge.

Richardson, W.H. 2010. *Blogs, Wikis, Podcasts, and Other Powerful Web Tools for Classrooms.* Thousand Oaks, Calif: Corwin. and London: Sage.

8

YOUNG LEARNERS

Children have to be educated, but they have also to be left to educate themselves.
ERNEST DIMNET, priest and writer

Play is the work of the child.
MARIA MONTESSORI, educator

Aims

In this chapter, we will try to give you some answers to the following questions:
- What impacts does technology have on children's lives and learning?
- What are the needs of young language learners and what is the role of foreign languages in the curriculum?
- What types of digital resources and tools are appropriate for young learners to use and/or create?
- How can young learners be safe online?

Introduction

The chapter opens by defining what we mean when talking about 'young learners'. We then move on to look at the role of technology in the lives and education of young learners and to discuss children and language learning generally, comparing different ways of engaging young learners. We then explore immersive language learning approaches with a task that suggests using aspects of the ICT curriculum to teach English. The final section addresses the question of online safety for young learners.

Defining young learners

'Young learners' is a very general term that can mean any child from pre-school (aged two to three) to mid-teens. Clearly, teenagers and pre-school children are very different in almost every way. Even within the primary school age range (five to eleven), there is considerable difference between the younger and older children in terms of attitudes, developmental stage, first language ability, and literacy. The extent to which foreign language teaching is part of the primary school curriculum varies across the world. However, it is probably true to say that as English continues to maintain its position as the language of global communication, there is a global trend to start introducing it earlier. In some countries, children begin learning a foreign language (usually English) from the earliest years of school. In others, foreign language teaching starts in the middle primary school years (around seven or eight years of age) at a time when children should have basic literacy in their expert language. In some countries, foreign language learning barely figures in the primary curriculum. In addition to mainstream school-based language learning, children may take part in private language classes or language clubs. In this chapter, our main focus is children under the age of thirteen, particularly between the ages of seven to eleven, although we occasionally consider learners on either side of this age range.

In this chapter, we are concerned with children learning foreign languages in the classroom (or non-classroom settings such as language clubs) rather than in ecological contexts such as migration or multilingual environments. In some ways, the problems of teaching English to young learners are similar to those of teaching older teenagers or adults; however these are compounded by the role of language in the school curriculum and the life of the child. There are additional factors to consider, in particular, the developmental (and linguistic) stage of the child, so that the foreign language teacher is not making demands of a child in the foreign language when the child has not yet reached an appropriate developmental stage in her/his expert language. As an aside we would like to note the use of the term 'expert language' rather than 'first language' or 'mother tongue'. In many contexts, children come into school with more than one language. Sometimes this may be because the language of the home is different from that of the wider community, or because the home contains speakers of more than one language. In other cases, the language of the education system is different from the language(s) of the home and community and children learn the 'official' language through their schooling. In either case, as the child grows, one of these languages will become the child's preferred and 'expert language'. Teachers of foreign languages to children should be aware that their curriculum may be adding to a child's already complex linguistic capabilities.

As with all school subjects, there are national variations in terms of how far the curriculum is determined by national and local policy. Young children will often be learning a foreign language at the same time as they are developing their initial literacy and numeracy skills and because of this, as Cameron (2001) points out, there may be a tendency to patronize young learners by assuming that they can learn only very simple language such as colours or numbers. However, Cameron argues that children are capable of following their genuine interests even in a foreign language and this is important because it enables children to see the relevance and value of learning language. To a large extent, the 'needs' of young foreign language learners are determined by the school curriculum which tends to assume that children should learn language because it may be useful for future employment or study. When thinking about the ways in which working with young learners are different from teaching adults or older teenagers, the main areas to consider are development (cognitive, linguistic, social, etc.) and the primary school setting/curriculum. In addition, when thinking about using technology with young learners, it is important to consider how the role of technology in the life of a child is different from the role that technology might play in the life of an adult.

Children and technology

Whilst it might appear (as we explained in Chapter 2) that children have a natural affinity with technology, this cannot be taken for granted especially with regard to use of digital tools for education. Furthermore, children's use of technology is controversial. Some people, for example Prensky (2001), argue that using **digital technology** changes the structure/working of the brain and that this is beneficial whilst others, for example Carr (2011), using digital technology changes the structure/working of the brain, argue that this is detrimental. In fact, there is no clear evidence that technology itself affects brain structure or function, although it is known that the brain is plastic (i.e. that it can be changed) and that experience/learning can enhance brain development. For example, studies have shown that London cab drivers (who have to pass a demanding street navigation test known as 'The Knowledge') show increased development of some areas of the brain, although this appears to be at the expense of other aspects of memory (Woollett and Maguire 2011). However 'The Knowledge' requires several years of intensive study into a single specialist area and it cannot be assumed that generalized use of technology will have similar effects. Nevertheless, it is known that screen-time, such as television viewing, can have a negative impact on children's language development and on other aspects of learning (see Sigman 2005) On the positive side, researchers such as Mitra (2005) have found that children given technology can appear to teach themselves. Mass exposure of children to digital technologies is simply too recent to be certain about the effects on learning and development. Even the generation that Prensky calls 'digital natives' are only in their twenties and did not, as children, have the same level of exposure to digital tools as the children of today. A third perspective is provided by people such as Sigman (2012), who argues that children now have too much 'screen time' or Louv (2008) who believes that modern children suffer from 'nature deficit disorder' and need to spend more time in natural environments, such as woodland. We would not argue that teachers should not use technology with young learners, but teachers should certainly be aware that the debate exists and, whilst children often enjoy using technology, parents and headteachers may have legitimate concerns.

Another area of concern regarding children and technology is about online safety. Much of the discourse about children and technology is about fears that, for example, paedophiles may use social networking sites to find and groom potential victims. There are also concerns about exposure to violent video games (although some researchers argue that these fears are overstated) and worries about children engaging in **cyber-bullying**. Some of the tools that might be taken for granted with older students cannot be used with young learners. For example, in other chapters we have suggested using social networking tools, such as Facebook or Twitter. Usually, the terms of service state that users must be over thirteen years of age in order to register for an account. This means that even though many children do have Facebook accounts (Consumer Reports 2011), it would be unethical for teachers to use Facebook with children under thirteen.

The role of technology in the school curriculum is currently the subject of heated debate. Where ICT forms part of the school curriculum, in the UK at least, the focus has tended to be on teaching children to use software, especially office programs such as word processing, presentation software, and spreadsheets, alongside using the internet as an information source. Some groups, such as the Royal Society (2012) are now arguing that the focus should be on programming and that what is needed is a computer science curriculum rather than ICT. The problem that this poses is that a certain level of competence with basic software such as word-processing and understanding how to use the web is necessary in order to access both information and education in the modern age. The issue here for language teachers is that clearly it is not the responsibility of the language teacher to teach ICT skills, much less programming, but if the ICT curriculum is entirely replaced by computer science then children may lack the skills they need to take part in activities such as video creation or online writing. This debate may take some time to resolve (if, indeed, it can be resolved), but one possibility is for English to be used as a medium for teaching computing, and we explore this idea later in this chapter.

Another debate about the role of technology in the curriculum concerns the question of what it means to be 'literate' in the digital age. We have touched on this question in Chapter 6: authors such as Kress (2010) or Jewitt (2009) argue that in the 21st century literacy is multimodal and includes images, video, text, and sounds. Gee (2011), disagrees with this and uses the word 'literacy' to mean text-based literacy only. Not only is there disagreement about what it means to be literate, it is also unclear how and when children develop '**digital literacy**'. Plowman et al. (2010) show that the home is an important site for children's learning to use technology, yet the resources and activities available in the home are highly variable and may not be at an appropriate developmental level for the child (such as games which require levels of numeracy or text literacy that the child has not yet attained). However, it cannot be assumed that home use of technology will impart the skills, awareness, and knowledge of 'digital literacy', whatever that may be. Buckingham (2007) argues that digital literacy requires children to be able to create as well as to consume digital media and this is certainly a view we support and try to encourage in this book. However, in the context of the school curriculum, there may be a contradiction between this view and the belief that school ICT should focus on programming. If the questions of what constitutes 'multimodal digital literacy' and how it should be taught in the dominant language of the curriculum are not resolved, then it is even less clear how this aspect of modern communications should be covered in the foreign language curriculum.

Tactile interfaces

One of the affordances of the latest digital technologies, and one that is particularly appropriate for children, is the **touchscreen**. Tablet computers and smartphones have highly sensitive **capacitive screens** which respond to the slightest touch.

Touchscreens becomes large when fitted to interactive whiteboards (IWBs) in classroom settings. Touchscreens are wonderful for young learners as they allow the children to use their bodies in learning. An early whiteboard project (Brna and Cooper 2002) showed how children using IWBs could draw on the board and engage in collaborative activities, such as writing or the creation of pictures and music. Although IWBs are not without problems, as Wall, Higgins et al. (2005) show, they allow children to drag and drop items on the large screen or to write with their fingers on the large surface, so that an onscreen language game can become a whole-body experience. When, as we show in Chapter 10, in settings such as lecture theatres, IWBs can make teaching more teacher-centred, when used with young learners, they can enable children to become more active in their learning.

For those children in a setting where the language of education uses the Roman alphabet then learning to form the characters needed to write in English will happen when they learn to write their expert language. Those who come from different writing systems, however, will need to learn how to write Roman letters. This will, of course, be easier with some writing systems than others. Most literature on teaching language to young learners pays little attention to handwriting. Cameron (2001), for example, mentions the need for a multi-sensory approach to writing and for children to feel and draw letter shapes, but there is little about how to teach letter formation to children. This seems strange to us: if children fail to learn good habits in letter formation, it will have an adverse impact on their handwriting in later life as their writing speed increases. Even though computers are used for much writing nowadays, there are still times in life (particularly examinations) when handwriting is needed and important.

Task 1	**Handwriting games**

Search online for 'handwriting games'. Two that we suggest for iPad are LetterSchool or iWriteWords (details to be found on our website www.oup.com/elt/teacher/tell).

- Look at screenshots of these products. What are children asked to do?
- These activities can be done on paper so why use technology?

These letter formation apps ask children to draw inside the shape of a letter. They show the correct path that a pen should follow, sometimes with tokens to collect. Children can draw with a finger, but could also use a stylus, mimicking a pen. The games help children to learn how to shape the letters correctly so that good habits are formed. The technology introduces a game element with the collecting of tokens and it can also give aural and visual feedback. Using the iPad allows unlimited attempts and, importantly, mistakes are erased, whereas on paper incorrect attempts remain and can look 'messy'. On the iPad the child need have no fear of making mistakes.

Tablet computers offer a number of exciting opportunities for young learners, particularly with regard to games and electronic books. The tablet sits easily in the hand or on the table and the touchscreen interface has a more natural feel than mouse input. Tablets also include cameras, microphones, and speakers, which means that they can be used for an exciting range of activities, as we discuss further in the final chapter.

Children learning language

Intuitively and anecdotally it appears that children learn languages much more easily than adults. Parents (at least, those who are language teachers) observe their offspring acquiring language without overt tuition and those who take their children to live abroad notice that the children seem to absorb the language effortlessly, whilst the parents need hours of classes, but never sound as proficient as the youngsters. This apparent facility with language learning has led to people making parallels between children's linguistic acquisition and their use of technology. Papert (1993), for example, hypothesized that a technology-mediated environment could help children to learn mathematics as easily as language, whilst Prensky's 'digital natives' idea is based on the assumption that children acquire fluency with technology in the same way as they do with language. Many people have argued that children have a **'critical period'** for language learning, usually before adolescence, and that because of this foreign languages should be introduced to children in the primary classroom. However, Pinter (2011) dissects the research in the area of child language acquisition and finds that the 'critical period' is only true for the physical skill of pronunciation. Children who learn a foreign language early (particularly through migration or a multilingual environment) have a more 'native-like' accent than adult language learners, but in areas such as comprehension, vocabulary, syntax, or fluency child learners do not outperform adolescents or adults. They simply sound as though they are better at the foreign language.

Engaging young learners

Apart from developmental differences, one of the greatest differences between adults and children (or teenagers) in terms of foreign language teaching concerns the reasons why the language is learned. As Knowles et al. (2005) point out, adults generally choose to engage in learning and have clear reasons for making that choice. Adults therefore need to be able to see how the new learning is relevant to their aims in undertaking the study. For example, adults may choose to take English classes because they see this as important for career development. Adult learners understand how English is relevant to their needs, will want the class to be focused on the aspects of English that will be useful to them, and will be strongly motivated to succeed. Too much 'fun' may seem like a pointless and time-wasting distraction to adult learners. For learners who are still within the compulsory education system, however, English (or another foreign language) is simply another curriculum subject and may appear (to the learner) irrelevant to the child's life, particularly if the child lives in a community where there are few or no English speakers and little need for the language. Even when lessons include topics that are of interest to children, such as football or pop music, the curriculum subject still appears irrelevant because, of course, children can discuss and follow these topics in their expert language. However, one of the benefits, at the moment, of online tools and environments for teaching English to children is that they allow teachers to bring real world uses of English into the classroom.

Task 2	**Manchester United**

Go to www.google.de and choose 'google.de offered in Deutsch'. Search for 'Manchester United'.

- Are all the first page search results in German?
- Which results are offered in English?
- How might this be useful for a teacher of English?
- Are there any drawbacks to using materials obtained in this way?

When we tried this task, the second result on the page was the official Manchester United website, which is in English (although the site does offer a few alternative languages including French, Spanish, and Japanese). For anyone who is interested in Manchester United, the club's official website is a natural destination, and it contains the most up-to-date information about the club and players. The website is therefore a more authentic text than an English language textbook chapter about Manchester United, which will be out of date almost as soon as it is printed. Moreover, any learners with a real interest in ManU will be able to find information which is relevant to that interest and will have a strong motivation for deciphering the English in which the information is wrapped.

If an activity using a live website such as the official ManU page is to be realistic, learners need to use the site as it is. This means that it is difficult for teachers to prepare detailed material such as worksheets in advance because site content changes rapidly and unpredictably. One way to use a live website in the classroom is to adapt Deller's (1990) newspaper reading comprehension activity in which she suggests that, instead of teachers making comprehension worksheets for newspaper articles, the teacher gives the newspapers to groups of learners and asks them to create comprehension questions for other groups. Similarly, learners can make questions about the websites for each other. This allows different groups of learners to use different websites that perhaps better fit their interests (not everyone is a fan of Manchester United). It also means that the learners will be working with language at their own level, even if much of the website content is too advanced, the questions they prepare will always be up to date (websites change frequently and even questions created the day before the lesson may be no longer relevant to the content).

As mentioned earlier, children often lack the personal motivation of adults when it comes to classroom language learning. This means that teachers of children need to make use of games and fun activities that would be inappropriate for teaching adults. Where adults who are focused on the instrumental learning of a language might be annoyed by games, children can be motivated. Gee (2007) is a strong believer in the benefits of video games for learning. He argues that, in a game the player can take on a new identity as, indeed, gamers do when playing large-scale games such as World of Warcraft. Gee points out that when children play games, they often have to read and understand texts and these may be challenging, but because they are essential for the game, players persist and make sense of texts which might be beyond a player's classroom reading ability. 'Video games' is a blanket term that covers a very wide range of possibilities. Some games take only a few minutes to play, whilst others have no end point. Many video games are unsuitable for young children – not always for obvious reasons. There are a number of multiplayer combat games that could provide excellent opportunities for speaking and listening, for example, but it is clearly not appropriate for children to be shooting each other, even in the cause of language learning. However, even gentle games such as multiplayer farm-building games, which involve no violence, often cannot be used with young learners because they require players to use social networking tools (for example, Farmville is based in Facebook). As we pointed out earlier, this creates ethical problems for teachers. However, there are online games and virtual worlds designed especially for children.

Task 3

Club Penguin

Club Penguin is a virtual world, now owned by Disney, which aims to provide a safe online environment for children. It is available in English, French, German, Portuguese, or Spanish.

- Go to the ClubPenguin website.
- Read through the information for users and parents.
- Consider what makes this site safe for children to use.
- If you have time, create an account and spend some time inside the environment.
- What activities are available for children in Club Penguin? How might it be useful for language learners? How could teachers incorporate Club Penguin into the classroom?

Obviously, as this company is now owned by Disney, child safety is taken very seriously. Safety is maintained by requiring a parental email address (although, of course, this can be circumvented as you will have done if you created an account). Club Penguin also maintains safety by employing moderators and providing a 'panic button' for any child who feels threatened. All of these measures mean that as a teacher you can take your class into Club Penguin (with the permission of parents) with an expectation that you will all be in a safe environment. One thing to watch out for, though, is that parents should not sign up for 'membership'; they should authorize a free account only. Membership can prove expensive as there are opportunities to spend real money on virtual gewgaws within the game.

Club Penguin allows participants to interact with each other, to build and decorate igloos, and to play mini-games. Participants mix freely and do not use their real names so it can be difficult to keep track of a class if they are working on individual computers. One way around this would be to have a class penguin (using an electronic whiteboard or projected onto a screen) and ask children for suggestions about where to go, what to do and, crucially, what to say to other penguins. Similar activities can be undertaken with the children in small groups. Alternatively, children can explore the environment individually but with 'scavenger-hunt' type tasks, such as 'talk to three new people', or 'find someone who has a pet rabbit in real life'. When they are in Club Penguin children are masked by the penguin identity; they do not have to reveal themselves, but the penguin needs to use the target language. It gives the learners a reason to use the target language, but in a non-threatening and emotionally safe environment. An important point to remember is that the language work surrounding a task such as a visit to Club Penguin need not end when the learners leave the virtual world. Children can take screenshots of their penguins and adventures and use this for further writing and speaking activities.

Immersion

One of the hypotheses about language learning is that people learn language more effectively when they are 'immersed' in it, as is the case in what Lightbown and Spada (2006) call 'natural language settings'. As Lightbown and Spada point out, the crucial difference between 'natural settings' and curriculum-based learning is that the focus is on communication rather than accuracy. What matters is the content, what the speaker has to say, rather than the way in which it is said. Papert, 1993, also picked up on this when hypothesizing that the 'Mathland' of Logo would help children to learn mathematics through communication. When children are first learning to talk, their learning is driven by communication and usually they are rewarded when the communication is successful. For example, an infant who asks for a piece of fruit by pointing at an apple and saying 'nana' is likely to be rewarded by being given the apple, rather than being denied the fruit until he or she has correctly said 'Please mummy may I have an apple?' although parents often insist on courtesy words such as 'please' before delivering the reward. Parents scaffold infant language development by rewarding successful communication whilst modelling 'correct' or more complex language forms. (Bruner (1978) calls this the 'communicative ratchet'. In structured, curriculum-based settings, however, the opposite generally applies and the 'reward' – for example, marks or positive feedback – is only delivered when the utterance is in the correct form.

Various teaching approaches attempt to tackle the divergence between 'natural' and curriculum-based language learning. These include the communicative approach and task-based learning. In school settings, an alternative approach is to mix content from the wider curriculum with language teaching, sometimes called **CLIL** (Content and Language Integrated Learning) when used. This is an important area, but too broad to discuss in detail here. However CLIL research and approaches are given thorough coverage by Pinter (2011). See suggestions for further reading at the end of this chapter.

When the entire curriculum is taught through the medium of the target language, the approach is known as '**immersion**'. There are some settings in which immersion happens automatically, for example amongst children from migrant families whose home language is not that of the education system. In others, immersion and CLIL are intentional within the education system in order to improve acquisition of the target language. There is logic to this approach: children have to learn all curriculum subjects, so why not combine one or more with foreign language teaching and get two sets of learning for the price of one? However, as Lightbown and Spada (2006) demonstrate, CLIL and immersion approaches can lead to less effective learning of the content unless learners have (or have had) considerable instruction in their expert language. It is also more likely to be successful when the foreign language demands fit within a learner's '**zone of proximal development**' (Vygotsky 1978); in other words, when they are what the learner is ready to learn. Teachers using a CLIL approach need to be aware that each lesson is a language lesson as well as a content lesson and plan accordingly so that there are both language and content learning objectives.

Computing is one curriculum area that might be used for a CLIL approach to teaching English. One advantage is that so much of the language of computing is English or is common across languages. However, children can also use programming skills to build games and activities that make use of English as in the task below.

Task 4

Scratch programming

Scratch (see our accompanying website for details) is a visual programming language that is free to download and is designed to teach children basic programming skills. The program has a drag-and-drop interface so children do not have to learn and type text commands.

- Go to the Scratch website and click on the 'projects' page. What could your learners do here?
- Are there any examples of games/projects that could have language learning objectives?
- Go to the 'forums' page. How might the forums be useful to language learners?
- Scratch is available in a wide range of alternative languages; how might these resources support CLIL learning of Scratch?

Scratch can be used to make games and simulations. These might not necessarily include explicit language, but some contain written instructions or character dialogue. Projects can also include making a soundtrack; often this is music but it could be spoken. The types of games could include ones with a specific language focus, if that is what the learner chooses (or is asked to make). One benefit of children making their own games is that they can make something that appeals to their own interests, so those who like 'shoot-'em-up' games can make, for example, a game to shoot words that end in *-ing*. Those who do not like shooting games can make something with a different type of game play.

The 'projects' page of the website contains completed Scratch projects. Users can play the completed games and find inspiration for their own work. They can also adapt existing projects and this can be one way of getting started with Scratch programming. Of course, children can upload their own finished projects to the website for comments or for others to download and adapt. Each project on the website is surrounded by text; some of it is explanatory saying how the project was conceived and giving instructions for play, whilst other text is comments/feedback for other users. *Scratch* is an example of an online **community of practice** (Lave and Wenger 1991) in which users can learn from each other both by observing/adapting each other's work and by reading/posting in the forums. Novice users can start with observation/adaptation and by reading the forums. As they become more expert, they can post their own projects and contribute to the community forums. The forums also offer answers to many of the problems and challenges that learners face when working out how to program with Scratch. Participation in the community allows learners to use English in a natural fashion but the availability of other languages means the learners (may) also have support resources available in their own languages if the English simply becomes too challenging.

Stories

Another holistic way of approaching language is through stories (Cameron 2001). Stories are a common feature of childhood, both in the home and in school. Story-telling is the oldest literary form and one that is still used every day with young children when parents and other family members tell or read stories. Stories present language in context, often mixing narrative and dialogue and, although they are often delivered orally, they may also be written so can allow practice of all four skills. Moreover, the structure of a story often follows a familiar pattern, especially with traditional stories. For example, a story usually begins by introducing the characters and setting ('Once upon a time there was a little old woman and a little old man who lived in a little cottage with a big garden') followed by a statement of the problem ('In the garden was an enormous turnip. One day, the old woman decided to make turnip soup. She tried and she tried, but she couldn't pull up the enormous turnip'). Core phrases are repeated, sometimes with a call and answer pattern ('The old woman called the old man, "Old man, can you help me pull up this enormous turnip?" They pulled and they pulled, but they couldn't pull up the enormous turnip. The old man called the dog …'). There are several attempts at resolving the problem; many traditional stories have patterns of three. In the end, the problem is resolved ('All together they pulled and they pulled and UP came the enormous turnip!') and there is a statement of closure ('So they all had turnip soup for supper').

The familiarity of story structure and patterning supports learners even when at least some of the language is unfamiliar. The children know that a key event or snippet of dialogue will be repeated (perhaps in slightly) different form and will anticipate the repetition; they may even join in as the repetition becomes familiar. Stories generally also lend themselves to a wide range of follow-on activities.

Task 5

The Enormous Turnip

Search a slide-or-video sharing site, such as YouTube, for the story *The Enormous Turnip*

- Review some of the results that are presented.
- Which ones are suitable for your classroom and why?
- How might you include this in your classroom and what other activities (digital or non-digital) could you use to follow the story?

When we searched for electronic versions of this story, we found several versions on both YouTube and SlideShare. We also found a version called *The Enormous Carrot* (by Lynne Garner) as an iPad app and another version in an iPad collection of stories. In other words, this is a popular and widely available story. Almost all the versions that we found available for free consist of text and images; there were no animations or clickable features. On the other hand, one of our doctoral students (Bin 2008), who developed an electronic story book for young learners of English, found that although children love clickable features, they have a tendency to click randomly to find the animations, and this can detract from the story. In all versions the text is read aloud, but in some versions (for example Lynne Garner for iPad), there is the option for the child to read the story alone. Sometimes the text is highlighted as the story is read. Some of the versions add extra detail and this may reduce their suitability for a class learning a foreign language. One of the advantages of electronic stories is that the children can return to the story themselves, again and again, even if the written text is above their reading ability.

For most benefit, electronic stories should be embedded in a series of classroom activities. Another of our doctoral students (Recio Saucedo 2008) used electronic English storybooks with a class of very young learners in Spain. She used the stories within a methodology that included retelling, drawing, colouring, and cooking (one of the stories was *The Gingerbread Man*). Even though the children were only three and four years old they were able to retell parts of the story (retelling in Spanish what they had heard in English) and use some of the English words.

Task 6	**Storybook making**

Look at an online storybook-making site such as Storybird (you can find details and other suggestions on our website). Then think about these questions and, if possible, discuss with a colleague:

- For which groups of learners would the storybook makers be appropriate?
- How do/would you use story writing (electronic or traditional) in your classroom?
- What is the difference between writing a story and making a book?
- What aspects of language could your learners develop by making storybooks?
- How does/would storybook making fit into a scheme of work?
- How would you introduce a storybook making activity to your learners?
- What would be the benefits, to your learners, of making an electronic book?
- For your learners, would there be any drawbacks to making an electronic book instead of a paper-based book? If so, what?

Book making (storybooks or non-fiction) is an established activity for young learners. It allows learners to articulate and externalize their knowledge by creating a product which can be shared with other learners or with people outside the classroom (for example, parents, next year's class, or younger learners in the school). However, producing good quality books tends to be time-consuming for both learners and teachers. Typically, there will tend to be several drafts of the story and accompanying pictures before a fair copy can be produced. After that, the teacher often needs to laminate and bind the books. Electronic storybooks do not need binding as they can be read onscreen, but if anyone (for example, a parent) really wants a printed copy these can often be ordered online for a price. The onscreen books have a professional appearance, especially if ready-made images are used. It can be very motivating for learners to see their work professionally presented in this way and it is less time-consuming to make electronic books than to make books with paper, crayons, and card. However, there is a risk that the polished **output** of electronic books might cause learners to feel that hand-made work is not good enough.

In addition to making storybooks, children could make cartoon animations (see Chapter 6). Retelling a story with puppets is a traditional activity, but this can be videoed and added to the collection of story versions on YouTube. Other retellings of the story can take place via microblogging. Children could also make games about the story, perhaps using a tool such as Scratch.

Safety and protecting children

At several points in this chapter, we have mentioned issues regarding the safety of children in digital environments. Environments especially designed for children incorporate measures to ensure safety, but other services, for example video upload sites, often do not. We have mentioned that environments such as social networking services generally have age restrictions and, however useful a service such as Facebook might appear, it is simply unethical for teachers to use it with children under the age limit. The age limit for social networking services is often set at thirteen, so that it complies with US law (COPPA), but this age limit still seems (at least to us) to be on the low side. Parents may have strong views about their children using social networking services and open social networks are probably best avoided with young people under the age of sixteen, even though the learners may be using them outside school.

The most feared problems with regard to children's online activities are access to inappropriate material, such as explicit or violent content, and concerns that children may be targeted by predators. However, child-to-child bullying is a common problem (Lenhart et al. 2011) and teachers need to be aware of this. Examples of 'cyber-bullying' include making videos of victims (easy to do with a mobile phone) and uploading them to a site such as YouTube, making fake social network profiles, and constructing hate websites. Bullies may also use text-messaging, email, and instant messaging to target their victims (Kowalski et al. 2008). It is, understandably, extremely unpleasant to be a victim of cyber-bullying, particularly as the harassment continues into the home (into the pocket, in fact); victims may be receiving unpleasant texts even after they have gone to bed. Moreover, unlike in-person bullying, the victim may not be able to escape by changing school. Bullying tactics such as fake social network profiles may be picked up by classmates in the new school and the harassment may continue. One of the major factors in the rise of cyber-bullying is the perceived distance and anonymity of the internet. One of us, conducting research into online chat with young teenagers, noticed that the first discussion of the project contained a lot of verbal abuse and unacceptable language. This occurred because the young people, although using their real names, had not completely understood that the conversations were recorded and would be shared with teachers (the discussion was deleted and firm warnings issued to the class). They felt that they could say what they liked with impunity, even though they were physically in a classroom together and using a commercial VLE.

Task 7

Edmodo

Find the Edmodo site (see details on our website) and watch the introductory video.

- What is Edmodo?
- How does Edmodo provide a safe environment for children?
- How might you use Edmodo with your learners?
- What can you do to prevent the service being used for bullying?

Edmodo is a social media service especially for education. Using Edmodo (or a similar service) allows teachers to make use of social media activities with learners in an environment that is private, protected, and not subject to age restrictions. Teachers can see all interactions between learners, which means that any sign of bullying or abuse can be caught early. This is different from commercial VLEs which were often designed primarily for higher education and generally allow learners mechanisms for communicating privately.

Edmodo originally described itself as a 'microblogging service for education'. There are many activities in this book for which we have suggested using Twitter or Facebook. For those working with young learners, Edmodo can be used for these kinds of activities, but in a controlled environment. The interface is designed to be similar to popular social networking services, which means that pupils feel that they are using a genuine social network rather than a school VLE. As the introductory videos demonstrate, Edmodo can be used to gather and host a wide range of materials, which means that it can be used as the base for class projects, such as video dictionaries (see Chapter 6) or blogs (see Chapter 5).

Summary

In this chapter, we have tried to draw together children's language learning and the issues and debates surrounding children's use of technology. The online world offers tremendous potential for young learners, particularly in relation to language use and learning. In addition, learning language through the use of technology can be a helpful way to enhance children's digital literacy and even a vehicle for learning some basic programming. However, there are genuine risks for children in online environments, so teachers need to make sure that all sites and services used are appropriate to the ages of the children. and that interactions between children can be monitored.

Further reading

Lightbown, P.M. and **N. Spada,** 2013. *How Languages are Learned* (4th edn.). Oxford: Oxford University Press.

Pinter, A. 2011. *Children Learning Second Languages.* Basingstoke: Palgrave Macmillan.

9

ASSESSMENT

Examinations are formidable even to the best prepared, for the
greatest fool may ask more than the wisest man can answer.
CHARLES CALEB COLTON, writer

Aims

In this chapter, we will try to give you some answers to the following questions:

- How does technology affect assessment?
- What are the advantages and disadvantages/arguments for and against using technology in assessment?
- How can technology be used in the assessment of language learning?

Introduction

This chapter opens by considering the different reasons for assessing learners and goes on to look at how technology affects assessment and the arguments for using technology to assist it. We then consider the issues of reliability and validity before discussing the possible impact of assessment on teaching (known as '**washback**'). We go on to explore the different stages of the assessment process and consider the role(s) that technology might play in each phase. The final section examines some of the pitfalls inherent in technology enhanced/assisted assessment and suggests how they can be avoided.

The different purposes of assessment

Assessment is an essential component of education systems. The term 'assessment' is extremely broad and covers several different types of activity with different purposes: in most formal education settings, learners are assessed at several points. The main purposes of assessment include:

- diagnostic – to determine the needs of a learner
- placement – to assign learners to groups or classes
- proficiency – to assess how 'good' a learner is at something
- achievement – to award a grade or certificate

- formative – to give feedback to learners and determine the direction of future learning opportunities
- summative – to establish what a learner has achieved at the end of a course of study
- quality assurance – to evaluate teaching

Assessments may come at the beginning of a programme of study in order to put students into groups (placement testing) or to find out what they need to learn (diagnostic testing). They may take place at any time during the course in order to establish how well students are learning and what they need next (**formative assessment**). Assessments may take place at the end of a programme of study to see how much students have learned (**summative assessment**). Some assessments are formal such as written examinations or assessment coursework. In these situations, everybody knows that an assessment is being conducted and usually a grade is awarded (achievement). Other assessments are informal, such as small in-class tests, or homework marked by teachers. In these cases, neither learners nor teachers may perceive what is happening as 'assessment' because grades are not formally recorded; however learners will receive formative feedback that will help to improve their performance in future.

The purposes of assessment are not mutually exclusive so that assessment intended for one main purpose often provides information that can be used for secondary functions. For example, learners can be given formative feedback on end-of-course assessments (to help them do better at the next level) and continuous assessments during a course may be used by teachers not only to give formative feedback, but also to contribute to the summative grading of a student.

Assessment can also be for accountability, i.e. for checking the quality of teaching that an individual or institution provides. In many cases, the summative and/or formative tests used on a course can be used for quality assurance. For example, in the UK, secondary school 'league tables' are produced and published in newspapers. These tables are based on the results of the national GCSE and A Level results. Although these exams are summative and provide individual qualifications for the students, the accumulated results are used to assess and compare the performance of schools. This makes the exams 'high-stakes' in two senses: firstly, for the individual students, the exams are their school-leaving qualifications and determine whether or not they will be able to continue with further study; secondly, for the schools, the exams determine their rankings in comparison with neighbouring schools.

Another role for assessment is 'gatekeeping'. This is where a minimum test score is set as a baseline criterion for entry, for example, to a course of study at a university. Institutions may have their own entrance tests or they may ask for minimum grades from proficiency examinations, such as GCSE (General Certificate of Secondary Education). Two of the best known gatekeeping examinations in English language teaching are the Test of English as a Foreign Language (**TOEFL**) and International English Testing System (**IELTS**). These tests are administered by independent bodies, but used by educational institutions, typically universities, to decide whether students have an adequate level of English for academic study. At the time of writing, the IELTS threshold for UK universities is a score of six, although some courses ask for a higher overall score. The IELTS or TOEFL score that a student achieves may also be used as an indicator of whether he or she would benefit from in-sessional support with academic English, so although the main function of the test (from the university's perspective) is gatekeeping, the results may also be used for diagnostic purposes.

In recent years, there has been a move towards Assessment for Learning (AfL) (Black and Wiliam 1998). This is a teaching approach that enables personalization of learning, but provides frequent assessments that enable targets to be set for individual learners. The underpinning principle of an AfL approach is that learners should know what they need to learn. In addition, they should know how far they are progressing towards the desired outcomes and what they need to do in order to achieve their targets. This means that teachers need to be explicit about intended learning outcomes, not only in their lesson plans, but also with learners, and provide frequent opportunities for learners to find out about their progress and future targets. Not all AfL assessments need be formal; as we have shown earlier, teachers continually assess and provide feedback on the progress of their students as a matter of course.

How does technology affect assessment?

When technology is introduced as a **mediational tool** in the processes of assessment, it has clear impacts on the ways that work is shared in the activity, on the culture and rules of the activity, and it sometimes changes the purposes of the activity. In terms of the workload of assessment, in some cases parts of the work are transferred from people to technology. An example is computerized marking: where work can be marked electronically, there is no need for a human marker. However, this in turn changes the nature of the judgements that can be made, since computer programs work best with clear answers and cannot usually make the subtle decisions of which human markers are capable. Technology allows or creates some assessment practices which are otherwise difficult or impossible. An example of this is plagiarism (which we have covered extensively in other chapters). Technology makes plagiarism both easier to commit and easier to discover. However, use of plagiarism detection tools may uncover instances of unintentional similarity which would previously have gone unnoticed. The use of similarity checkers can also be seen as creating an assessment culture in which all students are viewed as potential cheats and certainly raises the level of anxiety amongst students.

Technology may also change the types of skills and knowledge that can be assessed. Some types of software, for example, **screen recording** or **eye tracking** may make it easier to assess process. The process of writing can be difficult to observe, but use of screen-recording software can show how a writer has created and edited their work; for example Soong et al. (2010) show how the use of computer-mediated dialogues can give insight into learners' thinking and ideas. The history information in a wiki provides information about what each member of a group has contributed to a collaborative project. However, technology may also constrain assessment. A policy decision to use only computerized marking may lead to the replacement of open-ended questions with, say, multiple-choice.

We believe that there are three main arguments for the use of technology in testing and assessment. However, these arguments certainly do not indicate that technology should be used for all assessment; as with all uses of technology in education, the prime considerations should be the needs of the learners, the desired outcomes, and the affordances/constraints of the learning context. The starting points should always be these questions:

1 What do we want to know about the learner's knowledge and/or skills?

2 What is most effective way to gain that knowledge?

Argument one: technology is part of real life

We have discussed in other chapters the concept of 'digital literacies' and it seems logical that where 'digital literacy' is part of the knowledge or skills to be assessed, the assessments themselves should be digital.

Task 1	**Assessing digital literacy**

Over the last week, in what ways have you used technology to accomplish tasks that involve the language skills of speaking, listening, reading or writing? In how many of these cases has the electronic option become your main way of undertaking this task? If your learners have the same patterns of behaviour, what are the implications for assessment of those skills?

It is very likely that for at least some of these tasks, the online option has become the default. For example, phone text messaging is now more popular than phone (voice) calls (OFCOM 2012). Indeed, one of us has found that a text message is the most effective way of asking teenage offspring to be quiet late at night. We have discussed the need for language teaching to include skills and language forms associated with text messaging and it seems difficult to imagine these could be assessed without using text messages.

An assessment should have some level of task authenticity which Leung and Lewkokicz (2005: 214) define as 'the extent to which a test ... relates to the context in which it would normally be performed in real life.' We would extend this definition to include the tools that would normally be used to perform a task. As we have pointed out several times, technology is an essential part of the way that tasks are accomplished. We have mentioned text messaging, but email and other forms of CMC (for example, social media) are also part of our everyday communications tools. Where computers are available, very few people choose to hand-write essays or other long documents, and preparing a presentation using only flip charts seems antediluvian now that electronic slides have become ubiquitous. The internet is used as a primary information source, for everyday shopping, for booking travel, and so on. Furthermore, government departments are trying to provide services online and this means that, increasingly, people need to read and navigate electronic text in order to access government services.

Given that technology is so much a part of how we read, write, and communicate, it is reasonable, possibly even essential, that technology is used in the testing of reading, writing, and communication skills in order to make the assessments as authentic as possible. This is particularly true, of course, when technology is also part of the teaching of those skills. If language teachers ask students to write digital texts as part of their learning, it is arguable that the students should be assessed through the production of digital texts. This does not only apply to the types of text which people often regard as 'new' or 'digital' (for example, blogs). If all essays are written using a word processor, for example, then the students may be placed at a disadvantage if the examination requires them to handwrite their essays. They will be accustomed to planning a text onscreen and then filling in the sections and to being able to cut or copy and paste text, and to instant correction of spelling errors. Writing an essay by hand requires different skills to word-processing, such as the ability to work from a plan rather than creating and adapting the plan during the writing process within the main text. Presentational features such as spelling also become more important when texts are written by hand as mistakes cannot simply be erased without trace.

Argument two: technology can make assessment more efficient

The argument that technology will make assessment more efficient is particularly compelling for policy makers. However, it should be noted that 'more efficient' does not necessarily mean cheaper; it may simply mean replacing expensive markers with equally (or more) expensive programmers. That said, tests which make use of right/wrong answers (multiple choice, gap-filling, short answer, etc.) can be marked very quickly by computers. Computer-based formative self-assessments can be taken by students at any time and without peeking at the answers (hard to resist when the answer is at the back of the book). Computer-based tests can also compile the results and give a grade automatically, feeding the results back to the teacher. Digital, audio, or video allows students or examiners to record unlimited samples of oral language for assessment. This gives digital equipment an advantage over tape-based recording; in addition, digital recording is cheaper and the files are easier to store and to access. They are also easier to delete, but that is another issue.

Digitally written essays are easier to read than hand-written essays and, if the text is submitted electronically, comments can be added using the tools described in Chapter 7. This makes the feedback easier to store (and to reproduce if necessary). In addition, it is possible to create 'comment banks' for frequently used comments (such as 'check your spelling' or 'reference needed here') so that the marker does not need to write the comment in full each time it is needed. This makes the marking process more efficient, although a consequence may be that at least some of the feedback may be less personalized for the student.

Argument three: technology creates new possibilities

Every kind of tool has affordances and constraints – things that you can do with it and things which you cannot do (or perform only with difficulty).

An example that we have mentioned frequently is checking for plagiarism. Before the advent of plagiarism software, there were only two ways that students that were likely to be caught plagiarizing. Either a tutor would recognize copied text, or there would be some way in which it was obvious that the candidate could not have written the plagiarized work (for example, if the language was above the ability of the candidate).

More interesting examples of the possibilities offered by electronic testing are the 'sophisticated tasks' suggested by Boyle and Hutchinson (2009). These are multimedia, multimodal tasks which can incorporate sound, video, and images as well as text, and can make use of semi-tactile inputs such as drag and drop. Threlfall et al. (2007) reported on tests that used 'sophisticated tasks' to assess ICT capability in school. These tests were conducted using a locked virtual environment designed to simulate a suite of everyday applications such as word processing, email, spreadsheets, image editing, and web browsing. Learners received task rubrics via 'email' and then had to carry out a series of actions, such as choosing an image, editing it, importing it into a document, and then adding appropriate text via copy and paste in order to create a leaflet. Each action was recorded by the software to provide evidence for a grade to be generated automatically. These tests were not without problems, but test designers were trying to do something in a radically different way; they were trying to assess complex processes in a field where the process is important, but normally only the product can be assessed.

Another example of technology making possible something that cannot easily be done with traditional means is **computer adaptive testing** (CAT).

Task 2	**Adaptive testing**

1 Go to Oxford English Testing (http://www.oxfordenglishtesting.com) and look at the placement test.
2 How does this test work? How does it adapt to the level of the learner?
3 What are the benefits of an adaptive test?

Computer-adaptive tests (CATs) have been around for as long as people have been using computers for education and can be a type of AfL. The principle underlying CATs is that the test adapts to the candidate, so that the questions become more difficult or easier depending on the candidate's previous answers. This can then deliver learning opportunities that are personalized to the individual. In the case of the Oxford Test, the next set of learning opportunities is provided by teachers, but CATs are also the basis of so-called Intelligent Tutoring Systems (ITS), in which a computer acts as a tutor using information from the CAT to create the next set of learning tasks. These systems can, in principle, work well, especially with learners who have specific educational needs, but in practice the implementation is often less successful than the promise. Jervis and Gkolia (2005) provide an analysis of one implementation and found that although the learners quite liked the system, they felt that the teacher was a more effective educator. CATs are expensive and so schools need to think carefully about how the system will be used and supported before making the investment. However, one principle of CATs – tasks that become more difficult as the user progresses – has also been realized in several apps for smartphones and tablets, and these can be a useful support for learners.

Types of assessment

Common types of tests in language learning and teaching include multiple-choice questions, cloze and gap-filling, short answer questions, composition writing, and oral interviews. Listening tests commonly use recorded (usually but not always scripted) conversations or lectures with multiple-choice, or short-answer questions. Reading tests/assessments tend to use items of text, ranging from a bus ticket to a lengthy newspaper article, with multiple-choice or short-answer questions.

Task 3	**Traditional or electronic?**

In the past year or so, what assessments have you used with your learners and what kinds of support materials, such as texts for reading, did these employ? Could any of these assessments have used electronic tasks or materials? If so, what would be the benefits (if any)? What might be the drawbacks?

Most types of traditional assessment can be presented electronically or 'blended', so that the tasks contain different types of materials; for example, a reading test could present both text and questions electronically. However, it might be better to present the text on paper and the questions electronically so that the candidate can look at both the text and the questions without having to scroll the screen or flip between windows. Electronic presentation is particularly suitable for tests of listening (where facilities are available) as students can listen individually on headsets and, where appropriate, move backwards and forwards in the text. Assessment of writing (although not handwriting) grammar, vocabulary, and spelling can all be electronic, but assessing speaking is more problematic.

Other types of assessment include using student-created resources such as video, audio, diaries, blogs, and **portfolios**. Portfolio assessment precedes technology, of course, but the use of e-portfolios widens the types of materials that can be included. Digital video, photography, and audio tools make it very easy for students to record and reflect upon their learning; they could also use these, and other technology tools, to prepare presentations for assessment. We discuss e-portfolios in more detail below.

Reliability and validity

Two important issues in assessment are reliability and validity. Reliability means, simply that the results of the test are consistent. A reliable test should give the same results every time it is used, so that if a person takes the same test on two different days then he or she should achieve more or less the same score. However this doesn't quite work in reality because people get better with practice and may be affected by their emotional states or by external factors, such as the weather. Multiple-choice, cloze, gap-filling, and certain types of short-answer question test are highly reliable. Essays, presentations, and other forms of assessment which rely on qualitative judgements on the part of markers are less reliable, although the reliability is improved by the use of multiple markers and carefully written assessment criteria.

Validity means that an assessment should test what it is intended to test. It is possible for a test to be perfectly reliable and yet totally invalid. For example, the question, 'If Asma has fifteen apples and she gives three to Bashir, how many apples will she have left?' may be intended to test subtraction; however, in order to answer the question, the student has to be able to read and understand the language of the question, so it is as much a test of English as it is a test of arithmetic. On the other hand, the question may be included in a test of English language, in which case the student can only answer the question if he or she can perform the arithmetical operation. Weir (2005) believes that that an assessment should be considered valid only if the marks or grades are an accurate reflection of the candidate's knowledge and skills. This is an interesting argument, but a candidate's performance can be affected by many different factors (as mentioned above), so a mark that does not give an accurate reflection of ability does not necessarily mean that the test was completely invalid, although it would be evidence for a reduction in its validity.

In language testing, it is quite common for the skills of reading, writing, speaking, and listening and for elements such as grammar and vocabulary to be tested separately. However, it is very difficult to isolate the skills and elements in reality, so it is important to think very carefully about the validity of a test. This becomes particularly important when technology is considered in relation to assessment because it is important to make sure that what is being tested is language knowledge or skills rather than familiarity with technology. On the other hand, one justification for using technology in assessments is that many everyday activities are mediated by digital tools: it could therefore be argued that where learners are accustomed to using technology for certain types of tasks, a failure to use technology in the assessment reduces the validity of the test.

Washback

'Washback' (also called 'backwash') is the effect that an assessment has upon learning and teaching (Alderson and Hamp-Lyons 1996, Alderson and Wall 1993, Andrews, Fullilove, and Wong 2002, Green 2007, Hamp-Lyons,1997). A common phenomenon, especially with high-stakes tests, is 'teaching to the test' whereby teachers focus on the test skills and knowledge to the exclusion of other topics and skills. This can lead to some significant conflicts in the curriculum, especially where there is a mismatch between the topics and pedagogy laid down by the curriculum designers and the assessment that learners will eventually have to take. For example, if the curriculum dictates a communicative teaching method but the national examinations are based on grammar, translation, and reading comprehension, teachers will need to teach grammar, translation, etc. if their students are to succeed in the exams. However much teachers might believe in **communicative language teaching**, if the methodology conflicts with the assessment, there is a risk that the demands of the assessment will take priority.

Task 4	### Washback and technology

If you think about the high-stakes language assessments that your learners will have to take in due course, what knowledge and skills will be needed to do well in the tests? What impact does this have on your teaching? What are the implications for using technology in your teaching and assessment?

Washback has significant implications for teachers who want to incorporate more use of technology in their teaching, especially if the goal is to provide more collaboration and interaction. Interactive media fit very well within a communicative or task-based approach to language learning, but if communication is not valued by the assessment system, this is likely to discourage teachers from making use of technology. Even if teachers do introduce interactive media, this may be resisted by those students whose primary goal is excellent exam results. In these cases, it may be worth looking at some of the drill-and-practice types of software and apps that we have identified in this book. Some of these can be authored by students themselves, which means that the teacher can promote interactivity, whilst the students see a clear link to the structural knowledge required by the exams.

Technology in the process of assessment

Assessment may be seen as a process at each stage of which there are options for using technology. The first stage in the process is setting the challenges and invariably needs to be done by a human being. Although assessment software can be programmed with a bank of questions that will generate a random selection for each student, the questions themselves can only be written by a person. However, once the test items are written, technology may be used to deliver the challenges to the student. The benefit of this is that each student can have an individual test which may be tailored to his or her ability (as with CATs). If the question bank is large enough, the system can be used for large-scale assessments which are not carried out simultaneously, such as the computerized version of TOEFL.

Task 5	### Authoring

Go to a website that offers quiz authoring, for example Quizlet or Yacapaca – see our website for more suggestions and details.

- What can you do on an authoring website?
- What does an authoring tool offer to English language learners and teachers?
- What types of questions or tasks will work well with these tools?
- Try making a quiz or test for your learners.

Authoring tools allow teachers to create quizzes and tests. Some of these, such as Yacapaca, can be used for summative assessment (because they provide feedback to the teacher) whilst others, although very useful for AfL and formative assessment, cannot be used for summative purposes. Both Yacapaca and Quizlet include materials made by other teachers as well as the tools for teachers to make their own quizzes and assessments. However, finding a suitable authoring tool and learning is the easy part of authoring: the real challenge is in setting appropriate questions, as we explain in the 'questions and answers' task below.

The next stage, doing the task(s) is, the part of the assessment process that is undertaken by the student. In some cases, even when computerized marking will be used – for example, multiple-choice tests scored by optical mark readers – students have to use pen/pencil and paper to sit the test. In other cases, although the work will be marked by a person – for example, coursework essays – students may create the material for assessment using technology. Digital tools are extremely useful for any kind of assessment where students are asked to collect material over time, for example, with photographs, video, audio recordings, or with text. This kind of content can be included in a portfolio and there are a number of specialized **e-portfolio** tools available.

Task 6

Foliospaces

Find an e-portfolio site. We would suggest Foliospaces, see our website for details.

- What can learners do with the e-portfolio?
- What are the benefits to learners?
- How might e-portfolios be useful for language learners?

The point of a portfolio, whether real or virtual, is it that allows learners to assemble evidence that demonstrates what they have learned and what they can do. Ideally, e-portfolios should be portable, i.e. not tied to a specific institution, so that when learners leaves school or college they still have access to the portfolio and the material that it contains. If possible, they should be able to continue adding content so that the portfolio develops with them.

For language learners, an e-portfolio can be a way to collect evidence of language ability. The portfolio provides more detail than a simple performance grade; for example, a student may have high grades in, say, the writing component of an exam such as CAE, but those grades only demonstrate that the performance overall was excellent. However, the e-portfolio can include samples of different types of written text that demonstrate individual style. Similarly, the portfolio might include videoed presentations or role-play activities that show far more about how somebody uses spoken language (and handles different situations) than a simple grade.

Even novice learners or young learners can use e-portfolios to collect evidence of their learning as it documents their progress. Showing learners how far they have developed over the course can help to motivate them for future learning.

The next stage of the process is submitting the work. If an assessment is entirely electronic, for example, computer-based multiple-choice tests, then clearly the work will be submitted electronically. However, work that is carried out independently by students, such as essay writing or video creation, may either be submitted electronically or handed in personally (or posted in the mail). The benefits of electronic submission are the following:

- There is no need to spend time and resources printing work for assessment.
- It is easy to submit non-written work, such as video or audio.

- Written work can be checked for possible plagiarism.
- Where deadlines are critical, the time and date of submission can be recorded automatically.

The main drawbacks of electronic submission are:

- Some students may not have access to the submission tool (for example, due to **firewall** problems or internet failure).
- Only digital texts can be submitted electronically, so hand-created material must be photographed or scanned before submission.

After submission comes marking. Sometimes, marking is built into the design of assessment software, which can generally decide if an answer is correct, partially correct, or incorrect. There is an overlap between marking and feedback as the marking process will often generate information about aspects of performance that can be given to the examinee, so that performance can be improved in future. This may be a simple indication of which answers are incorrect, or it may include detailed advice about the aspects of the work that can be improved.

Task 7

Questions and answers

Look at quizzes A and B below. Which is the better set of questions? Why? What are the implications for marking?

A Match the words.

cat	puppy
dog	lamb
cow	calf
sheep	kitten

B Choose the best word to fill each gap.

The child ran .... down the hill.	happily
The water trickled .... into the bowl.	quickly
The baby slept .... in the cot.	noisily
Anna smiled .... at the flowers.	peacefully

The questions and answers in set A are unambiguous and there is only one possible option which would provide a correct answer to each question. In set B, however, more than one of the answers would fit each question. It is always important to make sure that assessment questions are carefully worded so that there is no ambiguity, but particularly so with electronic assessment. Set A can easily be marked electronically and the marking will be reliable. For set B however, the ambiguity means that it is not suitable for electronic marking and the results will not be reliable; it is not really suitable for human marking either, but that is because we have exaggerated the ambiguity. A human marker should notice the ambiguity in the test and be able to make allowance for it in the marking. The real message here is that if an assessment is to be marked entirely electronically, with no human input, then the questions must be set with considerable care.

Once the work has been marked, there needs to be an assessment judgement to determine what the marks mean. Digital tools may also be used to calculate the formula for awarding a grade and – where the assessment is delivered, completed, and marked electronically, – it is likely that the grading formula will also be built into the software. However, in other cases, making the judgement is a task that relies on evaluations made by people. This may be because complex criteria are used, but it may also be necessary for a human being to decide on the weighting that should be given to particular aspects of performance in the light of a student's individual circumstances. In all cases of formative assessment, and some cases of summative assessment, there is a process for giving feedback on the results (although some summative assessments report the grade only and do not give feedback on the details of performance). Simple reporting of the grade is easily done by technology, but does not make a significant difference to the process of assessment. However, although it may not be possible to create complex feedback electronically, digital tools may help teachers to deliver the comments to students.

Task 8   **Audio feedback**

Take a piece of learner work that you need to mark. Instead of writing comments on the paper, record the comments using an phone, an audio recorder, or a computer. How does audio recording affect the feedback that you give? How do you think your learners would receive audio feedback instead of written feedback?

It is likely (for those accustomed to audio recording) that audio feedback will be quicker to produce than written feedback. However, the main advantage is that you are likely to find yourself entering into a conversation with the student, especially if marking an extended text. This may mean that you address the student directly and give more detailed explanations than in written feedback. Although written feedback is easier to review, students who receive audio feedback (for example in Macgregor et al. 2011) seem to prefer audio, finding it more personal and easier to understand. As Macgregor et al., point out, audio feedback is not new. However, digital technologies make audio feedback easier to create, deliver, and store than tape recordings.

The final stage of the assessment process is storing the results. This is an aspect to which technology is well suited, as large quantities of data can be stored in databases and spreadsheets from which they can (usually) be retrieved easily on demand. However, there are important security issues to consider; it is important that confidential data, such as assessment results, be password protected (with strong passwords) and there should be secure backups.

Drawbacks of technology for assessment

At the risk of stating the obvious, probably the most important disadvantage of computer-based assessment is that computers cannot make judgements, except those that were anticipated by the test designer. For example, suppose a test includes a short-answer question where the correct answer is 'seagull'. The test could allow for 'gull' as an alternative answer. If spelling is not important in this instance, the test could also allow alternative answers such as 'gul', 'seegull', 'saegul', and any other misspellings that test-writer can think of (although potential answers may still include unforeseen misspellings). However, the student might give an answer such as 'herring gull', 'black-headed gull', or even 'larus' (the Latin name for the genus). These answers might be correct, but if the designer had not predicted them, the testing software will not accept them.

A related point, which we have already touched on in the discussion of marking, is that computer software cannot make complex judgements such as those required for marking essays. Much composition marking uses impressionistic criteria, which depend on the judgement of the reader. For example, in the writing component of the Cambridge Certificate of Advanced English, the criteria include aspects such as 'effect on the reader', relevance, organisation, use of 'cohesive devices', text structure, range of vocabulary and grammatical structures, register, and format (Cambridge ESOL 2008). At the moment, only a human being can make all of these judgements, although some, such as number and range of cohesive devices, can be counted electronically. Until we have true affective computing (see Chapter 12), software will not be able to evaluate 'effect on the reader', and we are not sure that this will ever be a possibility. Even the TOEFL writing test, which uses computer scoring on the practice version, uses humans to mark the 'real thing' for, as the Educational Testing Service (2010: 3) explains 'the computer scoring of the practice test does not factor in the meaning expressed in a response in the same way human raters do.'

Computer software is not yet good at assessing speech. Whilst speech recognition software exists and can be very useful, it is not sufficiently accurate or flexible to be used for any but the simplest assessment of oral language capability. Moreover, much speech recognition software is designed for converting speech to text. In order to achieve an accurate conversion, the software 'guesses' words based on the meaning of preceding text and some programs are extremely good at this. Whilst this may lead to a reasonably accurate written product, it does mean that it cannot be used to evaluate speaking skills as the software is designed to compensate for gaps in a speaker's ability.

We have noted that digital tools are extremely useful for recording oral assessments, such as interviews and presentations. However, it is also easy to edit or even delete digital files. On tape cassettes, it is possible to write identifying information on the label and to break the tabs so that it is impossible to overwrite the recording; but this kind of mechanical protection is not always available for digital files. Where digital recording is used, especial care must be taken with both labelling and security so that there is no possibility that the material will be edited, erased, or that the work of different candidates will be muddled. Again, this may seem an obvious point, but it could easily be overlooked if there is enthusiasm for 'going digital'.

Although it may seem logical for large-scale, high-stakes assessments, such as national examinations, to be electronic, there are considerable logistical difficulties, as was noted by Threlfall et al. (2007). One of the problems concerns the integrity of the examination. A computer that is used for a formal examination must be 'locked down' so that the examinee cannot access, for example, the internet. This is not an insurmountable problem (for example TOEFL test centres are able to do this), but it is difficult in an ordinary school. Some institutions are able to provide specialized examinations rooms, at least for the duration of the examination period, where internet access has been blocked from the computers. In addition, where there are large numbers of students taking an examination, a computerized test may require more machines than an institution is able to provide at any one time. This then leads to a need for randomized question banks, which must be extremely large if there is to be sufficient variation in order for the exam to be significantly different for each examinee. Another logistical complication is technical support. In a traditional examination, it does not cause problems if any examinee's pen runs out of ink or pencil breaks. The invigilator can simply provide a replacement and the examinee can continue without much interruption. With an electronic examination, however, an equipment failure can lead to, at best, a delay of several minutes. More seriously, it may result in an examinee losing the work completed at the time of the failure. Whilst technical failure is unlikely to be a serious drawback when students are being examined in very small numbers (for example, one at a time), it is a major impediment to the implementation of large-scale, high-stakes examinations.

Summary

In this chapter, we have tried to explore the effects of technology for assessment of language learning and some of the ways in which technology-enhanced assessment may be used. Technology offers some exciting possibilities with regard to assessment for learning, for interactive multimodal assessments, and for student-led portfolios. There are also strong arguments for providing 'task authenticity' when assessing tasks that would be normally be carried out using digital tools. However, as with all uses of technology for learning, it is not a panacea. Technology enhanced assessment needs robust technical support, especially when the outcome of an assessment has lasting importance for the learner; in some cases, it is possible that introducing technology into an assessment may affect validity.

Further reading

Carr, N. 2011. *Designing and Analyzing Language Tests: A hands-on introduction to language testing theory and practice*. Oxford: Oxford University Press.

Fulcher, G. and **F. Davidson.** 2007. *Language testing and assessment: an advanced resource book*. London: Routledge.

Hughes, A. 2003. *Testing for language teachers* (2nd edn.). Cambridge: Cambridge University Press.

Ioannou-Georgiu, S. and **P. Pavlou.** (2003). *Assessing young learners*. Oxford: Oxford University Press.

10 TEACHERS USING TECHNOLOGY

We live in a society exquisitely dependent on science and technology,
in which hardly anyone knows anything about science and technology.
CARL SAGAN, astronomer

Aims

In this chapter, we will try to give you some answers to the following questions:
- What kinds of skills do teachers need to develop in order to teach effectively with technology?
- Do they already possess some of those skills?
- Why might teachers feel resistance towards using technology? Can that resistance be overcome?
- How can teachers develop their skills in using technology in their classes?

Introduction

This chapter considers some of the ways in which teacher roles and skills in using technology have been portrayed in research. It asks whether researchers have tended to 'de-skill' teachers, who already possess many of these skills, albeit in the context of a traditional classroom. It then goes on to examine some of the reasons why teachers might resist and fear technology, and proposes ways in which they can overcome their fears by assuming control over their own professional development.

What skills do language teachers need in order to use technology for language teaching?

Despite the fact that many schools and universities worldwide now promote the use of technology in language learning classrooms, most of their attention is focused on student learning, rather than on the skills which teachers need in order to use technology effectively. If there is discussion of teachers' skills, it tends to focus on technical skills, such as knowing how to turn the sound up, or use Skype, or access and use some aspect of their institution's VLE (Virtual Learning Environment). When we have attended meetings about using technology at our own work places, the discussion has quickly turned technical to the exclusion of other considerations. Some researchers have, however, looked beyond the merely technical to the ways in which teachers need to combine technical and pedagogical skills in order to produce situations in which effective learning can take place. Hampel and Stickler (2005), for instance, proposed an influential model of skills which are needed by those teaching languages online. They suggested a pyramid of skills in which each skill needs to be acquired in turn, building on previous skills:

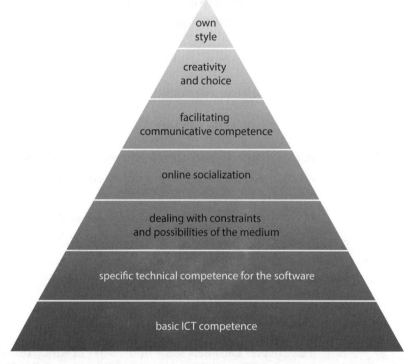

Figure 10.1: Skills pyramid (from Hampel and Stickler 2005)

In this model, they described teachers as first of all needing basic competence in using networked computers; they should be able, for instance, to handle the keyboard and mouse, word process, and use the internet. They should also be able to 'troubleshoot' common browser problems. It is interesting that even in the short time since this article was published, most people would think that the list of basic skills has expanded; we might now want to add the ability to download images, audio, and video files, and to have some rudimentary knowledge of social networking. The next level up the hierarchy is to have the skills necessary to use a particular software application for teaching purposes, whether it be commercially available educational software, such as Blackboard, Turnitin, or interactive white boards, and/or free and open source programmes, such as Skype, or software which allows you to set up virtual meeting rooms. The third level of skill is understanding what kinds of learning the software can facilitate, and what its limitations are. The fourth level was of great interest to Hampel and Stickler because they saw the main aim of technology as enabling learners to develop their communicative competence in a language by interacting with other language learners: they therefore felt it was very important that teachers had the skills to create online communities for learners who may not know each other outside the learning space. Teachers need skills to build a feeling of trust and security between their learners, to set rules of procedure and behaviour, and to encourage learners to interact with each other. Most teachers will have developed these skills in real world classrooms, but may need different or additional techniques to achieve the same results online. The fifth level takes place once the online learning community has been established, and concerns helping interaction to happen through good task design and tutor intervention. The sixth level has to do with having the searching, designing, and evaluative skills which are needed in order to choose, alter, or create the most appropriate digital learning materials for a particular group at a particular time. We will discuss these skills further in Chapter 11. The highest level of the skill pyramid suggests that very competent online teachers will have developed their own personal teaching style; they give the example of a tutor who became confident enough to delegate some of the tutor-initiated parts of the course to individual learners.

This is an appealing model for two reasons: firstly, because it focuses on teaching skills as well as technical skills and tries to see how technical and teaching skills might develop in tandem; and secondly because it echoes theories about how beginner teachers develop – from nervous concentration on their own performance and the tools of their trade, such as materials and control of the classroom, towards being able to focus on their learners instead, in the process developing an instinctive feel about what works for them and their particular group of learners (Berliner 1994). It has been criticized, though, by Compton (2009) and others, who say that the skills do not necessarily have to be developed sequentially, but can also be developed concurrently. They also argue that learning a language does not always require direct interaction with others in an online community; you can have interaction between the learner's mind and already-created language content which results in learning (Chapelle, 2005), such as when, for example, a student is listening to an audio **podcast** and filling in blanks in a text, or reading and perhaps singing along to the lyrics of a song while watching a performance on YouTube, or doing an online task which involves arranging words into a correct sentence. The Hampel and Stickler model does assume a certain view of learning, i.e. socio-constructivist, whereas we have seen in Chapter 1 that other views of learning, such as **constructivism**, **connectivism**, and even **behaviourism** have a part to play in learning with technology. The model also leaves out the ways in which using technology may affect language use, the '**socio-digital competence**' we mentioned in Chapter 1. Teachers need, for example, to develop awareness of the new genres which are emerging in digital contexts, and the new ways in which students combine written and spoken language. The model also skips rather lightly over the issue of how much teachers transfer skills they have learnt in real-life classrooms to virtual learning environments, and what new skills they need to learn. There is a general view that teaching skills cannot be transferred naturally from the conventional classroom to an online environment (see Compton 2009 and Wood 2005). However, we wonder if, in practical terms, some skills are rather more transferrable in practice than researchers may think. Task 1 considers this question from the point of view of forming an online learning community:

Task 1

Forming a learning community

In a classic article, Tuckman (1965) suggested that, when a disparate set of people meet together and start to form a group, they go through a series of stages as they become a group. He named these four stages 'forming, storming, norming, and performing'. His model has been used in a number of academic areas, including language learning. 'Forming' is when the group members first come together, establish relationships with each other and the group leader, create ground rules, and test the boundaries for how they are to perform tasks. 'Storming' is a stage when the group may be in conflict with each other, as they all want to do things their own way. 'Norming' is the stage when the group develops cohesion, accepts each others' idiosyncrasies, establishes roles, and discovers the most effective ways of working together. 'Performing' is when the group has become a single 'problem-solving instrument'. Group energy is channelled into doing the task.

Imagine that you are meeting a group of students online for the first time, and you are going to be their teacher.

- What kinds of activities would you see yourself doing with the students for each of the four stages?
- Do you think they would be totally different in kind from the kinds of activities you would do as a teacher in a traditional classroom?

To help with the 'forming' stage, you would probably introduce yourself and tell the students something about yourself, and then get the students to introduce themselves, posting photos. Perhaps you might do some 'ice-breaking' activities. There might be a 'virtual café' provided in your software where you could encourage students to chat about non-course matters so they could get to know each other better. You would probably give the students an outline of the course and the kind of activities they would be doing, and indicate what was expected of them in terms of online participation and collaboration. You might refer them to course documentation available online. The 'storming' stage would probably happen when students were performing their first activities in the course. You would need to make sure that everybody was participating, and support those students who were shy or confused about what to do. The support might be for expressing themselves or dealing with content, or it might be technical help. You might also need to diplomatically smooth out any conflicts of opinion or disagreements about the best way to proceed with tasks. You would probably not want to reply to every student post as that might interfere with group formation. Throughout the norming and performing stages, you would need to remind students of course requirements, clarify, perhaps point out language errors, encourage participation, give praise, and suggest useful resources or give help with language.

We would argue that there are many similarities with the functions and activities which teachers might carry out with their students in a traditional classroom to help students form an effective learning community. There are also, of course, new factors for teachers to deal with, such as expertise in using the technology, dealing with the challenges of asynchronous discussion, and in some contexts for online discussion, not being able to see or hear students. Online learning is taking place in a new environment and this affects learner behaviour and identity, as does the fact that some of the interaction has moved from face-to-space speaking to written communication. Students who are shy in a real life classroom can suddenly feel confident enough to contribute in this new 'space' and, vice-versa, students who are confident in class may 'lurk' in the online environment because they do not want to make fools of themselves by writing down errors (Kirsten Thomson, Leeds University – personal communication). However, teachers do not go into the brave new world of technology enhanced language learning with no skills at all. It is all too easy for teachers to feel totally 'deskilled' just because they may lack expertise with using the technology.

Another influential way of describing how teachers can support the forming of communities on line has been proposed by Salmon (2002, 2011). It bears some similarities to Tuckman's model, but is more specifically applied to distance and **blended learning**. She suggests a five stage process:

1 Access and motivation – making sure students can log on, motivating them to spend time and effort, 'handholding' nervous students and helping to convince them that this online course is going to be worth it.

2 Culture building – getting individual participants to establish online identities and find other people to interact with.

3 Co-operation – participants exchange course information with each other.

4 Collaboration – the beginnings of course related discussion between participants. Interaction starts to become collaborative.

5 Development – participants start to develop personal goals and explore how they can integrate CMC with other forms of learning. They reflect on the learning process.

Many of the activities which Salmon (2002) suggests for these stages will seem familiar to language teachers from their classroom experience, for example the 'ice-breaking' activities associated with Stage 1. This may make teachers feel more confident that they can adapt their current expertise in devising learning activities for dealing with online contexts. We do not want in any way to minimize the new skills teachers have to learn in using technology in their teaching, but feel that there also needs to be a positive emphasis on how much knowledge they already bring with them.

Teacher resistance

Will TELL be the only, or at least the dominant way, of learning languages in the future? Many of us in the present generation of language teachers would feel threatened by Kurzweil's (1999) prediction, summarized in Chapelle (2003: 4) that in the future, 'much of the instructional time learners spend will consist of interaction with a computer'. That prediction somehow makes us feel uncomfortable – the notion of students all labouring away individually at their computers, at a distance from each other and their teacher, never meeting up together in real life, and the teacher's role reduced to that of an administrator and overseer of software programmes is not an attractive one. The people responsible for promoting and maintaining the VLE in our own institutions said that, of course, this situation is technically possible, but whether it will happen is another matter. According to them, the deciding factor in whether it happens or not will be whether students want it, and whether they will be happy learning languages in a completely virtual environment. Even if it does not happen in such a total fashion, the role of teachers will have irrevocably changed and that can worry many of us. We will discuss teacher roles later on in this chapter.

Are most teachers a little bit resistant, in their heart of hearts, to using technology for all aspects of language learning? The history of institutional use of TELL at tertiary level, which has been closely monitored, tells us something about the process of 'digital immigration', i.e. of teachers starting to use technology. At present, of course, because of age differences, most university lecturers, like most school teachers, are 'digital immigrants' and most students are 'digital natives'. As Chapter 2 warns us, we should not assume that this is always so clear-cut a divide, and of course it will not continue to be true as digital natives enter the teaching profession. For the present, the pattern of adopting TELL methods at tertiary level tends to follow the same pattern in many places in the developed world. We would define 'developed world' as anywhere with the infrastructure and funds to install and operate an institution-wide **LMS** (Learning Management System), also sometimes called a **VLE** (Virtual Learning Environment). There are usually a few 'early adopters' of learning software, who start using it before their institution invested in an LMS or developed an overall policy advocating the use of technology in learning as a 'good thing'. Then, after some years of institutional promotion and training, most lecturers are using it to post material associated with a module, including audio and video resources. They are also using it to post messages about assignments and lectures. Far fewer use the collaborative tools available, such as discussion boards, wikis, and blogs, or the tools available to set online quizzes, surveys, and tests. A growing number use it for electronic submission of assignments, which could then be checked for plagiarism using software, such as Turnitin. One explanation we were offered for this pattern of use is that training courses for lecturers often stress how to post material onto a VLE. Another reason is student pressure and feedback, which tends to focus on being able to access materials and submit assessments online. However, we think there are other reasons behind this pattern of use which we can see in so many places.

VLEs and IWBs

There are two very striking features of VLEs in educational institutions. One is that they are so similar to each other no matter where in the world they occur, and the other is that they tend to be entirely 'teacher led'. The uniformity of what VLEs offer is due to the fact that the software has been almost entirely developed in Europe and Anglophone countries, such as the United States, and that a few 'big players' tend to dominate the market for VLE software and design, influencing others. These VLE designs assume Western models of learning – individualism, open and frank communication, and linear reasoning, – which might not be suitable for other kinds of society (Godwin-Jones 2012). Yet, while they allow for individual action, VLEs also tend to be quite static environments, full of 'spoon-fed' content, and shaped by instructor goals rather than responsiveness to students. Godwin-Jones suggests that VLEs are unlikely to be very attractive or stimulating to students, because they are 'far removed from the vibrant, ever-changing online world in which our students are fully engaged' (2012: 6). He also makes the point that such VLEs do not really prepare students for the technology needs of their future workplaces. But we also think that the way these VLEs are organized might prevent teachers developing the higher-level skills, such as creativity and choice, and developing a personal style, which we mentioned at the beginning of this chapter. In fact, it might be more correct to say that the VLEs are 'institution-led' rather than 'teacher-led', and this might be one of the reasons why many teachers do not fully engage with all the facilities which they offer. It is easy to post course material and assignments in a VLE, and students really appreciate being able to access these at a distance from the physical teaching space; but it is much more difficult to develop a **discussion board** or get students using a chat room, especially when these are very 'institutionally' controlled, and very unlike the fluid, multi-media social networking sites which students are familiar with in their private lives. There are many examples of discussion boards which are set up in VLEs and never receive a single posted comment, or only after the teacher has forced people to contribute, perhaps saying it will be assessed. In our own experience, the successful discussion boards have been ones controlled by students, which tutors never enter, or which they enter on an equal basis, for example, by contributing a reflection on a childhood experience on the same footing as everybody else who has been given the task to write about. Another possibility is for individual teachers to opt out of the 'corporate' LMS in order to use other free systems for creating modular pages, such as iGoogle and Netvibes, or discussion forums, such as Wikispaces, or file sharing, such as iGoogle. This of course, involves teachers in more work and may require some technological expertise, as opposed to institutional VLEs which do it all for you. However, much of this open software is easy to use. The software usually offers secure spaces to work in, but there is the risk that a particular software tool may disappear or become entirely commercial. One of the best experiences of a discussion forum one of us had was with an MA TESOL group in Oman, using a free software tool. The students took over use of the space, posting pictures of new-born babies and links to favourite songs, but also engaging in lots of communication with each other about where to find good articles, unpick difficult concepts, and arrange real life meetings to discuss assignments. Using an 'unofficial' software tool seemed to give us all the license to 'be ourselves' and form links as a group which were both personal and professional. Unfortunately, the software we used stopped being free after a few years. There is, however, a growing trend in using open educational resources to balance some of the restrictions of institutional VLEs, which seems likely to continue.

If the structure of VLEs can be off-putting to teachers, they can also find individual software tools difficult to integrate into their own, already developed teaching style. Perhaps this will not be a problem in the future, as trainees learn right from the beginning how to incorporate technology into their teaching, but it is a significant issue for many current teachers. For instance, one of the software tools which is now widely used in educational institutions who can afford it is the interactive white board (**IWB**). IWBs allow the teacher to display visual, audio and video material on a screen placed at the front of the class where formerly blackboards or whiteboards would have been in evidence, hence the name. The IWB reacts to a pen or to touch in the same way that a mouse would work on a computer. Teachers can prepare material in advance, using access to the internet to import images or other web material. They can use tools for writing and drawing, such as concealing part of an image or text and then revealing it, or underlining text, or writing labels and notes. They can display the results of student votes in graphic form. The pages created in class can be saved and printed out and given to students. A student can be invited to perform the teacher's function of operating the IWB. A number of publishing companies have adapted their coursebooks so that they can be used on the IWB, and adapted and modified by the teacher. The IWBs can also run other software programs. We have discussed some of the advantages of using IWBs with children in Chapter 9.

It is fair to say that there has been quite a lot of controversy over the past few years about IWBs, with a number of language teaching 'gurus' claiming that, despite their name, they are not really 'interactive' at all. They also suggest that IWBs, instead of promoting student-centred learning, in fact perpetuate teacher-dominated classrooms.

| Task 2 | **Technologically-damaged learning?** |

One of our colleagues, Sam Rich, wrote an amusing 'rant' against IWBs, arguing that they were no improvement on old fashioned blackboards, and in fact made teaching and learning less effective. The article subsequently appeared in *English Teaching Professional* under the title 'The Battle of the Boards'. Read some edited highlights of his arguments about what appears to be the opposite of TELL, i.e. 'technologically-damaged language learning' and then answer the questions which follow. Please bear in mind that he was acting as a 'devil's advocate', and that therefore he might have exaggerated a little in places in order to make a point:

If you have little access to an interactive whiteboard, or if, like most teachers worldwide, you have never even seen one, you might envy the lucky few who have these devices installed in every classroom. Please don't.

My objection to these things is not that they occasionally break down [...], or that some teachers find the technology daunting (they might at first, but really it is not that difficult to master) or that they are so expensive. [...] No, the objection in this article is that the traditional board (black or white) which the IWB is supposed to supersede is – in ways that really matter – better.

Until the technology advances rather more, [the IWB] can only be written or drawn on by one person at one time. Enthusiasts for the new boards are apparently excited that they can invite a student to the front and hand over the pen, but at a traditional board, depending on its size, you can have any number of learners working at once.

According to advocates for the new technology, you can bring democracy to the classroom by allowing all the students at once to pick options on electronic voting devices, and have their responses displayed in colourful, computer-generated graphs. [...] Far from being deeply democratic or participatory, the pedagogic model for the computerized board is of a (no doubt benevolent) dictatorship, or a priesthood, with its miracles – flashes, spotlights and zooms – to entrance the flock, [...] all slickly and seamlessly presented. There is a serious point here for teachers who want their learners to engage critically with how ideas are delivered and to take ownership of the learning process. […] And does the use of exciting multimodal displays really do much more than desperately drag the learners' attention toward the screen, when what we ought to be doing is to encourage (or allow) them to pay attention to each other?

- From what you have read about the learning and teaching possibilities of IWBs above, and/or heard about them, or experienced using them yourself, how far would you agree with the points made in the article above?
- How do you think teachers can avoid being 'led by the technology'?

In a way, this connects to our previous point about teachers feeling constrained in the ways they want to teach by the overall design of VLEs. In this case, a teacher feels constrained by what he perceives to be the limitations of a particular piece of software. The faculty learning technologist had an interesting reply to Sarn's concerns. She said that:

'My approach has always been that the *appropriate* use of technologies can be both empowering and liberating, but what is appropriate to one person's teaching style may not be appropriate to another's. Without a full understanding of a technology or the ability and skills to employ it creatively to one's own ends, it is easy to see it as a gimmick or a threat. Only a complete understanding allows us to reject what is inappropriate, as well as accept what may be appropriate.'

(Glenis Lambert: personal communication).

Others, for example Graham Stanley, (see our website for links to his work with IWBs) have pointed out that teachers are in control of IWBs, not the other way around, and that they can turn them off if they are not going to add pedagogically to an activity, such as pair work when you want learners to look at and talk to each other, rather than look at a board. Teachers can put pressure on software designers to develop the software so that it is more user friendly, and the designers (if they are commercially wise) will listen and do so. They also point to the fact that IWBs have many advantages over traditional black and whiteboards: they are good for distance students and disabled students; they cater for many different learning styles, including the tactile; they attract students' attention; and they allow easy access to the vast resources offered by the internet. In the past, teachers never relied on the blackboard alone to teach anyway, and as a replacement for traditional blackboards, IWBs can do so much more than traditional black or whiteboards ever could.

Teachers' roles

It appears to us from the example above that teachers' anxieties about using technology are mainly centred on two things: firstly, that the software will in some sense 'take over' and dictate how teaching is carried out; and secondly, that it may make the learning experience less effective than it was without technology. We have seen in the previous section that teachers should feel free NOT to use a particular piece of software if it is not appropriate for an activity; however we feel that teachers have another, deeper concern which relates to the ways in which their role in the classroom is being affected by technology. Teachers seem to be called different things in the 'technosphere', such as 'instructor', 'e-moderator', and 'tutor', which adds to their uncertainty about what their role is or might be.

In Chapter 1 we talked about the four roles which computers can play in learning: 'tutor', 'tutee', 'tool', and 'talk', but how do these interact with the roles of teachers? The 'tutor' role played by computers could be seen as particularly threatening as the wealth of resources available on the internet means that teachers are no longer the only 'experts' that learners have access to. Another question is whether we need to differentiate between the roles which teachers play in conventional classrooms with technology, and those they play in online distance learning. As 'blended learning' becomes more frequent, the boundaries between learning inside the real life classroom and outside it are blurring, so perhaps we do not need to. Teachers in real life classrooms, in addition to using technology in class, might ask learners to take part in a discussion group, or post on a wiki, or search for material online outside class. So such a distinction becomes difficult to make.

The different roles which teachers play in traditional classrooms have been defined by one influential practitioner (Harmer 2007) as: 'controller' of activities; 'prompter' for how to do activities and for language (for example, suggesting what could come next in a paragraph a learner is writing), encouraging and motivating; 'participant', for example taking part in a discussion; 'resource' for help, perhaps pointing learners to where they can find information rather than supplying it ourselves; 'tutor' to individuals or small groups. If we look at a list of tutor roles which have been suggested for distance learning (Dias 1998), we think that some of those roles are the same, even if they are expressed in different words or connected to different activities:

Distance-learner teacher roles	Traditional teacher roles
Integrator – setting goals	Controller
Salesperson – motivating others, capturing their interest	Prompter
Negotiator – getting people together	Tutor/Prompter
News reporter – informing students about developments or problems	Controller/Resource
Confidant – showing students what happens behind the scenes	Tutor
Nervous parent – worrying about security of students engaged in CMC, making sure they follow the rules of 'netiquette', etc.	
Teaches teaching – showing students how to give feedback to each other	
Trouble-shooter – providing technical advice	Resource
Human being – acknowledging mistakes	Participant
Student – teachers themselves learning something they did not know before the activity took place	Participant

Table 10.2 Comparing traditional and distance-learning roles of teachers

Where it is not so easy to see an overlap, this seems to be something to do with the nature of the medium ('nervous parent'), or something which demonstrates the increased possibilities students have to learn from each other through technologically enhanced language learning, ('teaches teaching'). The latter role is the one which teachers may find new and somewhat threatening. Technology enhanced language learning challenges teachers who feel uncomfortable with the less hierarchical relationship between teacher and students it encourages, or with the learner autonomy it fosters, or who do not like learning which is 'dispersed', i.e. happening in a number of different places, such as discussion forums, blogs and wikis (Comas-Quin et al. 2012). They would rather have learning which is taking place in one site, the classroom. Certain kinds of teacher appear to be more receptive to and willing to try TELL. Teachers who are already comfortable with student-centred approaches and communicative principles of language learning seem to be the most successful in using and integrating technology into their classroom teaching, as Wong and Benson (2006) found. The implication is those who train teachers to use technology may also need to modify the trainees' beliefs about student roles and models for language learning at the same time.

Educating teachers to use technology

A survey of 108 MA TESOL graduates from various tertiary institutions (Kessler, 2007) reported that they were rather dissatisfied with the formal instruction they were given in TELL and that they tended to find out the information and technical skills they needed informally by asking others, or by accessing blogs and websites giving advice about using technology in language learning and teaching. Our experience tells us that this situation hasn't changed much. One of the problems with formal instruction, Kessler maintains, is that it tends to make distinctions between pedagogical and personal uses of technology, for example, between IWBs and Facebook, thereby perhaps suggesting (wrongly) that the latter are not so relevant for learning and teaching. Kessler also says that his research revealed teachers to be more confident in using already existing software than in creating their own materials, or integrating them in their syllabus. They felt particularly anxious about materials for teaching speaking and listening skills. Chapter 11 focuses on some of the issues involved in material creation. Wang et al. (2010) found that language teachers being trained to use technology go through four stages. The first stage is 'wow – this is exciting', and the second, 'uh-oh' when some technical problems emerge, and trainees begin to realize the differences between online and classroom teaching. The third stage is the 'anxiety' stage when the trainees begin their teaching preparation and practice with real students. As the teaching practice goes on, trainees become more used to online teaching, and begin to move into the fourth stage of 'internalizing' the experience and become capable of evaluating how well teaching and learning were going, helped by the **moderator** and their fellow students to do so.

Task 3	**Polling and voting software**

We would like to explore how the stages described by Wang et al. happen, and also how much teachers educate themselves, as well as getting advice from trainers and colleagues. One kind of software which is widely available and often free allows you to conduct surveys, polls, and votes with your students, and for them to post opinions about hot and debatable topics of the day. Explore three or four examples of this software. Tricider, Urtak, PollDaddy, SurveyMonkey, and Answer Garden have been used by educators in the UK and the US, but there are dozens of others. You can also do a Google search for 'polling tools', or search the blog of an 'ELT technological guru' (see more below) which will provide you with other suggestions for voting software.

- Which of the tools most gives you the 'wow' factor? Why? What kinds of technological possibilities does it seem to offer which you couldn't do before?
- Explore your favourite tool some more. Are there any 'uh-oh' factors, which make you worried about your ability to use it for teaching? Try to find help via the resources on the internet to solve your anticipated problems. Do you know anybody who has used such a tool in your own teaching context?
- How would you see yourself using this tool in your syllabus? How would it help promote learning?

When we first see some new software, our first reaction, hopefully, is to be excited by some of its possibilities, (the 'wow' factor) although there might also be scepticism present at the same time. Most polling tools allow you to post controversial statements, such as, for example, 'women can't play football', to which students can agree or disagree, giving reasons. Other students, using a plus or minus sign, can add their own comments. Students can then vote on which of the comments they most agree with. Other possibilities are to give a list of options, such as 'Which of these films should get the Oscar?', 'Which topic do you want to cover next in class?' or 'Which of these features of English language learning do you feel least confident about?' The polling tools can then display the results of the poll in visual form, for example in pie charts or bar graphs. Some polling tools, such as AnswerGarden, allow you and your students to create a 'word cloud' of words and phrases which respondents can choose from to answer a question; this is a great way to introduce and practise vocabulary. The 'uh-oh' stage depends on how helpful the website promoting the software is at explaining how to use it and giving a demonstration. Things which some sites leave out are how to embed polls in blogs or wikis, and how to prevent people from voting more than once! Many people, when faced with the 'uh-oh' stage, and without an experienced colleague, will go online to consult a 'technological guru': these come and go, but for a number of years, Nik Peachey and Russell Stannard in the UK and Larry Ferlazzo in the US have pointed people to resources and given advice about the technical as well as the pedagogical aspects of particular software. It is helpful to search for such people on the internet and keep up to date with their blogs. There are also useful 'how to' videos on YouTube. This underlines the point made earlier that much 'teacher training' in TELL is self-directed and a matter of trial and error.

In exploring the polling software, you probably realized that two big advantages it offered were the chance for opinions to be given from outside the classroom, and also shared with others beyond that classroom. Furthermore, the information on voting can be displayed in visual form, which is easily digestible. This kind of software is interesting to use because it enables students to interact with each other and share knowledge on a much wider scale than would be possible in a traditional classroom. There are a wealth of possibilities for integrating it into a syllabus: generating and comparing ideas for when you should use a particular tense; brainstorming words to do with a particular topic; making statements about a particular character in a class reader, for instance 'In the story of the *Three Little Pigs*, we should feel sorry for the wolf, who is homeless'; creating options to vote on if covering a particular topic, such as sport, for example –'Which of these sports deserves to be included in the next Olympics?' If you were running a teacher-training course, you might want to make provocative statements such as 'Interactive White Boards are an expensive waste of money' for your students to comment on. Creative teachers will never lack ideas about how to use software if they are convinced it adds to the learning experience and is worth the hassle of getting to grips with the technological demands.

Continuing professional development

We have suggested that much of teachers' training in using technology may come from their own efforts, augmented and enhanced of course, by courses, conferences, and advice from more experienced teachers, both online and offline. We are going to suggest that e-portfolios could play a part in teachers learning how to use technology in their classes. The notion of tracking and reflecting on your development as a learner over time is not new and has been used for assessment purposes in the form of the portfolio, which typically consists of a collection of different tasks accompanied by an overarching reflection written by the learner on what he or she has learnt from doing the tasks, and how he or she has progressed. We have discussed the use of portfolios for assessment in Chapter 9. Portfolios have also become popular when applying for jobs, as a way of displaying achievements and experience (a rather different purpose for them). Software now exists (some examples are PebblePad and Pathbrite) for collecting together and displaying many kinds of texts – photos, videos, reflective blogs, teacher feedback, and so on – in one portable form, either for student assessment purposes or for work 'display' purposes. There is a lot of useful information on the JISC (Joint Information Systems Committee) website which explains in detail what e-portfolios are and how they can be used. (See our accompanying website for details). Generally speaking, teachers have preferred their students to collect together data in a variety of places, both in paper and electronic form, rather than using a software program, because they have found these programs are more concerned with 'display' rather than reflective learning. Sangheeta Paul a colleague at Majan University College in Oman, who is teaching English language skills for a BA in Business Studies, asks students to create a CV, take part in a mock job interview which is filmed, set up a meeting by email, including bookmarking participants' digital calendars, create an agenda, carry out and film the meeting, and also keep a reflective blog about what they have learnt from these experiences. Students then have a portfolio of different kinds of evidence to show future employers, some in digital form and some not. The portfolio, through the medium of the blog, also gives the teacher some insight into the learning path undertaken by individual students over the year. Our own tertiary institutions have numerous examples of these kinds of portfolios, which are particularly popular with medical and performing arts students, where theory and workplace placement practice are very closely associated, as they are for trainee teachers.

Task 4	**E-portfolios for professional development**

Explore one of the free software packages which help you to set up an e-portfolio: Pathbrite and Mahara are two current possibilities. You can also create e-portfolios on blogging sites such as WordPress. Think about how you might create an e-portfolio to show your learning path in using technology, perhaps beginning from the point of reading this book. What kinds of things might you want to put in the portfolio?

The essential part of an e-portfolio is the reflection on how the author has learned from the activities he or she has carried out. Those activities might include links to useful blogs and websites, activities you have done with your class, things you have read, conferences, workshops, and other training you have attended, and projects you are involved in with other colleagues. It is useful to look back over, for example, six months of recording the ways in which you have developed your understanding of how to use technology. Such an e-portfolio might be a useful way of encouraging autonomous learning on the part of teachers, in the same way that we encourage our students to be autonomous.

Summary

We hope that reading this chapter may have made teachers feel a little more empowered when using technology. In the hierarchy of skills for online teaching which we described at the beginning of this chapter, purely technical skills were portrayed as being fairly low level. We suggested that teachers already possess many of the higher order pedagogic skills in the model, and that these skills are at least partly transferrable to teaching contexts which use technology. We have also suggested that teachers are, after all, experts in 'how to learn' and they are well able to find ways of continually developing their own ability to use technology by, for example, seeking out online advice from ELT websites and individuals, or by using software to describe and remember their learning journey. Teachers often feel constrained by the limitations of institutional VLEs, but we hope that we have shown that there are ways in which teachers can opt out when they want to, and find strategies for using technology which fit their own individual teaching style.

Further reading

Godwin-Jones, R. 2012. 'Emerging technologies: challenging hegemonies in online learning'. *Journal of Computer Assisted Language Learning* 16/2: 4–13.

Hampel, R. and **U. Stickler.** 2005. 'New skills for new classrooms: training tutors to teach languages online'. *Computer Assisted Language Learning* 18/4: 311–326.

11 CHOOSING AND USING MATERIALS

Don't limit a child to your own learning,
for he was born in another time.
RABINDRANATH TAGORE, poet

Aims

In this chapter, we will try to give you some answers to the following questions:
- How can we incorporate TELL materials into a language learning syllabus?
- What criteria can we use for designing and assessing the learning potential of TELL materials?

Introduction

In the previous chapter, we considered the roles which teachers play in using technology. In this chapter, we focus on learners and what they might get out of TELL materials. We begin by looking at ways in which teachers might want to adapt and add to coursebooks, given the fact that most **ESOL** coursebooks still do not have much technology attached to them, apart from DVDs and CD-ROMS. We also look at the ways in which contexts for learning and roles of learners and teachers are likely to be affected by the use of TELL, because it moves opportunities for learning beyond the physical confines of the classroom and gives students more choice and autonomy in what, when, how, and where they learn. The second part of the chapter considers how teachers can judge whether particular software programs and Web 2.0 tools are really going to help students to learn language.

How can TELL materials support language learning?

Before we look at a practical example of ways in which teachers might add TELL components to a coursebook, it might be useful to recap what we have said so far about language learning and learners. We will then try to match those principles to how and why we might want to add activities to the coursebooks we use, using a couple of pages from the print version of *Project* (Hutchinson 2009) to illustrate the process.

Providing the conditions for language learning to take place

In Chapter 1, we said that some aspects of language learning involve repetition and memorization, and also made the point that learners, as human beings, react positively to reward. These features of language learning are associated with behaviourism. Computers can play a role in this kind of learning, but of course, this is not the only kind of language learning which is facilitated by technology. There is also a consensus that comprehensible language input of some kind is essential for language learning (Mitchell and Myles 2004). TELL can provide inexhaustible amounts of input, although there usually has to be intervention from teachers, software designers, and learners themselves to make it comprehensible. We also know that we analyse the structure of the language we are exposed to when we receive comprehensible input. We notice things about language forms (pronunciation, syntax, vocabulary) if they are made salient to us by others, and/ or they become relevant to us at a particular time because of communicative needs (Schmidt 1990). Another theory about how we learn languages is **connectionism**, which says that instead of constructing rules, we tend to look for associations between the language items we are exposed to, and the more we are exposed to these links, the stronger the association becomes. This is another argument for providing learners with lots of comprehensible input. Theories about output suggest that producing language, as well as receiving it, is a vital part of language learning. By producing language, learners get to grips with language forms and are pushed to develop them. They also receive help and correction from those who hear or read the language they are producing. TELL can provide many opportunities for learner output. Finally there is the role of interaction. This interaction can be intrapersonal, taking place in learners' minds as they analyse and produce language, or it can be between computer and learner, as in the example of children programming a turtle in Chapter 1. But most interest has focused on the part played in language learning by social interaction with other human beings, especially, but not solely, between learners and more expert language users, who can 'scaffold' their development. Learners receive feedback from those they interact with about their language use, which helps them to modify it and understand more about how the language works. Table 11.1 below gives just a few examples of ways in which TELL can support these different aspects of learning. Some of the examples describe teacher actions or possibilities already embedded in a software program; others describe student-initiated activities:

Type of learning activity	Examples of how TELL can support it
Repetition and memorization	– Using the repeat button on an embedded video or audio podcast in order to listen again to something not understood first time around. – Playing a 'find the hidden object' game with commands and explanations which are repeated, often in different contexts, for example rooms in a house. – Highlighting a word in a reading text, and asking a comprehension question which will make the learner revisit the word. – Having another 'go' at a task – the computer won't mind how many times you do it!
Input – making it comprehensible	– Including images with, or adding them to a spoken or written text to clarify meaning. – Providing hyperlinks to online dictionaries, explanations, or translations (or students search for them themselves).
Salience and noticing	– Highlighting language items, and adding commands such as: 'Click to hear the underlined words'. – Annotating parts of a reading text with 'sticky notes'. – Using a concordancing program to explore how a word or phrase is used in different contexts.
Output	– Writing blogs and emails. – Using MovieMaker to make a short video and posting it on YouTube. – Voting in an online survey.
Interaction	– Taking part in CMC, for example in discussion groups and virtual classrooms. – Doing collaborative projects such as wikis, podcasts, and making digital storybooks.

Table 11.1 Examples of how TELL can support different aspects of language learning

Providing for different kinds of language learner

We know that individual learners vary in the ways in which they approach learning, which is one reason why teachers always find themselves adapting coursebooks. No coursebook could ever hope to cater for all ages, personality types, and abilities of learner; for all kinds of learner interests; goals and motivations, for all classrooms all over the world, and for all kinds of learning style and learning strategy preferences. TELL can provide 'differentiated' activities for different kinds of learner. It broadens the spectrum of locations in which learning can take place, so that it is no longer confined to the classroom, but also involves using mobile devices and computers outside the classroom. Learners can work individually or together at their own pace. Not everybody in the class has to do the same thing at the same time in 'lock step', as used to be the case with coursebooks being used traditionally. The act of incorporating technology changes how we view the role of the coursebook.

Task 1

Adapting a coursebook

Imagine that you are about to cover the following two pages (36–37) of a coursebook for a class of 14-year-olds learning English as a second language. The students have very mixed levels of ability in English. They all have mobile phones and many of them have access to a computer at home. You can envisage this class as taking place either in your home country or a country you have taught in. The topic of the two pages is 'Looking after yourself'. The Teacher's Book states that the language learning aims of these two pages are: 'to practise the language of advice and to introduce vocabulary connected with health'. There is a grammar aim of teaching students how to use 'should/shouldn't' to give advice, and a pronunciation focus on the sounds /ɒ/, /ɔː/ and /əʊ/. All the four language skills are practised. There are also non-linguistic aims to do with teaching the students about health issues because their language learning needs to fit into their overall curriculum, which covers many subjects. The two pages are divided into five sections, 'Reading', 'Listening and speaking', 'Vocabulary', 'Listening and speaking', and 'Pronunciation'. Before looking at the suggestions we provide below:

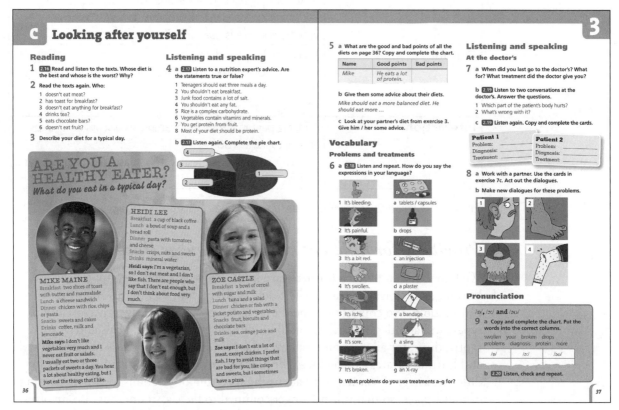

Figure 11.1 Project 4 (3rd edition), Student's Book. (Hutchinson, Oxford University Press, 2009)

- Think of one way in which you would use TELL for each of the sections, bearing in mind the age of the class and different kinds of learner.
- How could each TELL activity provide some of the favourable conditions for language learning as listed in Table 11.1?

There are so many possible ways in which TELL could be used to enhance the learning opportunities of this or any coursebook that we have limited ourselves to fuller suggestions for the first section, and then one suggestion for the other sections. Some suggestions might be:

For section one, 'Reading'

1 Students could search for a link on the internet to the topic of 'healthy eating for teenagers' and post it to a virtual noticeboard such as Pinterest, Wallwisher, Pindax, or Linoit. If you want to control which websites students have access to for reasons of time and security, you can use a tool like jogtheweb, which lets you select websites around a particular topic, and add comments to guide students. This facility is useful for students when creating webquests, too. The topic is likely to be of interest to teenagers, and allows them to work together or alone, outside class or in class, and at their own pace and reading level.

2 Students can join a Flikr group and post a photo connected with the topic with an accompanying tag. This activity is likely to appeal to students with a 'visual' learning preference.

3 The comprehension questions in 2 can be sent to students' mobile phones using a program such as StudyBoost, which makes use of text messaging. Students could read the text and answer the questions individually outside the classroom, by typing in the answers. Class time the next day could then be spent looking at the questions which students found difficult.

4 For activity 3 'Describe your diet for a typical day', students could contribute a description of what they eat in a typical day to a class wiki (and get comments from others in the class).

For section two, 'Listening and speaking':

5 After listening to the questions and doing the activities, groups of students could prepare and then record their own true/false questions, which could simply be variations on the questions in the book, for example 'Teenagers should eat one meal a day'. This would provide a focus on the target grammar form 'should/ shouldn't' and lots of repetition of this form. Students can record the quiz using the recording device on their mobile phones. The teacher could upload the recording as a podcast, if the classroom has a computer, or students could just play the recording to another group on speaker phone. An alternative is for students to make an online quiz using a programme such as Google Docs. The other members of the class could answer it at home. You could allow individual students to choose in which way they wanted to do the quiz.

For section three, 'Vocabulary'

6 Teachers or students could test each other on the vocabulary in this section by creating a 'wordsearch' for other students, using a programme like Armed Penguin or Hot Potatoes, or using other word game programs, many of which can be downloaded as an '**app**', such as Draw Something, or Hanging with friends (a version of 'hangman').

For section four, 'Listening and speaking'

7 In groups, students could role-play and film dialogues at the doctors for the health problems, perhaps filming outside the classroom and/or adding other health problems. They could also add sequences to the beginning and end of the film on how the problem was caused (with a caption 'one week earlier') and whether it was solved ('one week later'). They could even film the dialogues as a cartoon using an animation program like GoAnimate or Sockpuppets. The class could view all the dialogues and vote on the best film. This and activity five cater for teenagers' preferences for working with a peer group.

For section five, 'Pronunciation'

8 Students can practice the words using a voice recognition app, such as the ones we suggested in Chapter 3, or a pronunciation app. This app could be downloaded to their mobile phone.

Many of these activities seem to provide multiple opportunities for learning, according to Table 11.1. We would suggest that they cover the following: 1) input 2) output 3) input and output, and possibly repetition as students repeat the task to try to get a better score 4) input, output, interaction 5) input, output, interaction 6) input, output, repetition 7) input, output, interaction 8) output, repetition.

What does TELL mean for the future of coursebooks?

We have seen in Task 1 that incorporating TELL activities seems to separate learning activities into those which are better done on an individual basis outside the classroom, on a computer or mobile device – for example reading, writing, doing activities which focus on language forms – and activities which are better done on a group basis inside the classroom, such as speaking and listening, and setting up and doing collaborative project work. Another suggestion which has been made for how technology might change what is done in the classroom and what is done outside is the so-called '**flipped classroom**'(Tucker 2012). This envisages students receiving language presentation at home via teacher-made videos, and using class time for one-to-one advice from the teacher and group work. These changes, if they happen, will mean that teachers face new challenges, such as monitoring the work done outside class and managing the different learning paths which individual students are now able to take using TELL.

However, keeping track of student activity is not a problem. There are a number of programs such as Edmodo and Lore which allow teachers to see a record of what students are doing, give them feedback, and make awards for good work, whilst also giving students opportunities to share work and submit it for grading by the teacher. The recent interest in '**dogme**' learning (see Meddings and Thornbury 2009) – which encourages teaching without coursebooks, and places emphasis on students creating content and teachers highlighting ways in which students can make use of learning opportunities – seems to us to arise partly as a result of the new resources available using Web 2.0, although some would disagree with this view. For us, the coursebook acts as an essential 'spine' and 'work plan', drawn up by experts, which transparently states overall goals and objectives to a variety of people including students, teachers, parents, and educational authorities. This 'spine' is essential because it provides an important criterion for navigating and choosing amongst the vast array of possible TELL resources. It means that the resources the teacher chooses and the learners use build on each other in a principled and structured way, rather than being a heterogeneous assortment of 'fun' activities, or a matter of 'getting lost' in a sea of resources (Beatty 2010: 160). Incorporating TELL activities in order to flesh out the learning goals in the coursebook enables teachers to cater for learners with different needs and preferences, and it gives those learners more autonomy. The teacher is the 'strategist', directing students to resources which are appropriate for learning aims; students are 'tacticians', using those resources in individual ways to create a **PLP** (Personalized Learning Pathway). Free language-learning resources on the Internet are widely available to anyone who has the ability to connect to it, which is much less costly than purchasing supplementary books. To sum up our opinion on the relationship between TELL resources and the coursebook, we rather like a Tweet on #eltchat saying 'The coursebook's the scientific element of LT. It's up to us to humanize it.' Adding TELL activities enables teachers to build on their own students' interests and incorporate activities which motivate them (for instance, teenagers who like working with a peer group). It also means that teachers can use activities which reflect the cultural and learning beliefs of the context they are teaching in.

The last section seems to suggest that there is a 'brave new world' of endless resources out there which can be used to enhance the learning possibilities of the coursebook. However, there is a big 'but' out there, too; some of these resources are more effective and useful than others. How do teachers and learners evaluate these resources to find out if they are useful or not? How do they use Web 2.0 tools in ways which will maximize student language learning? The following sections of the chapter consider this question.

Evaluating language learning software

Evaluating software presents particular problems for teachers; unlike a coursebook, the whole thing is not transparently laid out in front of you, you may have difficulty in getting access to a fully operational version until you have bought it, and your level of knowledge of TELL may prevent you fully appreciating what the software can do. Hubbard (2006) and Chapelle (2001) provide some interesting criteria for evaluating software programs, although, as we will see, these have their limitations. Hubbard has been refining his evaluation framework over a twenty year period, and has incorporated many of Chapelle's insights about the relationship between software and language acquisition. His work has influenced the template which the CALICO Journal uses to review software. He says that there are three points in time at which evaluation can happen: when a teacher or institution is first choosing what to use, while it is being used, and after it has been used to see if it was effective or not. Most emphasis has tended to be on the first, selection stage; perhaps we need to think more about the other stages too. He suggests using six criteria for selecting a piece of software for use with language learners:

1 Technical preview – make sure that the software will run the way you want it to on the equipment which is available. Have you got the appropriate equipment?

2 Operation – go through the main parts of the software and get an understanding of how it works. Hubbard goes into some detail in this section and says you need to consider timing – is there a time limit on how long students have to give responses, or how long they see information? – as well as control – do students have freedom to move around the program? He also says that teachers need to consider user input – does the student click, or speak, or type a word, or more than a word? – as well as feedback – does the program just say if something is correct, or does it provide explanations, prompts, and help?

3 Teacher fit – try to infer the language teaching approach which the software reflects. Does it fit your own approach?

4 Learner fit – do the contents, skills, and language level of the software suit your students' needs, and those of the syllabus?

5 Implementation – could you integrate the software easily into the course or curriculum?

6 Appropriateness – this is a kind of summative judgment based on criteria 1–5. If the software were a human teacher, would you want that person teaching your students?

| Task 2 | **Software reviews** |

Read a review of some software application which you might be interested in using in your own present or future teaching context. You can find reviews in the technology sections of English language teaching journals, such as the *ELT Journal, English Teaching Professional*, and *Modern English Teacher*. Think about the following questions as you read:

- Does the review mention any of Hubbard's criteria for selecting software?
- Is the review useful? Would you have liked some more information? If so, about what?

The review probably covered many of Hubbard's criteria, especially those which are very practically concerned with how to use the software. However, it hopefully gave other information which does not seem to be covered by those criteria, such as what students actually learn in terms of language and thinking skills. The problem is that Hubbard's criteria were mainly designed for specially produced software used in 'tutor' mode, in which learners tended to be passive 'receivers' of instruction. The criteria may not work so well for all the possibilities which Web 2.0 now offers us in terms of 'tools', which may not have been specially designed for language learning, but which can be adapted by for that purpose. In this scenario, students have much more choice and freedom in the ways in which they use the tools, and they can interact and collaborate with each other. Web 2.0 tools, according to Bower et al. (2010: 178), are more in accord with 'the student-centred, interactive approaches being advocated by contemporary educational theory'.

Bower et al.'s article is actually about designing learning activities using Web 2.0 tools, but it is useful for evaluation purposes too. Hubbard's and Chapelle's models perhaps focused on how software programs can provide opportunities for language acquisition, as well as being designed so that they are easy for teachers and students to use. Bower et al. discuss three other important features of learning activities using technology – knowledge, pedagogy, and thinking skills.

Knowledge

They refer to a taxonomy by Anderson and Krathwohl (2001), which is based on Bloom's (1956) original and very influential taxonomy of skills needed for learning. They say that learners need to learn the following kinds of knowledge. (We have taken the liberty of adding suggestions about how these might apply to language learning:)

1 Factual knowledge – of the different language systems, such as syntax, pronunciation, vocabulary, etc.
2 Conceptual knowledge – of how bits of language combine together to express meaning and the rules which govern that process.
3 Procedural knowledge – of how to use language in different contexts.
4 Metacognitive knowledge – of how well one is using language, and how well others are doing so.

Pedagogy

They suggest that online activities can follow one of the following 'teaching and learning styles' (which we have discussed to in Chapter 1):

1 Transmission – information about language is given directly to learners.
2 Dialogic – through dialogue, learners extend understanding of the language beyond what they could have achieved on their own (Vygotsky's concept of the zone of proximal development).
3 Constructionist – where language learning occurs through developing a product (Papert 1986).
4 Co-constructionist – combines two. and three. Students learn language through making something together in a group, and interacting with others.

Thinking skills

Finally, they suggest that all kinds of learning, including language learning, involve students in learning a hierarchy of thinking skills, and they refer to Churches' 2008 reworking of Bloom's taxonomy of thinking skills for the digital age (remembering, understanding, applying, analysing, evaluating, creating). So for example, 'remembering', a lower order thinking skill, might involve 'social bookmarking' where learners save and exchange articles on a particular topic from their favourite websites and blogs, using tools such as Diigo or Delicious. 'Creating' a higher order thinking skill, might involve blogging, filming, podcasting, or writing a program.

Bower et al.'s suggestions give us some more angles on deciding if activities using technology have helped students learn language, and how this has been achieved. For instance, in Task 1, we suggested that activity 7, in which students make a film in a group, would be good for providing students with opportunities for language input, output, and interaction. We can now add that it would be good for developing procedural knowledge, that it would probably use a co-constructive pedagogy, and that it would develop 'creating' thinking skills. On the other hand, activity 8, in which students practice pronunciation using a mobile app, and which gives them opportunities for output and repetition, would probably deal more with factual knowledge, a transmissive pedagogy, and the 'remembering', 'understanding' and 'applying' levels of the thinking skills taxonomy.

| Task 3 | **Digital tools and thinking skills** |

A number of teachers have come up with suggestions about how Web 2.0 tools can help students develop the thinking skills they need to learn any subject, including language. Look at the table below (11.2), which links thinking skills, associated activities, and Web 2.0 tools. Explore one of the tools, and watch the explanatory video accompanying it, if there is one. How do you think that it develops particular thinking skills?

Thinking Skill	Tools	Activities
Creating	VoiceThread, WeVideo, Prezi, Screenr	Recognizing, listing, describing, identifying, retrieving, naming, locating, finding.
Evaluating	Blogger, Google Groups, Google +	Interpreting, summarizing, inferring, paraphrasing, classifying, comparing, explaining, exemplifying.
Analysing	Survey Monkey, Google docs, Zoho, Flisti	Comparing, organizing, deconstructing, attributing, outlining, structuring, integrating.
Applying	Pipes, Scribble Maps, Podomatic, Aviary	Implementing, carrying out, using, executing.
Understanding	Diigo, Google reader, Google advanced search	Checking, hypothesizing, critiquing, experimenting, judging, testing, monitoring.
Remembering	Wordle, Diigo, Google, Fotobabble	Designing, constructing, planning, producing, inventing, devising, making.

Table 11.2 Thinking skills for digital learning (slightly adapted from Anderson and Krathwohl 2001)

There are a number of other 'digital models of Bloom's taxonomy' available on the Internet which give examples of iPhone and iPad apps, as well as **Android** apps for each level of thinking skill. You can find these by googling 'Blooms digital taxonomy'. Our website also provides some suggestions and a link to an online version of Churches' suggestions for digital activities associated with levels of thinking. We were rather surprised to see Twitter (the instant messaging service which confines messages to 140 characters) in the 'understanding' section of a number of these taxonomies, because it is usually used for exchanging information and news. We could see that it might be useful for 'paraphrasing' and 'summarizing', but would generally place it more at the 'remembering' level for finding and listing information. These taxonomies are interesting because they encourage teachers and learners to try out Web 2.0 tools, but they are not infallible.

Evaluating language

The last feature, and many would say the most important one, to add to this framework of software design, teacher and student 'fit', pedagogy, acquisition, and skill learning is language. What kind of language are students exposed to, what language do they seem to learn, and what kind of language do they produce? What is their role in using the language learning tools?

Task 4

Learner language in a chat room

Shin (2006) gives the following two examples of a group of adult ESL learners of intermediate level at an American university using a free Web chat tool synchronously to learn English. They are either students at the university or spouses of students. Tom is the teacher. Read the examples, and then consider the questions which follow:

Example 1

The group have been discussing how they are adjusting to life on the university campus.

Lee   I think it is very systematic and have lack of tolerance

Chuck I don't know much about here, because I am just here about 4 weeks.

Lee   I don't find the proper adjective for TOLERENCE

Tom   Only 4 weeks?

Lee   Do you know what I mean?

Chuck Yes. I arrived in here four weeks ago

Tom   It's a shame when Americans in a UNIVERSITY setting aren't tolerant (there's the adjective).

Lee   YES, thanks. I'm an idiot. ^^

Lee   an

Lee   I mean it's just about some rules of CAMPUS life.

Tom   No, don't say that. My wife scolds me all the time when I say I'm an idiot about Chinese. It's not good for learning.

Example 2

Steven people here is very nice

Lee   For me, they are very exclusive.

Tom   Wow, very different opinions!

Tom   Sun, are most of the people in your department helpful, or less than helpful?

Sun	helpful
Steven	It is a little difficult for me to be familiar with here.
Sun	I have no problem except English and driving …
Jenny	^ ^
Lee	☺
Jenny	me too
Lee	Even between members in the same LAB, they hardly talking each other.
Tom	Ana, does your husband ever say anything about his colleagues?

- Do there seem to be other things going on in the 'chats' besides language learning?
- How do the learners help each other?
- What kind of role does Tom, the teacher, seem to play?
- There are quite a few language errors which no one corrects. What is your opinion of that?
- What do you think of the use of emoticons such as the raised eyebrow sign in ^ ^ and the 'smiley'?
- Thinking back to the evaluation features we have mentioned in this chapter, what do these two examples seem to show about language acquisition, knowledge, pedagogy, and thinking skills?

The students are having the problems adjusting to a new culture which often accompany language learning, and the chats help them to exchange opinions and realize they are not alone in experiencing difficulties. The group are very careful to be friendly to each other, to respond to comments, and to preserve each other's 'face'. Although there are differences of opinion, these never become heated. The teacher Tom, plays an important role in promoting an atmosphere of politeness and group unity. In the last turn of Example 1, he shows solidarity with the rest of the group, so he is not acting out any hierarchical role as a teacher. He promotes language use in three ways: by supplying language correction to students if they ask for it; by making sure everyone participates; and by using language in his turns which might be slightly above their level – for example 'scolds', 'colleagues', 'helpful'– and which will scaffold their learning. Although there are a number of language errors, this chat does not contain many typing mistakes, which can also be a feature of CMC 'chat'. The chat is about communicating meaning and becoming fluent in the language, so focus on form and correction would hamper it. Teachers tend not to correct oral discussion in the classroom for the same reasons. One argument in favour of emoticons might be that they allow less advanced or less talkative students to participate in the conversation. In Example 2, Sun and Jenny seem to fall into these categories. One would hope that their language production will increase as time goes on and they get more confident and learn more language. The fact that they are participating, even if it is in a limited way, means they are being exposed to lots of comprehensible input. They can also reread the chat at leisure after the live discussion has finished.

In terms of other features of TELL activities discussed in this chapter, there are opportunities for input, output, and interaction. The students can look at the transcript of the chat afterwards if they want to, and repeat and memorize new language. There has been a group noticing of the word 'tolerant'. In terms of knowledge, this activity has been particularly useful for procedural knowledge, although other kinds of knowledge are probably also being learnt. The pedagogy used is co-constructionist; students learn language through constructing something together (a conversation) and interacting with each other. Notice also the dialogic 'scaffolding' by the teacher. For thinking skills, there seems to be a focus on 'understanding' and 'applying', as students compare their experiences and explain the reasons for their opinions, and give examples, such as Sun's 'English and driving'.

Encouraging autonomous learning

Godwin-Jones (2011) has remarked that perhaps the biggest current challenge for teachers using TELL is to help students to become self directed learners. We have mentioned metacognitive knowledge, which involves an understanding of how well one is using language, and developing this self awareness is an important part of becoming an autonomous learner. Godwin-Jones says that important roles for teachers include giving students guidance on useful online tools and demonstrating how they can be used, as well as the problems and benefits attached to them. So teachers can introduce students, for example, to translation, dictionary, language and proofing tools, or ways of using the news for learning purposes such as VOA Special English (slowed-down news), the news in simple French from *Radio France Internationale*, using CNN transcripts, or learning vocabulary from BBC Words in the News. Language centres can help students to plan personal learning paths. There are a number of teachers who provide online suggestions of resources for students. A current example is Michelle Morissette (see details of links on our website). It is worth keeping up to date with who is offering this kind of helpful information for learners. Godwin-Jones also makes the point that learners should be 'autonomous, not alone' and that it is important that they interact in a peer network. If students are motivated to learn, and know how to direct and monitor their learning, they can turn any experience with technology into a language-learning opportunity. For example, what about the people all over the world taking part in multiple-player games, such as World of Warcraft and Runescape, and speaking to each other in English using headphones? These are examples of games which are not designed for language learning, but they are much more fun than many so-called 'language games' (Mawer and Stanley 2011). If learners have the motivation and techniques for using them as language learning tools, they could be very valuable.

Task 5

Using computer games

Download an 'escape the room' or 'adventure' game which is available for free online; Mawer and Stanley provide a number of suggestions. One we have used is an 'escape the room' game called MOTAS, or Mysteries of Time and Space, but there are many more (see details and suggestions on our website). Imagine you are a second language (L2) speaker of English who is very motivated to learn English.

- How might you use this game to develop your language skills?
- Would it be better to play this game in class and have a teacher's help?

Most learners, if they are habitual game players, will be aware of the conventions of 'escape the room' games; they involve collecting objects and solving puzzles to get out of one room and into another, and there are usually a number of rooms and levels to complete. The player clicks on an object and gets feedback about whether that object will help them get out of the room. When the learner goes into the first room, the objects are helpfully labelled. The player could learn the vocabulary while looking at images of the objects which the words refer to. When players click on objects, they could use a translation tool to understand the comments at the bottom of the screen. This particular game can be played in a number of languages, so players could go directly to the version in their mother tongue, if available. They could even play the whole game in their mother tongue and then in English, having benefited from the translation. Games can of course be used for learning other languages as well as English. It is likely that frustration will occur when they cannot solve a particular level. They can then access the 'walkthrough' online in English, and will be extremely motivated to read it, because it gives solutions to each level. The game provides lots of language input and reading practice. Students have to focus very closely on the meaning of short amounts of language in order to solve the puzzles. It is an example of 'dialogic' pedagogy in which the answers given by the computer scaffold the player to proceed to the next level.

Most teachers would feel rather uncomfortable with the idea of students taking up a whole class to play a computer game, which is probably best done out of class on one's own or with other students. However, teachers could model ways of using the game for language learning. They might devise a number of in-class tasks focusing on the vocabulary and syntax of the language used in the game, and provide suggestions about how and where students could find help in understanding the language used in the game. The moral of this task is that language learning opportunities can be found everywhere on the Internet, not just where you would expect to find them!

Summary

In this chapter, we gradually assembled a number of criteria for assessing how particular uses of TELL can help language learners. We considered how all these things – namely opportunities for language acquisition, exposure to different kinds of knowledge, appropriate pedagogical styles, and learning thinking skills – need to be present in TELL materials, and discussed how TELL can be incorporated into coursebooks. We also explored ways in which opportunities for language learning can be created with Web 2.0 tools and resources found on the internet, even in online gaming environments. Finally, we discussed how learners can be supported in seeking out their own language learning opportunities.

Further reading

Bower, M. et al. 2010. 'A framework for Web 2.0 learning design'. *Educational Media International* 47/3: 177–198.

Churches, A. 2008. 'Blooms taxonomy Blooms digitally'. *Educators' eZine*. Acessed on 12 August 2012 at: http://edorigami.wikispaces.com/Bloom%27s+Digital+Taxonomy.

Mawer, K. and **G. Stanley.** 2011. *Digital Play*. Peaslake, UK: Delta.

Tucker, B. 2012. 'The Flipped Classroom: Online instruction at home frees class time for learning'. *Education Next* 12/1: 82–83.

12 SUMMARY AND FUTURE-GAZING

I think there is a world market for maybe five computers.
THOMAS WATSON, chairman of IBM (1943)

Aims

In this chapter, we will try to give you some answers to the following questions:
- How does society accommodate new technologies?
- What does the future hold for technology and language learning?

Introduction

In this chapter, we will try to draw together the themes that we have addressed in this book and then consider what the future may hold for technology and language learning. We start with an overview of how new technologies are accommodated and assimilated by society and then look at the developments that we believe will be most significant. We conclude by arguing that technology is no longer something that is additional to the process of learning, brought in to 'assist', but has become part of the ecology of learners' lives.

Technology in society

When new technologies are introduced, they tend to be accompanied by claims that the innovations will transform the world, whether for good or ill. As Woolgar (2002) points out, this type of claim (which he calls '**cyberbole**' when talking about digital technology) has been made about every type of innovation from the printing press to the bicycle. In most cases, the technology does indeed have a transformational effect, but it tends to be incremental rather than immediate and it is often different from that which was predicted by the soothsayers. For example, the introduction of the printing press to Western Europe did not lead to the complete downfall of society, but it did contribute to the waning of the political and civil powers of the church. Claims made about digital technologies have included the following:

- Children and young people are 'digital natives' who think differently from adults and need more visual content, games, and rapid changes of pace than previous generations. (Prensky 2001)
- Technology reduces the attention span and causes people to think less deeply. (Greenfield 2005, Carr 2010)
- Video games make children more aggressive. (Sigman 2005)
- Video games enable players to take on alternate identities and provide rich learning opportunities. (Gee 2007)
- The internet is full of predators seeking to abuse children. (Many tabloid newspapers)
- The internet facilitates bullying. (Lenhart et al. 2011)
- Technology creates a participatory culture which reduces the power of traditional authorities. (Shirky 2008)
- Digital communications damage literacy and impoverish language. (Shaughnessy 2008)
- Digital communications enhance literacy and enrich language. (Crystal 2008)
- Digital communications tools allow us to communicate with people all across the globe.

As with all cyberbole, there are grains of truth in all of these claims, some of which we have examined in this book. Woolgar (2002) proposed 'five rules of virtuality', which, he argues, explain how new technologies are perceived when they are first introduced and how they are received into **socio-cultural** contexts.

Rule one: Uptake and use of the new technologies depend crucially on local social context

New technologies, of any kind, are tools that mediate activity within the context of culture. As we have already shown, the different elements in an activity system all affect each other. To a certain extent, culture will determine what needs to be done within an activity system and thus influence the tools that are appropriate. However, a tool that does not fit within an existing activity system is unlikely to be widely adopted. One example is the interactive whiteboard (IWB). As we have explained in Chapter 8, this has been one of the most successful technological innovations of recent years in the classroom. The fundamental reason for this is that it fitted neatly into the existing activity of teaching. When IWBs are first installed into a school the teachers, do not have to change their ways of teaching, although it will make certain aspects of the work more efficient. However, over time, the affordances of the IWB will have an impact on teaching and learning; the tool allows teachers to do things that were not previously possible and their teaching methods and culture will change.

Rule two: *The fears and risks associated with new technologies are unevenly socially distributed.*

Fears and risks regarding new technologies are not only unevenly distributed socially but will also fluctuate over time. For example, as we showed in Chapter 8, the lower age limit for most social networks is thirteen, but many children under that age have accounts, often with the knowledge of their parents. However, periodically there will be an incident involving a child and social networking (for example, stalking or bullying) that hits the newspapers and causes a short-term panic about the safety of children on the internet. As this incident becomes old news then the fear will recede. However, even at its height, the fear is likely to affect only (some) adults; young people are likely to be unconcerned.

Rule three: *Virtual technologies supplement rather than substitute for real activities.*

Although it may appear that people spend all their time nowadays attached to their digital devices at the expense of interacting with 'real people', in fact most of the things that people do online are extensions of their offline lives. For example, for people who are not celebrities, most of their social network contacts are family and 'real-life' friends. The virtual activity of conversing or exchanging photographs on the social network supplements other forms of contact such as face-to-face conversations, phone calls, and birthday cards. As Gee and Hayes (2011) show, many people use online activity as a way of learning more about 'real-life' interests (for example, one of us is an avid reader of a forum for tuba-players). Similarly, the introduction of new technologies into the classroom does not replace the ways of teaching that existed beforehand. As we mentioned above, when IWBs enter the classroom they offer additional options to the teacher and change in teaching approaches is incremental rather than sudden. We feel, however, that this rule should include the words 'tend to', as there are situations where technology makes possible activities that are not generally available in 'real-life', such as online role-playing games.

Rule four: *The more virtual, the more real.*

Woolgar argues that 'virtual' activity stimulates 'real' activity so the more people engage in online interaction, the more they also do it in real life. Thus, conversations on social networks bring us closer to our friends and family and make it more, rather than less, likely that we will arrange to meet in person. We would also argue that some of the activities we have suggested in this book, such as writing, making videos, or recording audio are very much 'real' and the availability of the tools for doing the tasks and services for publishing the products make it more likely that teachers and learners will engage in them. We believe, also, that the more learners use 'virtual' language, the more they will be able to use language in 'real-life' settings.

Rule five: *The more global, the more local.*

In Chapters 5 and 6 we have talked about the fact that publishing learners' work, such as writing or video online, makes the work available to an authentic global audience. However, the work that is done in creating the work will be local; it will take place in (or around) the classroom. In addition, it is likely that the main intended audience will also be local; for example, other pupils in the school, parents, people from the local neighbourhood. This is an illustration of Woolgar's fifth rule, which is a paradox of the internet: the easier it is to create something with global reach, the more likely people are to use the tools for activities that are mainly local in scope and intended for a discrete audience.

Looking to the future

Predicting the technology trends of the future is extraordinarily difficult. In part this is because trends are subject to fashion which means that, in some cases, there is no discernible reason why one type of device or service suddenly becomes popular. Each year, the Educause Foundation produces a report called 'On the Horizon' which attempts to predict the future of learning technology. It is interesting to track these over the past few years to see which predictions have continued to feature in the report, which have been achieved, and which have fallen by the wayside. The 2012 report (Educause 2012) identifies timeframes for likely adoption and amongst the predictions are:

- In one year or less – mobile apps and tablet computing
- Within two to three years – game-based learning
- Within four to five years – 'the internet of things'

It is interesting that mobile technologies have featured in the report for several years. The 2008 report focused on mobile broadband, but in subsequent years, attention shifted to devices. However, the 2012 report mentions apps, suggesting that the devices themselves are now so ubiquitous that they are, according to Bax's (2011) definition, normalized. We no longer think of the devices themselves as novel or interesting. What matters is the range of applications available – i.e. what we can do with our mobile phones.

Tablets did not feature in the 2011 report, whereas in 2012 the prediction is that they will be adopted within one year. On the other hand, the 2011 report predicted one year or less for the adoption of electronic books. This is interesting because, as we note in Chapter 4, dedicated **e-readers** have become extremely popular in the last year or so – to the point where online booksellers now report that they sell more electronic books than paperbacks (BBC News, 6 August 2012). However, it is also possible to read electronic books on tablets; Amazon's Kindle books can be read on the Kindle, **e-ink** reader, or on Kindle apps for smartphones, tablets, or PCs. Even though there are significant differences between e-readers and **e-book** apps on tablets, it seems that the Educause Foundation believes that tablets will become the main method of accessing electronic books. It will be interesting to see what happens.

Games

Games of various kinds have long been a staple of the language classroom. However, the proliferation of digital and online games leads to exciting opportunities for learners and teachers. Gee (2007) talks about the ways that games can help learners to assume alternative identities and about his belief that this facilitates learning. One aspect of this might be an identity as a speaker of a different language. In addition, Gee and Hayes (2010) show how games can be a starting point for many informal learning opportunities. They focus on The Sims which is a game that contains a lot of conversation but little language (the characters speak an artificial language called 'Simlish'). Gee and Hayes found players of the game The Sims who constructed complex storylines within the game, and then wrote fiction based on those stories, which they illustrated with screenshots, and then published online on fan-fiction or blogging sites.

In Chapters 3, 4, and 11, we have discussed how online and 'video' games can provide texts for listening/reading and environments for talk. As we have explained, many games are rich in language and provide opportunities for communication with other players. However, even games which are not language-rich (such as the The Sims, but there are others) can be useful to the language teachers. The rising popularity of smartphones has led to a proliferation of cheap (or free) **'casual' games**, which can be learned quickly and played in short bursts (rather than needing hours of dedicated play). Casual games may be designed to be played individually whilst others (discussed below) are played against online opponents. Although many casual games do not contain much English, many others have a narrative of some kind that can be used as stimulus for English language work. For example, a current favourite is Angry Birds produced by Rovio for smartphones and for tablets. The 'story' of this game is that pigs have stolen eggs from some birds. The birds are angry and vow revenge on the pigs which they achieve by firing themselves from catapults to destroy the pigs. The pigs build increasingly elaborate structures to defend themselves and, as the game progresses, different kinds of birds are introduced with different affordances such as dropping eggs or breaking into clusters. All of this makes for a game which is quirky and fun and widely played across different age groups.

The game narrative can be used as a starting point for emotive or descriptive writing from the perspective of either the birds or the pigs (e.g. 'how I felt when my eggs were stolen' or 'when we were so hungry that we had to steal eggs'). The narrative could also be a starting point for newspaper style reporting about the events or for a historical piece about the start of the hundred-year war between birds and pigs. Angry Birds is a 'physics' game which means that it is designed to replicate (approximately) the way that physical objects behave in the real world in terms of trajectory, collisions, levers, and so on. This means that there is a certain amount of mathematical and technical content in the game. An affordance of this is that it could be used in a light-hearted way with learners of academic or technical English. For example, a group of engineering students on an in-sessional EAP course might prepare and deliver a presentation about building bird-proof defence structures.

Casual games on smartphones are useful for teachers because they are cheap and widely available. Angry Birds, for example, costs less than £1 for the full iPhone version and is free for Android phones. Even games that cost money often have a 'lite' version that is free and, indeed, this is true of Angry Birds. Activities planned around the game make use of the devices that are already in students' pockets, but without asking students to pay additional money.

Players who are truly absorbed in a game can enter into what Csikszentmihalyi (2008) calls a 'flow state' where nothing else seems to matter. The flow state, also known as 'being in the zone' does not only apply to game players; Csikszentmihalyi observed it in sportspeople, musicians, and artists. It is the flow state that allows the phenomenon that Gee (2007) observed, whereby game players will tackle material that they would not consider reading in, for example, a classroom or a textbook. Similarly, players in the flow of a game may be willing and able to tackle language that they would be inclined to resist if were presented on a worksheet. Games can provide language that is situated, that is, it makes sense within the context of the game and the gameplay provides a reason to use the language. However, as Angry Birds demonstrates, even games without significant language content can provide a focus for language work and we expect that as more learners bring smartphones into the classroom, the possibilities for using games for language learning will increase.

Mobile devices

Casual gaming is only one example of how mobile devices such as smartphones and might be used in the classroom. As we explained in Chapter 2, smartphones are becoming more common in all parts of the world and, in some regions, cellphone technology has allowed 'technoculture' to bypass the desktop computer phase. Mobile devices have brought the web and social networking to areas that the wired internet could not reach. Smartphones are more than simple communication devices. They have already replaced **PDAs** (such as electronic diaries, address books and notepads) and are now fast replacing calculators, cameras, camcorders, dictionaries, encyclopaedias, MP3 players, satellite navigation systems and handheld game consoles. Smartphones are also moving in on the world of newspapers, magazines, maps, books, and TV. Jenkins (2006) talks about 'convergence culture' in which there are no longer clear distinctions between constructs such as TV, phone, internet, etc. The smartphone is a clear example of a convergence device. However, convergence does not apply only to technology, but also to roles. With digital media there are no longer clear distinctions between producer and consumer; Web 2.0 means that anyone can create and publish content and some 'amateur' bloggers and 'YouTubers' have generated huge audiences for their work. Although this started to happen before the rise of popular smartphones, it is the smartphone more than any other device that has facilitated the convergence of production and consumption. Many of the activities that we have suggested in this book take advantage of this facility to create and publish. We believe that the ability to publish to an authentic audience (rather than just the classroom) is tremendously powerful for language learners.

However, smartphones also change the relationships between students, teachers, and technology. Until very recently, electronic tools in classrooms were institutionally provided, managed, and controlled. However, this is no longer the case. Institutions still provide some technology (mainly desktop and **laptop** computers), but the majority of digital tools now in the classroom are in the pockets and bags of the learners. It is still common for schools to ban mobile phones in the classroom (and there are good reasons for this), but this will become increasingly difficult as learners use their phones for more and more tasks. For example, if students use their phones to take notes, rather than using a paper notepad, then it is not easy for the teacher to demand that the phone be switched off and put away. Teachers can make use of learners' access to mobile technology, for example, we have suggested above that casual games can be a learning resource. Learners' phones can be used for video (watching or making), for activities that involve looking up information (for an example, see Chapter 8), for drill-and-practice tasks, and many other activities – not least, communication! However, making use of learners' phones means that teachers have to accept that they do not have control over the classroom technology and must trust their learners to manage the devices and use them appropriately. Furthermore, as nobody can be expected to have expertise in all the smartphones on the market today, teachers have to accept that learners know more about the technology in their hands (their own personal devices) than the teachers do.

The other balance of power changed by mobile phone technology is the access to and 'ownership' of the internet. Wired internet has heavy infrastructure demands and there are parts of the world where, due to geography and/or economics, it has not been possible to build that infrastructure. Cellphone networks are cheaper and easier to build and this, as we mentioned above, has increased the reach of the internet. Although the internet is still dominated by western/developed countries, this is changing rapidly as the internet becomes more widely accessible in countries such as China and India. This is undoubtedly a good thing, but one of the arguments often advanced for TELL (and we have done it ourselves) is that the internet is a rich source of English. However, increasingly, people are able to use their own languages and writing systems in environments such as websites and online social networks. This can lead, as we have pointed out in Chapter 11, to reduced authenticity when these tools are used in English for English language teaching. When a tool or resource is not available in a learner's own language, there is a convincing reason to use English, even when learners who share an expert language are communicating with each other (as in a mono-lingual foreign language class). An increase in the variety of internet-enabled languages is clearly desirable in general terms as it makes the online world more accessible, but teachers will need to find creative and convincing ways to use these tools in English once the simple use of the tool loses authenticity. We hope that we have provided some ideas as a starting point.

Tablets and e-readers

As explained earlier, dedicated e-readers are not the same as **tablets**. However, one interesting question applies to both types of device, and that question concerns the future of reading strategies. A study by Diemand-Yauman et al. (2011) found that people appear to remember more information from a text that is written in a font that is slightly difficult to read. The study used textbooks rather than electronic devices, but one of the affordances of all digital reading devices is that the font style and size may be changed to suit the reader. A possible consequence of this might be that people learn less effectively from electronic texts than from (slightly challenging) paper texts. More research is necessary in order to find out. However, what is certain about electronic texts is that they can include additional information, such as dictionaries. For example, on devices that use the Apple **iOS** system, there is an integral dictionary. If a reader touches (and holds) a word in any text on the phone or tablet, a menu pops up giving the option to 'define'. Clicking this option takes the user to the dictionary and a definition of the word. There is no need for the reader to understand how to use a dictionary, nor to have one available. Similarly, electronic texts include a search function. This means that it is no longer necessary for a reader to scan a text in order to find key items of information. If you know what you are looking for, then you need only type the word or phrase into a search box. There are implications here for the teaching of reading strategies and, as the use of electronic texts continues to become embedded in our everyday lives, teachers and researchers will need to consider what strategies are needed in order for learners to become effective readers of those texts.

The Johnson et al. report (2012) considers tablets to be a completely new type of device. This is partly due to the capacitive touchscreen interface, which responds to gentle touch and so can be stroked, pinched, or swiped, and the **accelerometer**, which means that the device can respond to being tilted or turned upside down. However, the impact of the tablet is not only in the hardware, but also in the apps. The tablet is a truly convergent device. Tablets can be used as books, notebooks, for audio/video recording, and much more. In addition, the internet is integrated into tablets in a way that is not true of laptops and PCs, or even of netbooks (mini-laptops designed for email and the web). Tablets function best when connected via WiFi or a cellular network to the internet because then, for the user, there is no distinction between local and global, between what is stored and running on the device and what is outside the device. Many services (such as Twitter or YouTube), which to a PC are websites accessed through a web browser, are apps in their own right on a tablet. Tablets (like mobile phones) know where they are in real space (either through the WiFi setup or **GPS**), which means that they can be used for location-based activities, such as following a trail. As a tablet is almost all screen, it can be laid flat on a table for group based activities, and most are now equipped with front-facing cameras that can be used for video-calling services such as Skype. In short, the tablet is an extremely versatile device. Furthermore, because tablets are light enough for children to carry easily, they can be used to link home and school. Work can be started on the tablet in school and then taken home to complete with parents. One study, the 'Homework' project (Luckin 2009) which tested this approach, found that it improved children's learning and helped to engage parents. However, one drawback of tablets is that most have limited data storage and rely on 'the cloud' if users want to store more data than the tablet can hold.

Cloud computing

'**The Cloud**' refers to remote data storage or services. What this means, is that data is not stored on a personal computer or on the servers of an individual institution, such as a school or enterprise, but instead is stored in 'cyberspace' on banks of computers (called servers) owned by a company that specializes in data storage. Many of the Web 2.0 services and tools that we have suggested in this book are cloud-based: YouTube, for example, or Google Docs. The benefits of these cloud services are that they can be accessed by anyone, from anywhere, and often provide powerful tools that would be difficult or expensive to run on personal computers. In addition, there are a number of cloud-based services for file storage, synchronization, and sharing: for example, iCloud from Apple, Microsoft's Skydrive, or the independent Dropbox. These services allow users to store files, which can be synchronized to and accessed from a range of devices such as a home computer, a work computer, a tablet, and a phone. Usually, the service is installed as a folder to each device, and it means that a user can work on a document at work, continue using a tablet or laptop on the commute home, and then continue at home without having to transfer the document manually. The files are automatically synchronized (as long as the device is online). Files can also be shared through the cloud service so a group of people working on a project together may use a cloud folder to store and share project documents. Each user will have access to all the documents in the folder and the documents are automatically kept up to date for everyone. This is clearly an easier and more efficient way of working than exchanging documents by email; as all documents are synchronized there is less confusion over different versions and there is no need to wait for files to be circulated.

However, there are some important points to be considered with regard to data security. One question is about ownership of the data: does it belong to the person who uploaded it or does it belong to the company that owns the servers? For a small-scale project this may not be important, but in other situations, where the data or documents have commercial (or research) value, it could be crucial. There are also concerns about the security of the data and whether a cloud provider has adequate controls in place to prevent unauthorized access. This is a particular worry when essential and/or confidential documents are stored in the cloud. Because of this, some institutions have policies preventing use of cloud services. This is an example of the phenomenon we noted in Chapter 10, whereby institutional or sometimes governmental policies are in conflict with the direction of technological development. This can be difficult for teachers who are forced then to make choices between resources that suit their pedagogical purposes and those which comply with institutional policy.

Overall, cloud services, both interactive Web 2.0 media and file storage/sharing, are useful and convenient. They provide constant and instant access to data (as long as users are online). Cloud storage can, in principle, provide backup facilities for organizations such as schools which might not be able to provide and maintain their own servers. For teachers who want to engage in collaborative class projects with a school in another location, cloud services and storage can prove ideal. Moreover, the cloud is pervasive: users can access their data and services whenever they need; data is no longer tied to location.

'The internet of things'

The pervasiveness of the internet reaches its zenith in the concept of 'the internet of things' (see our website www.oup.com/elt/teacher/tell for more details). This is more of a vision than a reality at present, but we are starting to see its emergence. The vision is that all kinds of physical objects are, in one way or another, connected to the internet. This may be through using **radio tags** attached to the objects, or it may be through wireless or phone connections. Another possibility is codes that can be read by and thus interact with mobile phones. An example that we have seen is a product that comes with an instruction to download an app onto the phone and then, when the phone camera is pointed at the product, a video is displayed on the phone. We find the possibilities tremendously exciting; this development could allow the entire classroom to become interactive. Objects in the classroom or in paper books could talk to learners through the medium of their phones. One research project that is testing the idea of an interactive physical learning environment is the French Digital Kitchen at Newcastle University (see our website for details). This is described as 'a situated language-learning environment where the kitchen communicates with users, instructing them step-by-step in how to cook French cuisine and teaching aspects of French language'. Equipment and objects in the kitchen contain sensors that track what students are doing, so that instructions (in French) can be given at appropriate points. Touchscreens allow students to ask for translations or for instructions to be repeated. The project is continuing and has yet to be fully evaluated, but the interim results seem very promising and we feel that this approach has a lot of potential for language teaching. However, we suspect that cost may be a barrier to wide adoption in schools.

Summary: Techn-ecology

Mobile phones, tablets, cloud computing, and 'internet of things' bring together the real and the virtual; there is no longer a clear distinction between 'cyberspace' and real space. Other distinctions that we used to take for granted, such as 'home' versus 'classroom', are also becoming blurred as personal digital devices, such as phones or tablets, become part of the classroom. These are no longer independent contexts and are further bound together by applications such as VLEs that can take the classroom directly into the home. As Facer (2011) points out, our understanding of concepts such as 'school', 'teacher', and 'curriculum' may change as technology becomes more embedded in our personal lives and in society. Luckin (2010: 18) argues that 'learners are not exposed to multiple contexts but rather ... each learner has a single context that is their lived experience of the world and which reflects their interactions with multiple people, artefacts and environments'. Her view is that context is not something that is fixed, but consists of interlinked elements with connections mediated by technology. Luckin argues for an ecological approach to learning contexts that takes into account learners and the resources that surround them, both physical and virtual, including teachers, technology, and peers.

For language teaching, this change in the nature of context is extremely important. As we have shown in Chapter 11, language education has come to acknowledge that the context of the classroom is not the same as the context of the 'real world' in which authentic language is situated. However, digital technologies bring the real world into the classroom and take the classroom into the world. We believe that when teachers can acknowledge digital technologies as part of the learner's ecology of resources, the possibility for technology to enhance learning can become reality. We hope that through this book we have shown the impact of technology on both language and learning. We have shown how language is used in activities that are mediated by technology and also how technology can be employed in order to use language. We believe that technology and language share a rich interface that can truly enhance language learning.

Further reading

Facer, K. 2011. *Learning Futures: Education, Technology and Social Change.* Abingdon: Routledge.

Luckin, R. 2010. *Re-designing Learning Contexts: Technology-Rich, Learner-Centred Ecologies.* Abingdon: Routledge.

GLOSSARY

accelerometer: Devices such as smartphones and tablets contain an accelerometer chip which tells the device which way up it is and when it is moved or tilted. This allows the development of, for example, games where the player has to tilt the phone to move an object around the screen.

activity system: Considers goal-oriented activities as taking place within a complex system involving community, rules and shared workload. The activity in question is mediated by tools, one of which is language.

affinity spaces: A semiotic social space in which people interact socially and develop interpersonal relationships.

Android: An operating system, made by Google, for smartphones and tablets.

APA: American Psychological Association

app: Abbreviation for 'application' but generally used to refer to a program for a smartphone or tablet.

Assessment for learning (AfL): Students know at the outset of a unit of study what they are expected to learn. The teacher and student work together to get to that point, continually evaluating progress.

asynchronous CMC: CMC in which participants are not online at the same time. Examples of asynchronous CMC are discussion boards, email and commenting on YouTube.

audiolingual method: A method of teaching language based on behaviourist principles. Students were exposed to model sentences, often in a language laboratory, which they repeated and memorised. There was little or no explanation of grammar rules.

authoring software: Software that allows non-experts to create programs such as games or classroom exercises.

avatar: An image that represents a participant in an online environment (for example, in a game). An avatar may resemble the person that it represents or may be a fantasy image of some kind.

behaviourism: A theory which suggested that certain traits in human beings could be trained through a system of repetition and positive feedback for correct performance.

bibsonomy: A system (usually a website) for sharing references and links, also known as 'social bookmarking'.

blended learning: Combines face-to-face learning/teaching with online learning and teaching.

blog: Short for 'weblog', a blog is a website where you can post your thoughts (or pictures). Posts are displayed in chronological order. A blog is similar to an online diary.

browser plug-in: A program that works with a browser (such as Internet Explorer, Safari, etc.) to provide additional website functions.

capacitive screen: A touchscreen which works by creating a very low-intensity electrical connection with skin. A capacitive screen is very sensitive but needs direct skin contact.

casual games: A game which does not require a lot of time to play. Casual games usually have levels to complete (instead of following a storyline) and a level can generally be completed in a few minutes. They include puzzles and games based on cartoon-style characters.

channel: A mode of communication (for example, visual or aural).

chat facility: A chat room that is built into another program.

chat room: A program for synchronous computer-mediated communication (CMC).

CLIL: Content and Language Integrated Learning. An educational approach to teaching and learning in which a language which is not the learners' mother tongue is used for teaching both content and language.

CMC: Computer-mediated communication

coherence: How readers or listeners connect ideas in a piece of discourse and make sense of it. Often used in contrast to the term *cohesion*, which describes how stretches of language are connected by linguistic devices such as discourse markers.

communicative competence: Knowledge of language rules, and how these rules are used to understand and produce appropriate language in a variety of sociocultural settings.

communicative event: Interaction with others. The ways in which the interaction is carried out and language is used are influenced by factors such as topic, purpose, setting, participants and message form. The term is associated with Dell Hymes.

communicative language teaching: An approach to language teaching based on the goal of enabling learners to communicate with others for real life, meaningful purposes.

community of practice (CoP): A group of people who come together to carry out activities in daily life, the workplace or education. Such groups have a common endeavour, shared routines and a repertoire of shared linguistic practices. Members of the community can learn from each other while participating in joint activities.

computer adaptive testing (CAT): A computer system that gives the learner a set of tasks to do and then adjusts the level for the next set, making the tasks more or less challenging depending on the performance of the learner. CATs designed for teaching are also known as Adaptive Tutoring Systems, Intelligent Tutoring Systems or Intelligent Learning Systems.

conferencing: A system that allows a number of people in different locations to talk together at the same time. Systems include telephone conferencing, video conferencing, and web conferencing.

connectionism: The theory that knowledge and learning rely on the gradual strengthening of a network of associated memories.

connectivism: A theory of learning based on the idea that knowledge exists in the world rather than in the mind of an individual. That knowledge can be accessed through participating in group activities.

constructionism: The theory that learning happens most effectively when learners are involved in making tangible objects in the real world. The theory is associated with Seymour Papert, and expanded on constructivism.

constructivism: Refers to a learning process which allows a student to experience an environment first-hand. The student is required to act upon the environment to both acquire and test new knowledge.

critical period hypothesis: A theory that suggests that there is a particular period in language development when the brain is more predisposed to success in acquiring language.

cyberbole: Term coined by Woolgar (2002) to describe the way that people tend to exaggerate the possible benefits or drawbacks of new technologies.

cyber-bullying: Bullying that takes place via digital technologies, such as sending abusive SMS messages.

cyberspace: A general term referring to the internet and online games and the various ways that people can communicate in online environments.

desktop: A computer that needs to be used on a desk. Usually there is more than one component so, for example, the keyboard, screen and main computer box are detached from each other.

device: Used as a catch-all word for electronic equipment such as computers, tablets, phones, game consoles, e-readers etc.

digital fiction: Fiction that is written to take advantage of the affordances of digital texts; for example, by including hyperlinks that allow readers to choose alternative narrative paths.

digital immigrants: see digital natives.

digital literacy: The ability to interpret and create digital texts.

digital media: Media that make use of digital technology including video, web-based materials, smartphone apps, social networking, and digital audio.

digital migrants: People using technology which is new to them in some way.

digital natives: A false dichotomy coined by Prensky (2001). 'Digital natives' refers to children and young people who have grown up with technology whereas 'digital immigrants' refers to people who started using technology as adults.

digital technologies / tools: Software and/or hardware used to accomplish specific tasks; for example, 'presentation tools' are used to create and deliver presentations.

digital text: Text that is intended to be displayed on digital screens. Digital text includes websites and ebooks and may contain interactive elements such as hyperlinks.

discourse thread: Contributions over time to an online discussion which are all about a particular topic.

discussion board: An online forum for discussion and conversation. Conversations are threaded so the first contribution (post) opens a new thread and subsequent posts are part of that thread.

disrupted turn adjacency: Speech often consists of predictable pairs of adjacent utterances, such as question and answer. Computer mediated communication can disrupt these pairs, so that other utterances can appear in the middle of such pairs.

distance learning: Educational provision in which the learners do not physically attend the institution that provides the teaching. Formally known as 'correspondence courses'.

dogme: A communicative approach to language learning which encourages teaching without the use of published textbooks.

download: To transfer material from a website or other remote source to a computer or mobile device.

EAP: English for Academic Purposes

ebook: An electronic book.

e-ink: Digital ink that is used in specialised e-readers. An e-ink display has no light behind the screen which means that it does not strain the eyes but, like a paper book, cannot be read in the dark without a separate light source.

ELT: English Language Teaching

emoticon: Also known as a 'smiley' this is an image that is produced using punctuation marks, for example :-). In some systems this is automatically converted to an image.

e-portfolio: A personalised website in which people can record their individual achievements with supporting evidence such as video or written documents.

e-readers: Devices that use e-ink to display electronic books.

ESOL: English for Speakers of Other Languages

eye-tracking: Software that follows the movements of a user's eyes. This kind of software is often used in the evaluation of other computer programs because it allows researchers to see which parts of the screen the user looks at.

firewall: Software that controls internet traffic in and out of a computer. and prevents access to unauthorised websites.

flaming/ flame war: An exchange of angry messages in a *CMC* context such as an email list or discussion board. The messages tend to become increasingly heated and insulting.

flipped classroom: An approach to teaching whereby students watch recorded lectures or presentations at home and engage in related activities whilst in the classroom.

folksonomy: A system of classification based on user 'tagging'. *Bibsonomy* (see above) is a type of folksonomy.

formative assessment: Methods used by teachers during the learning process in order to evaluate learning. The information obtained is used to modify teaching and learning activities in order to improve student learning.

game console: A device that is designed and used for playing video games. A game consoles may be connected to a larger screen such as a television or it may be handheld with an integral screen.

genre: A type of discourse produced for a particular purpose, such as a menu, political speech or advertisement. It will tend to be structured in a certain way and have predictable linguistic features.

go viral: Something such as an email or a video 'goes viral' when it is spread rapidly by individual users who forward the email to each other or include the email or video in their social network posts. Once something has 'gone viral' then it will be seen by an enormous number of people and it is impossible to prevent its further distribution.

GPS: Global Positioning System: a GPS device receives signals from satellites which provide information about physical location.

grammar-translation method: A language teaching method derived from the way Greek and Latin were taught in the past. It typically involves translating whole texts word-for-word and memorising grammar rules and lists of vocabulary.

grey literature: Written material such as technical reports and working papers from research groups and government agencies which is often not published through conventional channels and is therefore more difficult to access.

hardware: The parts of a computer system or device that can be touched physically.

Harvard system: A systematic way of citing references. These are partially mentioned in brackets in the body of the text, avoiding footnotes, and then fully mentioned in an alphabetical list at the end of the text.

hyperlink: Links within digital texts that allow users to move from one part of the text to another. Hyperlinks may be attached to words or to images. Usually hyperlinks are identified by using a different text colour.

i+1: Refers to one of Stephen Krashen's theories of how language is acquired by exposing learners to language input which is slightly above their current level of knowledge. The 'i' refers to 'input' and '+1' refers to the next stage of language to be acquired.

ICT: Information and Communications Technology. This term is used in the UK as the name of the curriculum subject which deals with use of digital technology.

IELTS: International English Language Testing System

immersion: A method of teaching a second language in which the second language is the medium of instruction.

input: Language forms which are made available to learners in aural or written form, and which give them the opportunity to acquire language.

instant messaging: A program that allows users to send messages to each other whilst they are logged in. Popular IM programs include *Skype* and *Windows Live*.

interactive fiction: See digital fiction.

iOS: The operating system that controls Apple phones and tablets.

IP address: Internet Protocol. The IP address identifies an individual computer on the internet. It consists of a series of numbers (for example: 31.185.200.156).

IWB: Interactive White Board. A large display system, connect to a computer, that can be used in a classroom instead of a blackboard or whiteboard.

L2: Second language

language skill: An ability to process some aspect of a language, for example, place word stress on the correct syllable or listen for gist information. Usually contrasted with **language strategy**.

language strategy: Often used in the sense of an action taken to compensate for a lack of particular language skills. Some writers separate strategies into communication (interaction) and learning (cognitive and metacognitive) strategies.

laptop: A computer designed for portability with integral keyboard and screen. It may be used on the lap but this is not advisable.

learning journal: A diary in which students record their progress in learning some aspect of the target language on a regular basis.

lexis: The words in a language. Often used as an alternative term for vocabulary.

LMS: Learning Management System – a type of software used in educational institutions. An LMS may be used only for management and record-keeping or it may be integrated into a VLE.

mediational tool: Physical or cognitive artefacts that people use to achieve their goals within an activity system.

microblogging: A form of blogging where the post length is restricted to a very small number of characters. Twitter is a microblogging tool with a maximum post length or 140 characters.

mind mapping: A visual representation of the way that ideas relate to each other – may be created on paper or by using software.

moderator: A person who facilitates a discussion.

more able peer: A fellow student who knows more than the learner and is thus able to support or scaffold their learning.

multimedia: Combines audio, images, video and text.

multimodal communication: Delivery of information via different modes including aural and visual. For example, a software interface uses words and icons to convey meaning.

open-access journal: A journal which is available online to readers simply by accessing the internet. It is often, but not always, free of charge

orthography: A standardized system used for writing a particular language. It includes rules about spelling, punctuation and capitalisation.

output: The language produced by learners of a language.

over the air (installation): Installation of software on a mobile or portable device without plugging the device into a desktop or laptop computer.

PDA: Personal Digital Assistant: a pocket sized device with functions including diary, notebook, address book and calculator. PDAs have been largely superseded by smartphones.

peer-reviewed journal: A journal containing articles which have been evaluated by experts in the field to ensure they meet certain standards.

personal media player (PMP): A pocked sized device for playing music and/or video. An iPod is a PMP. Smartphones include PMPs.

phonology: The sound system of a language.

plagiarism: Closely imitating another writer's language and ideas and representing them as one's own original work.

PLP: Personal Learning Pathway (also Personal Learning Plan). A way of structuring learning opportunities to suit the needs of particular individuals. The individuals are often the ones who are in control of planning and managing their own learning.

podcast: Derived from a combination of 'broadcast' and iPod this is an audio file intended to be downloaded onto a PMP.

portfolio: When the term is used for the assessment of learning, it refers to a collection of different tasks completed by the learner over a period of time and often accompanied by an overarching narrative describing what has been learnt through doing the tasks.

pragmatics: The study of how language is used in relation to user, context and topic. It focuses on the speaker or writer's purpose in communicating.

privacy settings: The options on a social networking system that determine how much personal information can be made public or revealed to other users.

productivity software: Software for managing time or workload, for example, electronic calendars.

radio tags: A Radio Frequency Identification (RFID) chip can be incorporated in a tag or label. An RFID tag can be attached to an object and then used to track its whereabouts or progress to provide other information.

reference management software: Software to collect and format bibliographic information.

rhizomatic: Uses a botanical metaphor, that of the rhizomatic plant, to describe how knowledge online is accumulated and connected in constantly changing ways by communication between numerous individuals. The term is associated with Deleuze and Guattari.

scaffolding: Support provided by a more knowledgeable individual to enable a learner to communicate or complete a task.

screen recording: Video recording of a series of actions on a computer/phone/tablet. Useful to demonstrate how a program should be used or for researchers to see how users work with a program.

screenshot: A photograph of a computer/phone/tablet screen. Every operating system has a method of capturing screenshots. Also known as 'screengrabs' because they 'grab' an image of whatever is displayed on the screen at that moment.

semantics: Branch of linguistics focussing on the meaning of words.

semiotic social space: Physical or virtual locations where groups of people who share a common interest meet in order to share create meaning. Informal learning is a common outcome. The people do not necessarily interact socially.

SMS: Short Message Service: the 'proper' name for phone text messaging.

social bookmarking: See bibsonomy.

social constructivism: Focuses on learning which takes place as a result of the learner's interactions in a group.

social cues: Non-verbal information that directs or supports the flow of communication.

social media: Allows users to interact with each other and/or with the owner/ editor of the resource. Social media include social networks such as Twitter, Facebook and YouTube and also the user commenting facilities now found on many websites.

social networking: Online systems that allow people to make connections with each other. For example, Facebook users have 'friends' and Twitter users 'follow' each other.

socio-cultural theory: A theory that suggests that learning occurs through dialogue. Knowledge is constructed through face-to-face interaction, for example between child and carer. The theory is associated with Lev Vygotsky.

socio-digital competence: Understanding what is appropriate to use in different social contexts and knowledge domains, in terms of both technology and language.

speech act: A way of describing speech events which perform particular functions, such as inviting, describing and questioning.

speech-recognition software: A program that converts speech to text, mainly used by people with disabilities that make it difficult to write with a keyboard or pen.

summative assessment: Methods used to evaluate how much students know and can do at a particular point in time, often for purposes of external accountability.

synchronous CMC: *CMC* in which all participants have to be online at the same time. Examples include chatrooms and Skype.

syntax: The grammatical arrangement of words, showing their connections and relationships with each other.

tablet: A very small portable computer with a touchscreen.

tag: A label that indicates the categories to which an item may belong. Items may have multiple tags.

technolect: Language used in online/digital settings.

TELL: Technology Enhanced Language Learning

text messaging: Short messages, up to 160 characters sent and received on mobile phones.

texting: Sending text messages.

the cloud: Cloud computing means that data is stored in a number of remote locations rather than on a single computer. Data that is stored 'in the cloud' is not kept on the user's own device but is accessed through, for example, a website and generally the data can be accessed from any computer or device.

TOEFL: Test of English as a Foreign Language

touchscreen: A screen that can be controlled by touch. Users may use their fingers or a pen-like tool called a 'stylus'.

troll: A person who makes offensive posts on forums or other social media with the intention of causing conflict or distress.

tweet: To make a post on Twitter.

upload: To transfer material from a computer or mobile device to the internet.

virtual classroom: A web-conferencing system designed for teaching. Virtual classrooms usually contain a whiteboard that can be also be used for presentations, text chat, audio and video.

visual literacy: The ability to interpret meaning from information presented in the form of still or moving images.

VLE: Virtual Learning Environment. An online system used in education settings which provides a range of tools and resources including: space to upload teaching materials, discussion boards, student tracking, assessment, etc.

voice board: A discussion board in which users can record voice messages as well as using text.

washback: The effect of a test on teaching. A less commonly used term for the same concept is *backwash*.

web 1.0: 'Traditional' websites which are written by website owners (or authors) and read by users.

web 2.0: 'Read-write' websites which consist largely or entirely of material posted by users (for example, blogs or social networking sites).

web forum: See *discussion board*.

webcam: A camera attached to a computer that can be used for webconferencing.

web-conferencing: See conferencing. Web-conferencing takes place via a website.

wiki: A type of website that can be edited quickly by users.

world English: The term describes the fact that a large proportion of the world population use English to communicate in some contexts. The term covers all such uses without discriminating between native and non-native speakers.

ZPD: zone of proximal development – Language or tasks which are beyond a learner's current ability to produce or perform alone, but which can be accomplished by the learner with scaffolding support from other people.

BIBLIOGRAPHY

Abu Bakar, N. and **K. Ismail.** 2009. 'Using blogs to encourage ESL students to write constructively in English'. *ASEAN Journal of Teaching and Learning in Higher Education.* 1/1: 45–57. Accessed 16 September 2012 at http://www.ukm.my/jtlhe/VolumeView.aspx?vid=1

Adami, E. and **G. Kress.** 2010. 'The social semiotics of convergent mobile devices: new forms of composition and the transformation of habitius' in G. Kress (ed.) *Multimodiality: a social semiotic approach to contemporary communication.* London: Routledge.

Alderson, J. C. and **L. Hamp-Lyons.** 1996. 'TOEFL preparation courses: a study of washback.' *Language Testing* 13: 280–297.

Alderson, J. C. and **D. Wall.** 1993. 'Does washback exist?' *Applied Linguistics* 14: 115–129.

Anderson, L. and **D. Krathwohl.** 2001. *A taxonomy for learning, teaching and assessing: a revision of Bloom's taxonomy of educational objectives.* New York: Longman.

Alonzo, M. and **M. Aiken.** 2004. 'Flaming in electronic communication'. *Decision Support Systems* 36: 205–213.

Andrews, S., J. Fullilove, and **Y. Wong.** 2002. 'Targeting washback – a case-study'. *System* 30/2: 207–223.

Badger, R. and **G. White.** 2000. 'A process genre approach to teaching writing'. *ELT Journal* 54/2: 153–160.

Baron, N.S. 2008. *Always on: language in an online and mobile world.* New York: Oxford University Press.

Bax, S. 2003. 'CALL past, present, and future'. *System* 31: 13–28.

Bax, S. 2011. 'Normalisation revisited: The effective use of technology in language education'. *International Journal of Computer-Assisted Language Learning and Teaching* 1/2: 115.

Bayne, S. and **J. Ross.** 2007. 'The 'digital native' and 'digital immigrant': a dangerous opposition'. Paper presented at the annual conference of the Society for Research into Higher Education (SRHE). December 2007.

Beatty, K. 2010. *Teaching and researching computer-assisted language learning.* (2nd edn.) Harlow: Longman Pearson.

Bennett, S., K. Maton, and **L. Kervin.** 2008. 'The 'digital natives' debate: a critical review of the evidence'. *British Journal of Educational Technology* 39/5: 775–786.

Bennett, S. and **K. Maton.** 2010. 'Beyond the 'digital natives' debate: Towards a more nuanced understanding of students' technology experiences'. *Journal of Computer Assisted Learning* 26/5: 321–331.

Bere, M. and **M. Rinvolucri.** 1981. *Mazes: a problem-solving reader.* London: Heinemann Education.

Berliner, D. 1994. 'Teacher expertise' in B. Moon. and A. Shelton Mayes (eds.). *Teaching and learning in the secondary school.* London: Routledge.

Bin, I. K. 2008. *An interactive multimedia story for EFL young learners: design, evaluation and children's responses.* PhD thesis: University of Leeds.

Bishop, D.V.M. 1998. 'Development of the children's communication checklist (CCC): a method for assessing qualitative aspects of communicative impairment in children'. *Journal of Child Psychology and Psychiatry* 39: 879–892.

Black, P. and **D. Wiliam.** 1998. *Inside the black box: raising standards through classroom assessment.* London: King's College London.

Bloch, J. 2008. *Technologies in the second language composition classroom.* Ann Arbor, MI: The University of Michigan Press.

Bloom, B.S. 1956. *Taxonomy of educational objectives. Handbook 1: The cognitive domain.* New York: David McKay Co Inc.

Bower, M. et al. 2010. 'A framework for Web 2.0 learning design'. *Educational Media International* 47/3: 177–198. Accessed 16 September 2012 at http://www.tandfonline.com/doi/pdf/10.1080/09523987.2010.518811.

Boyle, A. and **D. Hutchison.** 2009. 'Sophisticated tasks in e-assessment: what are they and what are their benefits?' *Assessment and Evaluation in Higher Education* 34/3: 305–319.

Brown, C. and **L. Czerniewicz.** 2010. 'Debunking the 'digital native': beyond digital apartheid, towards digital democracy'. *Journal of Computer Assisted Learning.* 261/5: 357–360.

Bruner, J. S. 1978. 'The Role of Dialogue in Language Acquisition' in A. Sinclair, R. J. Jarvella and L. W.J.M (eds.). *The Child's Conception of Language.* New York: Springer-Verlag.

Buck, G. 2001. *Assessing listening.* Cambridge: Cambridge University Press.

Buckingham, D. 2007. *Beyond technology: children's learning in the age of digital culture.* Cambridge: Polity.

Callow, J. 2005. 'Literacy and the visual: broadening our vision'. *English Teaching: Practice and Critique.* 4/1: 6–19. Accessed 16 September 2012 at http://edlinked.soe.waikato.ac.nz/research/journal/view.php?article=true&id=77&p=1

Cambridge ESOL. 2008. *CAE Handbook* Accessed 21 September 2012 at https://www.teachers.cambridgeesol.org/ts/digitalAssets/109740_cae_hb_dec08.pdf

Cameron, L. 2001. *Teaching languages to young learners.* Cambridge: Cambridge University Press.

Campbell, A.P. 'Weblogs for use with ESL classes'. *Internet TESL Journal* 9/5 Accessed 4 November 2011 at http://iteslj.org/Techniques/Campbell-Weblogs.html

Canale, M. and **M. Swain.** 1980. 'Theoretical bases of communicative approaches to second language teaching and testing'. *Applied Linguistics* 1/1: 1–47.

Carr, N. 2010. *The shallows: how the internet is changing the way we read, think and remember.* London: Atlantic Books.

Carrington, V. and **R. Robinson.** 2010. *Digital literacies: social learning and classroom practices.* London: Sage.

Castagnaro, P. J. 2006. 'Audiolingual method and behaviorism: from misunderstanding to myth'. *Applied Linguistics* 27: 519–526.

Chan, K. K. and **J. Ridgeway.** 2006. 'Students' perception of using blogs as a tool for reflection and communication'. *Asean Journal of Teaching and Learning in Higher Education* 1/5: 45–57. Accessed 4 November 2011 at http://www.dur.ac.uk/smart.centre/publications/

Chapelle, C. 2005. 'Interactionist SLA theory in CALL research' in J.L.Egbert and G.M.Petrie (eds.). *CALL research perspectives.* Mahwah, NJ: Lawrence Erlbaum Associates.

Chapelle, C. 2003. *English language learning and technology.* Amsterdam: John Benjamins.

Chapelle, C. 2001. *Computer applications in second language acquisition: foundations for teaching, testing and research.* Cambridge: Cambridge University Press.

Child, D. 2004. *Psychology and the teacher* (7th edn.). London: Continuum.

Churches, A. 2008. 'Blooms taxonomy Blooms digitally'. *Educational Origami Wiki.* Accessed 12 August 2012 at http://edorigami.wikispaces.com/Bloom%27s+Digital+Taxonomy

Cole, M. and **Y. Engeström.** 1993. 'A cultural-historical approach to distributed cognition' in G. Salomon (ed.). *Distributed cognitions, psychological and educational considerations.* Cambridge: Cambridge University Press: 1–46.

Comas-Quinn, A., B. de los Arcos, and **R. Mardomingo.** 2012. 'Virtual learning environments (VLEs) for distance learning: shifting tutor roles in a contested space for interaction'. *Computer Assisted Language Learning* 25/2: 129–143.

Compton, L.K.L. 2009. 'Preparing language teachers to teach languages online: a look at skills, roles, and responsibilities'. *Computer Assisted Language Learning* 22/1: 73–99.

Consumer Reports. 2011. That Facebook friend might be 10 years old, and 'other troubling news'. *Consumer Reports Magazine June 2011.* Accessed 10 September 2012 at http://www.consumerreports.org/cro/magazine-archive/2011/june/electronics-computers/state-of-the-net/facebook-concerns/index.htm

Cooper, B. and **P. Brna.** 2002. 'Supporting high quality interaction and motivation in the classroom using ICT: the social and emotional learning and engagement in the NIMIS project'. *Education, Communication & Information* 2(1/2): 113–138.

COPPA *Children's online privacy protection act.* Accessed 21st September 2012 at http://www.coppa.org/

Cormier, D. 2008. 'Rhizomatic education: Community as curriculum'. *Innovate* 4/5. Accessed 20 October 2012 at http://www.innovateonline.info/pdf/vol4_issue5/Rhizomatic_Education-__Community_as_Curriculum.pdf

Coulby, C., J.C. Laxton, S. Boomer, N. Davies, and **K. Murphy.** 2010. 'Mobile technology and assessment – a case study from the ALPS programme' in *Work-based mobile learning: concepts and cases. A handbook for academics and practitioners.* N. Pachler, C. Pimmer, J. Seipold (eds.). Peter Lang: Oxford.

Crowhurst, M. 1991. 'Interrelationships between reading and writing persuasive discourse'. *Research in the Teaching of English* 25/3; 314–338.

Crystal, D. 2011. *Internet linguistics: a student guide.* London: Routledge.

Crystal, D. 2008. *Txtng. The Gr8 Db8.* Oxford: Oxford University Press.

Crystal, D. 2006. *Language and the internet.* (2 edn.). Cambridge: Cambridge University Press.

Csikszentmihalyi. 2008. *Flow: the psychology of optimal experience.* New York: Harper Perennial.

Cunningham, A. 2005. 'Vocabulary growth through independent reading and reading aloud to children' in E. Hiebert and M. Kamil. (eds.). *Teaching and learning vocabulary.* Mahwah, NJ: Lawrence Erlbaum: 45–68.

Deane, M. 2010. *Inside Track: Academic research, writing and referencing.* Harlow: Longman.

Deleuze, G., and **F. Guatarri.** 1987. *A thousand plateaus: Capitalism and schizophrenia.* London: University of Minnesota Press.

Deller, S. 1990. *Lessons from the Learner.* Harlow: Longman.

Dias, J. 1998. 'The teacher as chameleon: computer-mediated communication and role transformation.' in P. Lewis, (ed.). *Teachers, learners and computers: exploring relationships in CALL.* Tokyo: JALT: 17–26.

Diemand-Yauman, C., D. Oppenheimer and **E. Vaughan.** 2011. Fortune favors the Bold (and the Italicized): Effects of disfluency on educational outcomes. *Cognition* 118/1.

Doult, W. and S.A. Walker. 2013. 'He's gone and wrote over it': The use of wikis for collaborative report writing in a primary school classroom.

Dubois, M. and **I.Vial.** 2000. 'Multimedia design: the effects of relating multimodal information'. *Computer Assisted Learning* 16: 157–165.

DuQuette, J-P. 2011. 'Buckling down: initiating an EFL reading circle in a casual online learning group'. *JALTCALL Journal* 7/1: 79–92. Accessed 16 September 2012 at http://www.jaltcall.org/journal/articles/7_1_DuQuette.pdf

Educational Testing Services. 2010. 'Frequently Asked Questions about TOEFL® Practice Online'. Accessed 6th September 2012 at http://www.ets.org/s/toefl/pdf/toefl_tpo_faq.pdf

Facer, K. 2011. *Learning Futures: education, technology and social change.* Abingdon: Routledge.

Field, J. 2008. *Listening in the language classroom.* Cambridge: Cambridge University Press.

Field, J. 2000. 'Not waving but drowning. A reply to Tony Ridgeway'. *ELT Journal* 52/2: 110–18.

Fitzgerald, J. and **T. Shanahan.** 2000. 'Reading and writing relations and their development'. *Educational Psychologist* 35: 39–50.

Flowerdew, J. and **L. Miller.** 2005. *Second language listening: theory and practice.* Cambridge: Cambridge University Press.

Fulcher, G. 2003. *Testing second language speaking.* Harlow: Longman.

Gabriel, Y. 2008. 'Against the tyranny of PowerPoint: technology-in-use and technology abuse' *Organization Studies* 29/2: 255–276.

Garry, M. et al .2007. 'Photographs can distort memory for the news'. *Applied Cognitive Psychology* 21: 995–1004.

Gee, J. P. and **E.R. Hayes.** 2010. *Women and gaming: The Sims and 21st century learning.* New York: Palgrave Macmillan.

Gee, J. P. 2003. *What video games have to teach us about learning and literacy.* New York: Palgrave Macmillan.

Gee, J. P. 2004. *Situated language and Learning: a critique of traditional schooling.* London: Routledge.

Gee, J. P. 2005. 'Semiotic social spaces to affinity paces: from The Age of Mythology to today's schools'. In D. Barton and K. Tusting (eds.). *Beyond communities of practice.* Cambridge: Cambridge University Press.

Gee, J. P. 2007. *Good video games and good learning: collected essays on video games, learning and literacy.* New York: Prentice Hall.

Gee, J. P. 2007. *What video games have to teach us about learning and literacy (revised and updated).* New York: Palgrave Macmillan.

Gilbert, E. 2006. *Eat, Pray, Love.* London: Bloomsbury.

Godwin-Jones, R. 2011. 'Emerging technologies: autonomous language learning'. *Language Learning and Technology* 15/3: 4–11.

Godwin-Jones, R. 2012. 'Emerging technologies: challenging hegemonies in online learning'. *Computer Assisted Language Learning* 16/2: 4–13.

Goh, C. and **A. Burns.** 2012. *Teaching speaking skills: a holistic approach.* Cambridge: Cambridge University Press.

Goh, C. 2002. 'Exploring listening comprehension tactics and their interaction patterns'. *System* 30/2: 185–206.

Goh, C. 2000. 'A cognitive perspective on language learners' listening comprehension problems'. *System* 28/1: 55–75.

Goldstein, B. 2008. *Working with images.* Cambridge: Cambridge University Press.

Grabe, W. 2009. *Reading in a second language: moving from theory to practice.* Cambridge: Cambridge University Press.

Grabe, W. and **F.L. Stoller.** 2002. *Teaching and researching reading.* Harlow: Pearson Education.

Green, A. 2007. 'Washback to learning outcomes: a comparative study of IELTS preparation and university pre-sessional language courses'. *Assessment in Education: Principles, Policy and Practice* 14/1: 75–97.

Greenfield, S. 2003. *Tomorrow's People: how 21st century technology is changing the way we think and feel.* London: Allen Lane.

Hall, E.T. 1966. *The Hidden Dimension: man's use of space in public and private.* London: the Bodley Head.

Hampel, R. and **U. Stickler.** 2005. 'New skills for new classrooms: training tutors to teach languages online'. *Computer Assisted Language Learning* 18/4: 311–326.

Hamp-Lyons, L. 1997. 'Washback, impact and validity: ethical concerns'. *Language Testing* 14/3: 295–303.

Harmer, J. 2007. *The practice of English language teaching.* (4th edn.). Harlow: Pearson Longman.

Hedge, T. 2000. *Teaching and learning in the language classroom.* Oxford: Oxford University Press.

Helsper, E. and **R. Eynon.** 2010. 'Digital natives: where is the evidence?' *British Educational Research Journal* 36/3: 503–520.

Herring, S. 1999. 'Interactional Coherence in CMC' *Journal of Computer-Mediated Communication* 4/4) Accessed 19 September 2012 at http://jcmc.indiana.edu/vol4/issue4/herring.html

Hoare, S. 2007. 'Students tell universities: Get out of MySpace!' *The Guardian.* Accessed 19 September 2012 at http://www.guardian.co.uk/education/2007/nov/05/link.students

Holes, B. and **J. Gardner.** 2006. *E-learning: concepts and practice.* London: Sage.

Horowitz, R. and **S. J. Samuels.** 1987. *Comprehending oral and written language.* New York: Academic.

Hubbard, P. 2006. 'Evaluating CALL software' in L.Ducate, and N. Arnold. (eds) *Calling on CALL: from theory and research to new directions in foreign language teaching.* San Marcos, TX.: CALICO: 313–338.

Hudson, T. 2007. *Teaching second language reading.* Oxford: Oxford University Press.

Hughes, A. 2003. *Testing for language teachers* (2nd edn.). Cambridge: Cambridge University Press.

Hutchinson, T. 2009. *Project student's book.* (3rd edn.). Oxford: Oxford University Press.

Hyland, K. 2009. *Teaching and researching writing.* (2nd edn.). London: Pearson Education.

Internet world stats. 2012. *Internet World Users by Language.* Accessed 19 September 2012 at http://www.internetworldstats.com/stats7.htm

JANET. 2011. *JANET Acceptable Use Policy.* Accessed 19 September 2012 at https://community.ja.net/library/acceptable-use-policy

Jenkins, H. 2006. *Convergence Culture: where old and new media collide.* New York: New York University Press.

Jewitt, C. 2009. Introduction. In C. Jewitt (ed.) *The Routledge Handbook of Multimodal Analysis.* Abingdon: Routledge.

Johns, A., K. Hyland, et al. 2006. 'Crossing the boundaries of genre studies: commentaries by experts'. *Journal of Second Language Writing* 15/3: 234–249.

Johnson, A. 2004. 'Creating a writing course utilising class and student blogs'. *Internet TESL Journal.* Accessed 4 November 2011 at 10/8 http://iteslj.org/Techniques/Johnson-Blogs.

Johnson, B. 2010. 'Apple iPad: the first review'. *The Guardian.* Accessed 21 September 2012 at http://www.guardian.co.uk/technology/2010/jan/27/apple-ipad-tablet-first-review

Johnson, N. A., R. B. Cooper and **W. W. Chin.** 2009. 'Anger and flaming in computer-mediated negotiation among strangers'. *Decision Support Systems* 46: 660–672.

Johnson, L., S. Adams and **M. Cummins.** 2012. *The NMC Horizon Report: 2012 Higher Education Edition.* Austin, Texas: The New Media Consortium.

Jones, C., R. Ramanau, S. Cross, and **G. Healing.** 2010. 'Net generation or Digital Natives: Is there a distinct new generation entering university?' *Computers and Education* 54/3: 722–732.

Jones, J. and **D. Wiliam.** 2008. *Modern foreign languages inside the black box: assessment for learning in the modern languages classroom.* London: GL Assessment.

Keddie, J. 2009. *Images.* Oxford: Oxford University Press.

Kenning, M.-M. 2006. Evolving concepts and moving targets: communicative competence and the mediation of communication'. *International Journal of Applied Linguistics* 16: 363–388.

Kessler, G. 2007. 'Formal and informal CALL preparation and teacher attitude toward technology'. *Computer Assisted Language Learning* 20/2: 173–188.

Knowles M. S., E .F. Holton III and **R. A. Swanson.** 2005. *The Adult Learner* (6th edn.). Oxford: Elsevier.

Kowalski R.M., S.P. Limber and **P.W. Agatson.** 2008. *Cyberbullying.* Malden MA: Blackwell.

Kress, G. 2004. 'Reading images: multimodality, representation and new media'. Paper presented at: 'Preparing for the future of knowledge. Expert forum for knowledge presentation'. Accessed 19th September 2012 at http://www.knowledgepresentation.org/BuildingTheFuture/Kress2/Kress2.html.

Kress, G. 2010. *Multimodiality: a social semiotic approach to contemporary communication.* London: Routledge.

Kress, G. and **T. Van Leeuven.** 1996. *Reading images: the grammar of visual design.* New York: Routledge.

Kutner, L. and **C.K. Olsen.** 2008. *Grand Theft Childhood: the surprising truth about video games.* New York: Simon and Schuster.

Kurzweil, R. 1999. *The age of spiritual machines: when computers exceed human intelligence.* New York: Viking.

Lave, J. and **E. Wenger.** 1991. *Situated learning: legitimate peripheral participation.* Cambridge: Cambridge University Press.

Lenhart, A., M. Madden, A. Smith, K. Purcell, K. Zickuhr, and **L. Rainie.** 2011. *Teens, kindness and cruelty on social network sites.* Pew Internet Research. Accessed 19 September 2012 at http://pewinternet.org/~/media//Files/Reports/2011/PIP_Teens_Kindness_Cruelty_SNS_Report_Nov_2011_FINAL_110711.pdf

Lenski, S.D. and **J.L. Johns.** 1997. 'Patterns in reading-to-write'. *Reading Research Instruction* 37/1: 15–39.

Leung, C. and **J. Lewkowicz.** 2006. 'Expanding horizons and unsolved conundrums: language testing and assessment'. *TESOL quarterly* 40/1: 211–234.

Levelt, W. 1993. 'The architecture of normal spoken English' in G.Blanken, J. Dittman, H.Grimm, J.Marshall, and C-W.Wallesch. (eds). *Linguistic disorders and pathologies.* Berlin: De Gruyter.

Lightbown, P.M. and **N. Spada.** 2006. *How Languages are Learned* (3rd edn.). Oxford: Oxford University Press.

Louv, R. 2008. *Last Child in the Woods: saving our children from nature deficit disorder.* Chapel Hill: Algonquin Books.

Luckin, R. 2009. *Learning, context and the role of technology.* London: Institute of Education.

Luckin, R. 2010. Re-designing Learning Contexts: technology-rich, learner-centred ecologies. Abingdon, Routledge.

Lynch, T. 2009. *Teaching second language listening.* Oxford: Oxford University Press.

Macgregor, G., A. Spiers, A. and **C. Taylor.** 2011. Exploratory evaluation of audio email technology in formative assessment feedback. *Research in Learning Technology.* Accessed 21 September 2012 at http://www.researchinlearningtechnology.net/index.php/rlt/article/view/17119

Margaryan, A. Littlejohn and **G. Vojt.** 2011. 'Are digital natives a myth or reality? University students' use of digital technologies.' *Computers and Education* 56/2: 429–440.

Mawer, K. and **G. Stanley.** 2011. *Digital play.* Peaslake, UK: Delta.

Mayer, R. 2005. (ed) *The Cambridge handbook of multimedia learning.* Cambridge: Cambridge University Press.

McKay, S. 1993. *Agendas for second language literacy.* Cambridge: Cambridge University Press.

Meddings, L. and **S. Thornbury.** 2009. *Teaching unplugged: dogme in English language teaching.* Peaslake, UK: Delta.

Mitchell, R. and **F. Myles.** 2004. *Second language learning theories.* (2nd edn.). London: Arnold.

Mitra S. 2005. 'Self organizing systems for mass computer literacy: Findings from the "hole in the wall" experiments'. *International Journal of Development Issues* 4/1: 71–81.

Myers, G. 2010. *The discourse of blogs and wikis.* London: Continuum.

Mynard, J. 2007. 'A blog as a tool for English language learners'. *Asian EFL Journal.* Accessed 27 February 2012 at http://www.asian-efl-journal.com/pta_Nov_07_jm.php

Nardi, B. A. 1996. 'Activity Theory and Human-Computer Interaction' in *Context and Consciousness: Activity Theory and Human-Computer Interactions.* Cambridge, MA: The MIT Press.

Nah, K. C., P. White and **R. Sussex.** 2008. 'The potential of using a mobile phone to access the Internet for learning EFL listening skills within a Korean context'. *ReCALL* 20: 331–347.

Neville, D.O., B.E.Shelton, and **B. McInnis.** 2009. 'Cybertext redux: using digital game based learning for learning L2 vocabulary, reading and culture'. *Computer Assisted Language Learning* 22/5: 409–424.

Norbury, C. F., M. Nash, G. Baird and **D. V. M. Bishop.** 2004. 'Using a parental checklist to identify diagnostic groups in children with communication impairment: a validation of the Children's Communication Checklist—2'. *International Journal of Language & Communication Disorders* 39/3: 345–364.

OFCOM. 2012. *The Communications Market 2012.* Accessed 21 September 2012 at http://stakeholders.ofcom.org.uk/market-data-research/market-data/communications-market-reports/cmr12/

Paduraru, M. 2011. 'Online homework'. *IATEFL Voices* 222 September–October 2011: 4–5.

Paivio, A. 2006. 'Dual Coding Theory and Education'. Draft chapter for the conference on 'Pathways to Literacy Achievement for High Poverty Children'. The University of Michigan School of Education. Accessed 29 August 2010, at http://readytolearnresearch.org/pataysconference/presentations/paivio.pdf

Papert, S. 1993. *Mindstorms: children, computers and powerful ideas* (2nd edn.) Hemel Hempstead: Harvester Wheatsheaf.

Papert, S. 1986. *Constructionism: a new opportunity for elementary science education.* Unpublished proposal to the National Science Foundation.

Papert, S. and **I. Harel.** 1991. 'Situating Constructionism' in S.Papert. and I. Harel. (eds.). *Constructionism* Ablex Publishing Corporation. Accessed 16 September 2012 at http://papert.org/articles/SituatingConstructionism.html

Perfetti, C.A. 1991. 'Representations and awareness in the acquisition of reading competence' in L. Rieben. and C.A. Perfetti, (eds.). *Learning to read.* Hillside, NJ:Lawrence Erlbaum: 33–44.

Pinter, A. 2011. *Children Learning Second Languages.* Basingstoke: Palgrave Macmillan.

Plowman, L., C. Stephen and **J. McPake.** 2010. *Growing up with Technology: young children learning in a digital world.* London: Routledge.

Prensky, M. 2001. 'Digital Natives, Digital Immigrants'. *On the Horizon*: 9/5 Accessed 19 September 2012 at http://www.marcprensky.com/writing/Prensky%20%20Digital%20Natives,%20Digital%20Immigrants%20-%20Part1.pdf

Qi, L. 2007. 'Is testing an efficient agent for pedagogical change? Examining the intended washback of the writing task in a high-stakes English test in China'. *Assessment in Education: Principles, Policy and Practice* 1: 51–74.

Recio Saucedo, A. 2008. *Computer-aided storytelling : effects on emergent literacy of preschool-aged children in an EFL context.* PhD Thesis University of Leeds.

Rich, S. 2012. 'The battle of the boards'. *English Language Teaching Professional* 78: 54–56.

Richmond, S. 2012. 'iPad: how Apple started a tablet revolution' *The Telegraph* Accessed 21 September 2012 at http://www.telegraph.co.uk/technology/apple/9147868/iPad-how-Apple-started-a-tablet-revolution.html

Rollason, C. 2005. 'Why the internet age will not accept simplified English spelling'. Paper given at the conference 'International English for global literacy', University of Mannheim, Germany, July 29–31, 2005.

Rost, M. 2011. *Teaching and researching listening.* (2nd edn.). Harlow: Longman.

Royal Society. 2012. *Computing in Schools.* Accessed 21 September 2012 at http://royalsociety.org/uploadedFiles/Royal_Society_Content/education/policy/computing-in-schools/2012-01-12-Computing-in-Schools.pdf

Sadoski, M. 1985. 'The natural use of imagery in story comprehension and recall: replication and extension'. *Reading Research Quarterly* 20: 658–667.

Salmon, G. 2011. *E-moderating: the key to teaching and learning online.* (3rd edn.) New York: Routledge.

Salmon, G. 2002. *E-tivities: the key to active online learning.* London: Kogan Page.

Saville-Troike, M. 1982. *The Ethnography of Communication.* Oxford: Blackwell.

Shaughnessy, M. 2008. 'An interview with Jacquie Ream: what's happening with writing?' *Education News.* Accessed 24 August 2012 at http://www.educationnews.org/articles/an-interview-with-jacquie-ream-what039s-happening-with-writing.html

Schmidt, R. 1990. 'The role of consciousness in second language learning'. *Applied Linguistics* 11/2: 129–158.

Schellekens, P. 2007. *The Oxford ESOL handbook.* Oxford: Oxford University Press.

Shin, D.S. 2006. 'ESL students' computer-mediated communication practices: context configuration'. *Language Learning and Technology* 10/3 : 65–84.

Shirky, C. 2008. *Here comes everybody : how change happens when people come together.* London: Penguin.

Siemens, G. 2005. 'Connectivism: a learning theory for the digital age'. *Journal of Instructional Technology and Distance Learning* 2/1: 3–10.

Sigman A. 2012. 'Time for a view on screen time'. Archives of Disease in Childhood.

Sigman, A. 2005. *Remotely Controlled: how television is damaging our lives.* Vermilion: London.

Simpson, J. 2005. Learning Electronic Literacy Skills in an Online Language Learning Community. *Computer Assisted Language Learning* 18/4: 327–345.

Simpson, J. and **A. Walker.** 2014. 'New technologies for language learning and teaching' in Constant Leung and Brian Street (eds.). *Handbook of English Language Studies.* Routledge.

Skinner, B.F. 1974. *About behaviourism.* London: Cape.

Soong, B., N. Mercer, and **S. Er.** 2010. 'Revision by means of computer-mediated peer discussions'. *Physics Education* 45/3.

Stevenson, I. 2008. 'Tool, tutor, environment or resource: Exploring metaphors for digital technology and pedagogy using activity theory'. *Computers and Education* 51/2: 836–853.

Street, B.V. 1993. 'Introduction: the new literacy studies' in B.V. Street. (ed.). *Cross-cultural approaches to literacy.* Cambridge: Cambridge University Press 1–21.

Sutherland, J. 2010. 'We've lost our calm in a storm of 'busyness'. *The Times,* 21 August 2010.

Swales, J. 1990. *Genre analysis: English in academic and research settings.* Cambridge: Cambridge University Press.

Sze, P. 2008. 'Online collaborative writing using wikis'. *The Internet TESL Journal* xiv / 1. Accessed on 20 February 2012 at http://iteslj.org/Techniques/Sze-Wikis. html

Taylor, R. P. 1980. Introduction. In R. P. Taylor (Ed.), *The computer in school: Tutor, tool, tutee.* 1–10. New York: Teachers College Press. Accessed on 19 September 2012 at http://www.citejournal.org/vol3/iss2/seminal/article1.cfm

Thornbury, S. 2005. *How to teach speaking.* Harlow: Pearson Longman.

Threlfall, J., N. Nelson, and **A. Walker.** 2007. *Report to QCA on an investigation of the construct relevance of sources of difficulty in the Key Stage 3 ICT tests.* London: Qualifications and Curriculum Agency.

Tikkirou, M. and **S. A. Walker.** (submitted) 'Cypriot Students' Code-Switching in Synchronous Text-based CMC vs Formal Online Writing'.

Tribble, C. 1996. *Writing.* Oxford: Oxford University Press.

Tsui, A. and **J. Fullilove.** 1998. 'Bottom-up or top-down processing as a discriminator of L2 listening performance'. *Applied Linguistics* 19/4: 432–51.

Tucker, B. 2012. The flipped classroom: online instruction at home frees class time for learning. *Education Next* 12/1: 82–83. Accessed 16 September at http://educationnext.org/the-flipped-classroom

Tuckman, B.W. 1965. 'Developmental sequences in small groups'. *Psychological Bulletin* 6: 384–399.

Tufte, E. R. 2003. *The Cognitive Style of PowerPoint.* Cheshire, CT: Graphics Press.

Tufte, E. R. 2003. 'PowerPoint is evil: power corrupts. PowerPoint corrupts absolutely'. *Wired* 11.

Vandergrift, L. 1999. 'Facilitating second language listening comprehension: acquiring successful strategies'. *ELT Journal* 53/3: 168–76.

Vygotsky, L. S. 1978. *Mind in society: the development of higher psychological processes.* M. Cole, V. John-Steiner, S. Scribner, E. Souberman, (eds.). Cambridge, MA: Harvard University Press.

Walker, S.A. 2009. 'Confessions of a Reluctant Podcaster' in *Academic Futures: Inquiries into Higher Education and Pedagogy* edited by the iPED Research Network. Newcastle upon Tyne: Cambridge Scholars Publishing

Walker, S. A. 2007. 'What Does it Mean to Be Good at ICT?' School of Education Research Conference, University of Leeds 14th May 2007. Accessed 19 September 2012 at http://www.leeds.ac.uk/educol/documents/163464.pdf

Walker, S.A. 2003. *The Contribution of Computer-Mediated Communication in Developing Argument Skills and Writing-Related Self-Esteem.* PhD Thesis University of Leeds.

Wall, K., S. Higgins and **H. Smith.** 2005. '"The visual helps me understand the complicated things": pupil views of teaching and learning with interactive whiteboards'. *British Journal of Educational Technology* 36/5: 851–867.

Wallace, P. 1999. *The Psychology of the Internet.* Cambridge: Cambridge University Press.

Wallace, C. 1988. *Learning to read in a multicultural society: the social context of second language literacy.* London: Prentice Hall.

Wang, Y., N.S. Chen and **M. Levy.** 2010. 'Teacher training in a synchronous cyber face-to-face classroom: characterising and supporting the online teachers' learning process'. *Computer Assisted Language Learning* 23/4: 277–293.

Warschauer, M. 2010. 'Invited commentary; new tools for teaching writing'. *Language Learning and Technology* 14/1: 3–8.

Warschauer, M., K. Arada and **B. Zheng** 2010. 'Digital Literacies: Laptops and Inspired Writing'. *Journal of Adolescent & Adult Literacy* 54/3.

Warschauer, M., and **Kern, R.** (eds.). 2000. *Network-based Language Teaching: Concepts and Practice.* Cambridge: Cambridge University Press.

Warschauer, M. 1996. 'Comparing Face-to-Face and Electronic Discussion in the Second Language Classroom'. *CALICO journal* 13/2: 7–26.

Wecker, C. 2012. 'Slide presentations as speech suppressors: When and why learners miss oral information'. *Computers & Education* 59/2.

Weir, C. J. 2005. *Language testing and validation: an evidence-based approach*. Basingstoke: Palgrave Macmillan.

West, K. and **J. Williamson.** 2009. 'Wikipedia: Friend or foe?' *Reference Services Review* 37/3: 260–271.

White, G. 1998. *Listening*. Oxford: Oxford University Press.

White, R. and **V. Arndt.** 1991. *Process writing*. London: Pearson Education.

Wilson, J. J. 2008. *How to teach listening*. Harlow: Longman Pearson.

Wong, L. and **P. Benson.** 2006. 'In-service CALL education: what happens after the course is over?' in P.Hubbard and M.Levy. (eds.). *Teacher education in CALL*. Amsterdam: John Benjamin: 251–264.

Wood, C. 2005. 'Highschool.com'. *Edutopia*, 1/4: 32–37.

Wood, D. J., Bruner, J. S. and **Ross, G.** 1976. 'The role of tutoring in problem solving.' *Journal of Child Psychiatry and Psychology* 17/2: 89–100.

Woods, D. and **C. Hastings.** 2009. 'Data deluge will reboot our brains'. *The Sunday Times*, 13 December 2009.

Woolgar, S. 2002. 'Five rules of virtuality'. In S. Woolgar (ed.). *Virtual Society? Technology, Cyberbole, Reality*. Oxford: Oxford University Press.

Woollett, K. and **E. A. Maguire.** 2011. 'Acquiring 'the Knowledge' of London's layout drives structural brain changes'. *Current Biology* 21/24: 2109–2114.

Xuan T. D. 2012. 'Using internet resources to teach listening and speaking'. Presentation at ICT in Education Victoria Conference 2012, 26 May 2012. Accessed 13 September 2012 at http://ictev.vic.edu.au/proposal/2358/using-internet-resources-teach-listening-and-speaking

INDEX

Entries containing 't' or 'f' refer to information in tables or figures respectively.